The Social Dynamics of Financial Markets

CONTEMPORARY STUDIES IN APPLIED BEHAVIORAL SCIENCE, VOLUME 2

Editor: Louis A. Zurcher, *Ashbel Smith Professor of Social Work and Sociology, School of Social Work, University of Texas, Austin*

CONTEMPORARY STUDIES IN APPLIED BEHAVIORAL SCIENCE

Series Editor: Louis A. Zurcher
School of Social Work, University of Texas at Austin

Volume 1. **BUREAUCRACY AS A SOCIAL PROBLEM**
Edited by W. Boyd Littrell, Chairman, Department of Sociology, University of Nebraska at Omaha and Gideon Sjoberg, Department of Sociology, University of Texas at Austin, and Louis A. Zurcher, School of Social Work, University of Texas at Austin

Volume 2. **THE SOCIAL DYNAMICS OF FINANCIAL MARKETS**
Patricia A. Adler and Peter Adler, University of Tulsa

Volume 3. **COMPREHENSIVE EMERGENCY MANAGEMENT: EVALUATING THREATENED POPULATIONS**
Ronald W. Perry, Battelle Human Affairs Research Centers, Seattle

For Jacob Adler,

Who understood both the market and people

The Social Dynamics of Financial Markets

Edited by: PATRICIA A. ADLER
Department of Sociology
University of Tulsa

PETER ADLER
Department of Sociology
The University of Tulsa

JAI PRESS INC.

Greenwich, Connecticut *London, England*

Library of Congress Cataloging in Publication Data

Main entry under title:
The Social dynamics of financial markets.

(Contemporary studies in applied behavioral science; v. 2)
Includes bibliographies and indexes.
1. Stock-exchange—Sociological aspects—Addresses, essays, lectures. I. Adler, Patricia A. II. Adler, Peter, 1951– . III. Series.
HG4551.S63 1984 332.64′2 84-4340
ISBN 0-89232-435-X
ISBN 0-89232-475-9 (pbk.)

36 Sherwood Place
Greenwich, Connecticut 06830

JAI PRESS INC.
3 Henrietta Street
London WC2E 8LU
England

ISBN: 0-89232-435-X (cloth)
ISBN: 0-89232-475-9 (paper)
Library of Congress Card Number: 84-4340
Manufactured in the United States of America

CONTENTS

ACKNOWLEDGMENTS

Our aim in putting together this volume was to locate that small coterie of social science scholars who were willing to take a rare step and combine inter-disciplinary, theoretical and methodological skills to formulate a sociology of financial markets. We think that we have been successful in finding these "pioneers," but some of the credit must also go to several people who helped along the way. Allan Schnaiberg of Northwestern University showed an early interest in the project and offered suggestions of people working in this area of research. Mitch Allen and Marlie Wasserman provided advice, encouragement and comments on the publishability of the manuscript. Michael Klausner, a contributing author to the volume, was a driving force in seeing that it finally got underway and eventually was completed. His persistence and dedication made us continue with the project at times when we thought it would die. Jack Douglas' ever-present guidance, creativity and mentorship will forever be a role model for all our work. Lou Zurcher, editor of the series *Contemporary Studies in Applied Behavioral Science,* showed remarkable faith by urging us to publish the book at a time when it was still in a tentative form. Our colleagues in the Sociology Department at the University of Tulsa put up with our occasional moodiness, indifferences to important departmental matters and lack of personal contact when the book was being completed. Their financial, emotional and physical support was invaluable to us. Of course, all of our contributing authors had to put up with our incessant phone calls and nervous pleas during the final stages of the project; needless to say, they all came through and are the reason that this book appears in print. Connie Robins, who typed the final manuscript, and Florence Massey, who helped organize the references, worked long and hard to get the final draft done in record time. Finally, and most importantly, we want to thank our children, Jori and Brye, who had to adjust to early bedtimes, quick meals and busy parents at a time when they were not always equipped to understand why.

To you, our readers, we hope the book reflects the intellectual diversity and creative skills of our authors. If not, it is our fault for not being able to adequately convey and synthesize their ideas; if so, we all share in the credit and look forward to future social scientists continuing our research into financial markets.

Patricia A. Adler
Peter Adler
Editors

INTRODUCTION

Patricia A. Adler and Peter Adler

Remote and mysterious to some, the lifeblood of activity for others, today's financial markets touch the lives of millions of Americans, either directly or indirectly.[1] From the stock market, where securities are bought and sold, to the commodities market, where crops, livestock and metals futures are traded, our nation's financial markets provide the opportunity for almost anyone to become involved in a slice of the national or international economy. Whether it be through mass media reports, informal conversations, highly structured interactions or payroll deductions, the pervasiveness of this economic institution to the everyday financial lives of most Americans cannot be ignored.

Yet despite this widespread public participation, sociology has chosen to largely ignore the structure, dynamics and repercussions of people's involvement with financial markets. The irony here is clear. Sociology, the science of society, the depth study of human group and institutional life, has neglected this major institutional domain. What is the cause of this general dearth of sociological investigation and analysis of this arena?

Bruyn (1977) notes that sociologists, throughout the history of the discipline, have tended to bifurcate the social and business orders, as if they were two distinct, unrelated phenomena. Perhaps this is partly due to the traditional scholarly practice of "sticking with what one knows best," and therefore not encroaching on the seeming domain of another discipline. To remedy this deficit,

Bruyn calls for more systematic research and analysis into the field of ''social economy.''

ECONOMIC LITERATURE ON THE MARKET

Economists' treatment of financial markets have traditionally tended to be highly rationalistic, based on a search for universal models and laws. Historically, the classical economic supply and demand paradigm was the accepted view of market functioning, price fluctuation being seen as determined by objective business conditions. Here, not only was the value of any security or commodity determined by the precise overlap between the availability of goods and the public's desire for them, but the market itself served as an ''optimal allocator'' of funds (Baumol, 1965), bringing together individuals with money to invest and businesses in need of financing. Two important assumptions underlie this supply and demand model. The first relates to the decision making process of the abstracted human actor populating this market, and the second concerns the social structure of the idealized arena in which he or she acts.

In order to generalize on a universal scale, economists have depicted an abstracted view of the individual human actor and his ''averaged'' behavior pattern. Economists' ability to explain and predict economic trends is based on an image of ''economic man,'' that idealized individual whose actions form the base of market functioning.[2] Economic man has two remarkable qualities: (1) he is endowed with complete knowledge of all pertinent business, political, economic, etc. information which might affect his decisions about what course of action to pursue, and (2) he acts with the fullest rationality, carefully evaluating all possible outcomes and choosing a line of action which furthers his ultimate interests. These interests are assumed to be unidimensional, consisting of maximized financial gain, especially in the short run (Hayes, 1950; Hutchinson, 1938). The acting market participant is thus not only undeterred in his purposeful goal striving by conflicting motivations, but he also is endowed with the fortuitous knowledge of how his fellow actors will act. His behavior emerges as accurate and efficient.

Each economic man is surrounded by a coterie of people like himself, who similarly utilize rationalistic principles to further their immediate pecuniary gain. They then act together within an equally idealized social market system. For economists financial markets are characterized by ''pure competition'' which, as Boulding (1941:49–50) describes in his classic work, rests on four assumed conditions:

> 1. *Large Number of Buyers and Sellers.* The number of buyers and sellers must be so large in a 'perfectly' competitive market that the ordinary transactions of any single one of them do not appreciably affect the conditions under which other transactions are made. Obviously, the smaller the numbers of sellers selling any given commodity, the greater will be the effect of the transactions of any one seller on the fortunes of the others.

> 2. *A Homogeneous Commodity.* The second condition of a competitive market is that the units of commodity bought and sold by all buyers and sellers shall be identically similar . . . that is to say, the commodity sold by one seller must not be different, in the mind of a buyer, from the commodity sold by any other seller . . . then the buyer—or seller—is influenced in his choice of seller—or buyer—only by considerations of price.
>
> 3. *Close Contact of Buyers and Sellers.* This means that there must be *knowledge* on the part of each buyer and seller of the prices at which other buyers and sellers are willing to buy or sell. It means also that there must be opportunity to take advantage of that knowledge.
>
> 4. *No Discrimination.* The fourth condition is that the buyers and sellers must buy and sell freely among themselves. This means that they must be willing to enter into transactions with all and sundry. When a buyer announces that he is willing to sell at a certain price, these gentlemen must be willing to buy and sell to all comers.

Both the assumptions of economic man and of pure competition yield an image of the market arena as responsive to objective factors which are external to the events which transpire there. As the fundamentalist perspective holds, prices can be predicted through a calculation involving knowledge of inner corporate dynamics, price/earnings ratio, political events, national and international financial considerations, and a host of other factors. This simple supply–demand model dominated economic thinking about the financial markets up through the 1950s.

In the 1960s, interest became aroused among a few economists in the study of stock options (cf. Bachelier, 1964; Gup, 1962). Some of these early works, both separately and through joint inspiration, led to a new economic paradigm of the securities market: the Random Walk Hypothesis (cf. Alexander, 1961; Cootner, 1962, 1964; Granger & Morgenstern, 1963; Malkiel, 1973; Samuelson, 1965). The Random Walk Hypothesis and its successor, the Efficient Market Hypothesis (EMH), posited that it is impossible for investors to outperform the advances or declines of the general ebb and flow of the market by predicting price movements. Because the market is such an "efficient information processor," disseminating complete knowledge of relevant developments instantaneously to all participants (economic man), any news will automatically cause a stock's price to rise or fall (to become "discounted") before the investing public can have the opportunity to make a profit. Market price fluctuations thus wander in an unpredictably random manner, guided by the appearance of information as it randomly becomes available to the public.

This new doctrine, like its classical predecessor, is rooted in a highly abstract framework. While economists know that no real person acts like the idealized economic man and that many markets deviate from the conditions of pure competition, they nonetheless employ these abstractions to build their theories. Therefore, while their theories tell us something about the patterns (or lack thereof) of price fluctuation, they offer us little information or insights about what really goes on inside the workings of the market to produce such effects. Why, for example, if knowledge is complete and man is fully rational, don't people all interpret information the same way and all want to buy or sell the same commodity at the same time? Without more accurate, depth knowledge of how people actually acquire their information, interpret it and decide on their courses of action, we can neither understand how objective developments become translated into price fluctuations nor assess the validity of economists' universal laws and models.

PSYCHOLOGICAL LITERATURE ON THE MARKET

Psychological studies approach the market from the perspective of individual or group decision making. Katona (1951a,b), in his works addressing the general psychological dimensions of economic behavior, suggests that economic decisions are not always dominated by the characteristics of rationality, acquisition and competition, as economists would have us believe. Rather, our behavior and relationships are influenced by feelings and attitudes that are neither completely rational nor always consciously held.

Where the theories of another group of psychologists can be somewhat indirectly applied to the market as a behavioral arena, we see a perspective which stands in even sharper contrast to the economists' portrayal. The crowd psychologists (cf. Freud, 1922; LeBon, 1897; Mackay, 1932; McDougall, 1910) view the type of mass and crowd behavior that occurs in the market as a descension to a lower form of human functioning. These "primitivists" believe that when united either by proximity or by a solidifying rationale, people fuse together into a psychological group of the lowest common denominator. Here, the hereditarily baser instincts lodged in the repressed unconscious are unleashed. Casting off society's normative restraints, those possessed by the "group mind" are highly suggestible to the displays of charismatic individuals, being easily led into "extraordinary popular delusions and the madness of crowds." This irrational, almost uncivilized depiction of human behavior is as flawed by its abandonment of the informal mechanisms which guide the crowd and mass behavior of market participants as the economists' overly rational view. While it sheds some light on the mental decision making processes which lead into what Smelser (1962) calls "panic" or "craze" behavior, it does little to aid our broader understanding of the more mundane patterns and routines which comprise the everyday lives of market participants.

The only group of psychologists who directly address individual and group mental processes associated with financial markets have oriented their presentations toward a lay or "trade" audience. These "pop" psychologists (cf. Blotnick, 1978; Dreman, 1977; Maital, 1982), seeking to capitalize on the get-rich-quick ethos which pervades our socio-cultural environment, have applied psychological concepts to an analysis of speculative decision making. The idiosyncrasies of human nature combined with the random structure of price fluctuation (EMH) cause people to be both irrational and superstitious, they claim. Further, decisions made by groups become dominated by extremists, leading to a group-think force which spurs either greater risk taking or exaggerated caution. While these analyses are topical they do not offer a scientifically grounded approach to understanding the market's human element. It is to this task which we now turn our attention.

SOCIOLOGICAL LITERATURE ON THE MARKET

The field of sociology, with its breadth of analytical perspectives ranging from structural to situational, is ideally suited to guide the study of financial markets. All levels of analysis and types of concerns can be encompassed within its scope. While we have noted that contributions to the literature on social economy are scant,[3] a few important works by sociologists which address financial markets merit mentioning.

The earliest and most significant of these are the groundbreaking articles of Rose (1951, 1966). Rose began his interest in financial markets by examining how rumor affects attitudes and beliefs (what he calls the ultimate determinants of stock, bond and commodities options prices). He outlines and discusses the circumstances under which rumors arise and are spread, including inside information, tips and deliberately manufactured rumor. Finally, through an indirect index, the "measure of stickiness," he statistically demonstrates that rumors play a role in the determination of stock and commodities prices, at least in the short run.

His second, much more comprehensive piece endeavors to outline those social psychological factors which economists have traditionally overlooked in their analyses of financial markets. He divides these into two categories: (1) objective factors which would be considered *noneconomic* (i.e., propaganda, myths, rumors, incorrect news, etc.), and (2) the subjective effect of how people *perceive, interpret* and *act* on the information they obtain. He then isolates and discusses a variety of problems which fall into the social psychological domain including: the motivation underlying market participation; individual versus group interpretations of situations; how the "like" interests of economic men become the "common" interests of social men, and the nature of market crises. Rose's work serves as a valuable beginning to the insights sociologists can offer but, as he himself says, still leaves a vast realm unaddressed.

In 1957 the Chicago Mercantile Exchange became the setting for an in-depth participant observation study by Glick. Glick sought to contrast the specific workings of the market he studied with the rational objectivist model depicted by economists. His findings suggest that the market's formal social system is patterned after the idea of pure competition and rational economic behavior. Due to the pervasive uncertainty inherent in the market setting, however, an informal social system arises which partly complements, but largely supplants, the formal system. This informal social system reduces peoples' uncertainty by providing them with a stable social psychological environment which guides their actions. Traders' motivations are shown to be neither solely rational nor pecuniary, but emotional as well as unconscious, and oriented toward deriving gratification from the system of social relationships existing within the Exchange.

A final work from the sociological perspective was recently offered by Smith (1981). Based on a participant observation study, in-depth interviews and the aid of a key informant, Smith offers some interesting typologies of market participation. He begins by presenting four professional orientations, or trading philosophies, which guide market behavior:

1. the fundamentalist, or economic orientation;
2. the insider, or influence-based orientation;
3. the cyclist, or chartist orientation; and
4. the trader, or market action orientation.

Within each of these perspectives Smith elucidates four styles that market participants can follow: true believers; salesmen; rationalizers, and followers. While these descriptions offer some accurate insights into and typologies of the diverse spectrum of humanity which comprises securities markets, Smith's work is basically atheoretical, lacking in a broader scientific conceptual scheme or contribution. Its practical guide for the investor and cliched style place it within the realm of ''pop'' sociology.

Our work here gratefully acknowledges the debt of inspiration to Rose's and Glick's insightful writings on financial markets, opening this arena to sociological study and providing a cornerstone of quality analysis. We seek here to build on their foundations: where Glick's study is only concerned with the Chicago Mercantile Exchange we address the entire scope of financial markets, and where Rose's works deal with the dynamics of group interpretive behavior we seek to address a wider range of levels and institutional dimensions. We thus aim to offer a more expansive analysis of financial markets, applying the perspective of sociology to areas which have not previously fallen under its scrutiny. We will show how the sociological optic provides a range of different insights from previous interpretations of the markets, whether these stem from the economic, psychological or conventional business point of view. In so doing we will offer a multi-faceted and multi-leveled explication of that previously mysterious and unfathomable element of financial markets: social dynamics of human group behavior.

THE SETTING[4]

There are several kinds of financial markets, as noted earlier: securities, commodities and bond markets. Although chapter 7 addresses commodities trading, the majority of the discussions are concerned with the securities field. When just the term ''market'' appears then, the reader can usually assume that the intended reference is to the stock market. Of the many exchanges, the dominant market for trading in securities is the New York Stock Exchange (NYSE), located in Manhattan on Wall Street. Yet, while many of the chapters are based on studies of Wall Street, the conclusions they offer are not limited to this arena; many of the generalizations can and should be applied to financial markets more generally.

In order to lay the groundwork for our discussion of the market throughout the remainder of this volume, let us now define some of the terms we will be using and describe some of the kinds of people and perspectives we will encounter.

Types of Participants

A great diversity can be found among stock market participants, ranging from active ''pros'' (insiders) to hesitant ''lambs'' (outsiders). Most influential are the *major institutions* such as banks, corporations, trust funds, pension funds, mutual funds, index funds, hedge funds and insurance companies. Managed by a class of professional directors, these institutional investors wield enormous power and massive amounts of money. Second in influence are the *prominent individual entrepreneurs* and families who play the market, often controlling large blocks of stock. Maintaining regular knowledge of market movements, they sometimes act with a prescience that suggests inside information. *Stock exchange professionals,* including both seatholders (traders) and office brokers, are also heavily involved in daily trading, contributing significantly to the total number of transactions, although they deal in smaller quantities than the institutional groups. *Active outsiders* can be considered to form the bulk of the informed masses, keeping abreast of the latest developments by sitting in the brokerage houses, reading news and economic reports, and calling their brokers regularly. Their interest is usually in speculation through properly timed sales and purchases, although they probably keep a more secure portfolio as well. Last in influence are the relatively *inactive outsiders* who deposit surplus capital in the market for security, income and possible growth with the general business sector.

Collective Aims

These groupings of participants place their money in the stock market according to two general modes: *investment* and *speculation.* Investment refers to stock acquisition that is motivated by a desire for security: for the dividend income that is accrued, combined with a hedge against inflation and participation in the national economic development. Blue chip companies that pay a high yield are favored by this class, who may adjust their holdings occasionally but often maintain them intact from date of purchase until the time of financial need that forces dissolution of the portfolio. Investment-oriented purchases thus reflect a conservative outlook, channeling funds into "widows and orphans" companies that are universally acclaimed as pillars of the market and hence more apt to be chosen via sound business principles.

In contrast, speculation consists of transactions undertaken for the purpose of capital appreciation with the intention of being held on a temporary basis until an adequate profit is realized. Included herein are such practices as: buying on margin (putting up a fixed percentage and borrowing the rest from an investment bank through a brokerage house); trading on options (securing the rights for several months to a stock's future gains or losses through paying only a fraction of the purchase price); selling short (borrowing stock from a brokerage house to sell, in the hope that the value will fall so it can be rebought less dearly), and arbitraging (simultaneously taking a long and short position on a security or commodity in different markets to make money on the difference in price between one market and another). Unlike investment, which is conservative in nature, speculation involves the risk of gambling for great financial loss or gain. Estimates of the percentage of all transactions which are speculative in nature have run to 95% (Bond, 1930, pp. 8–9) with this form of trading constituting a major influence on stock price fluctuations. Thus, social psychological factors affecting speculators often cause price levels to depart greatly from intrinsic value, promoting the volatile "trader's market" and serving to expand the outer ranges of price swings by encouraging buying at high values (when optimism reigns) and selling low (when the market mood has turned pessimistic).

Participation Strategies

Drawing upon and cross-cutting the aims underlying investment and speculation is a trio of trading strategies guiding market participants: *fundamentalism; technical market charting* and *contrary opinion theory.*

The fundamentalist perspective, with its emphasis on concrete business soundness as the determinant of price fluctuation, dominates the rationale behind investment behavior. Espousing the credo, "true value will out," fundamentalists argue that the price of a firm's shares should reflect its real worth, as computed by current value, prospective earnings and dividend policy. When prices are accurately linked to earnings potential, the flow of money should be directed toward businesses best able to utilize it, thus serving as an incentive to management efficiency (cf. Baumol, 1965, pp. 35–60; Granger & Morgenstern, 1970, pp. 1–43). Fundamentalists thus draw on a classical economics model of stock market functioning, regarding short term price perturbations rooted in social psychological and technical trends as irrationally unpredictable and ultimately insignificant, to be nullified in the long run by the law of averages' tendency to restore equilibrium (true value).

The technical perspective provided by market chartists is more (although not solely) representative of the strategy powering speculative trading. Working from graphs of previous records, transaction volume and current stock prices, technicians have evolved a statistical science aimed at predicting future price behavior. Their formulas are intended to aid followers in interpreting, measuring and forecasting the strength of upcoming trends.[5] Rallying behind their credo, "the market is the market," chartists form their predictions for the market by studying the general reaction to it. Thus, rather than speaking causally of social, economic, political or business conditions accounting for market action, they attribute fluctuation to current levels of "market action," and to prior price patternings as multiple "tops," "bottoms," resistance lines and breakout points. For example, they commonly believe that if a price "barrier" has emerged through repeated topping at a particular level, once that barrier is passed, the momentum required to break through it will carry the stock's value considerably higher, until the next line of resistance is reached. They then immediately "put the word out" when such an event occurs, warning people to buy immediately in order to profit on this anticipated swing. The success of these forecasts is thus integrally related to their function as "self-fulfilling prophesies;" in effect they create price fluctuation by virtue of their very decree.

Contrary opinion theory draws upon the ideas of the previous two perspectives, providing market participants with a strategy for making individual decisions. Although contrarians admit the basic soundness of most fundamental business analyses, they assert that human judgment and communication are by nature problematic. At the point where original investment evaluations are made, this distortion is slight but when this opinion becomes expanded to great proportions by market promoters, "gurus," hucksters and the excitement of popular sentiment, information and judgments increasingly lose their validity. The task of the contrarian is to critically assess where the repertoire of rhetoric and slogans have driven reason away, replacing it with mass, contagious irrationalism, and to speculate against this dominant market pattern (Neill, 1963; Thurlow, 1967). Contrary opinion theory thus weds the traditional fundamentalist approach to a critical analysis of the psychological dynamics of crowds.

Evaluating these competing ideologies leads one to recognize that they all have a time span of strongest validity: technical considerations are more accurate for explaining short-term fluctuations, contrary opinion analyses recognize bubbles forming and play for their break over the middle-range term, and fundamental judgments usually come to fruition over a long-term span. Technicians, in their unbending rejection of concrete, factual influences fail to consider the greater reality framing the market, that this is not a world apart but one limited and affected by tangible trends and occurrences. In their concern to emphasize hard-core business causes, fundamentalists are overzealous in denying importance to the technicians' and contrarians' assertions that people respond to past and present market actions via a number of social psychological characteristics. Finally, although superficial resemblance can be drawn between fundamentalists' and contrarians' focus on sound business judgments, a more profound compatibility actually exists between fundamentalism and technical market charting: both are essentially "absolutist" (see Douglas, 1971) in nature, emphasizing the importance of totally objective criteria. Only contrary opinion theory attempts to integrate objective factors with the goal of this volume—an understanding of human group reactions to the market as an institutional arena. Let us now examine how this is done throughout this book.

OVERVIEW

Historical Perspective

Chapter 2 begins the book with a structural and historical analysis of changes and developments in the market over the last half-century. In it, Ritchie Lowry begins by examining the distribution of wealth as reflected in stock ownership. He notes that prior to the 1960s, individuals and family wealth dominated the stock markets, while now, institutional investors (insurance companies, retirement funds, corporations) own an ever-increasing majority of the outstanding shares. While this indicates a trend toward the shift of wealth in America (a trend which, it has been estimated, will continue), it also signals the development of professional fund managers. This group of managers is experiencing all the problems of professionalization. Lowry notes that although some guidelines orient these managers toward conservative trading practices, professional peer group pressures often encourage them to follow the crowd and "churn" (see chapter 9) accounts in order to perform no worse than other managers. The large blocks of shares in which they trade, and therefore the structure of the new markets, makes a form of technical speculation more likely. In contrast to the various other speculation and investment strategies, this type of trading leads to market instability. Lowry concludes that new strategies and new policies are required to respond to these problems.

Theories of the Market

In Chapter 3, Vincent Tarascio offers an economist's perspective on the stock market. He outlines the Efficient Market Hypothesis, the dominant economic theory of market price behavior, and contrasts it with the assumptions underlying fundamental and technical trading perspectives. He then introduces the controversy between three modifications of the EMH over the market's efficiency as an information processor and the perfection of its discounting mechanisms. Through a statistical test he shows that the market is basically efficient, following a random walk in nearly all cases as new information is haphazardly made public. On rare occasions, however, when the market overreacts to unexpected news, the adjustment is not perfect. Although price levels ultimately return or ''walk-back'' to their rational positions (''true'' value), these brief deviations and returns exhibit a non-random character upon which the shrewd speculator can capitalize. Tarascio's conclusion, however, is that these exceptions confirm the general random walk principle, which is that the speed with which insiders react to new information and thereby discount market prices makes it impossible for outsiders to profitably speculate in the market.

Michael Klausner draws out the relation between market behavior and various theories from the sociological and psychological literature in chapter 4. He begins by showing that in composition and behavior, market participants constitute a mass. As such, they are subject to the dynamics of contagion theory, including interstimulation, suggestibility and circular reaction. They also exhibit the characteristics of value added theory, especially during periods of craze and panic. Klausner then examines the influence of fad and fashion on the market, offering an historical analysis of investment fads over the last 40 years. Next he turns to a range of social science concepts, discussing the ways these can be used to understand financial market behavior. Convergence theory suggests that people possessing converging personality traits will behave as a unified mass when set off by certain conditions and environmental events. Cognitive dissonance theory explains a range of perceptions, interpretations and attitudes market participants form to achieve peace of mind in an unpredictably shifting market situation and how this leads them to counsel fellow participants. Social comparison theory sheds light on the process by which speculators compare beliefs about the market, fostering the creation of collective beliefs and actions. Lastly, contextual analysis illustrates the way stock price behavior is perceived to be affected by the industrial, market, national and international contexts within which they are located. This exposition of the relationship between sociological theory and investor behavior prepares the reader for its empirical exposition in the subsequent chapters.

Individuals, Groups and Organizations

Collective behavior theory provides the framework for Peter and Patricia Adler's look at the market's ebb and flow in Chapter 5. Their aim is to elucidate the human element in the market which intermediates between outside stimuli and price fluctuations. They begin by outlining the social psychological characteristics and behavior of market participants, including such individual and group traits as the ''sheep mentality,'' following ''like'' others and following opinion leaders (whether these leaders be specific individuals or the mysterious ''They''). The course of a dynamic market swing, whether it be a boom or a bust, is then traced from start to finish. Particular attention is paid throughout to the perceptions, interpretations and actions of key individuals, groups and institutions in contributing to the development or halt of these major market movements. The structural and dynamic differences of booms and busts are discussed with respect to the diverse forms of structural control, collective organization and human emotions found within these opposing swings. The Adlers conclude that there is a momentum to market price fluctuations which is caused by the uncertainty of most market participants and their tendency to "jump on the bandwagon" of first one trend and then another.

Wayne Baker takes a more narrowly focused look at the behavior of market participants in Chapter 6. His descriptive analysis of floor trading focuses on the dynamics of human interaction on the trading floor: between the point where the order to buy or sell reaches the floor of the exchange and when confirmation of the trade is received. Economists have traditionally looked on this as an insignificant aspect of market functioning, as having no impact on the nature of price fluctuation. Baker demonstrates the flaws in this assumption through his discussion of how the actual trading process is affected by the organizational structure of the exchange, the market mechanisms through which transacting occurs and the group process of trading. Of particular interest is his description of how patterns of informal roles and relationships supplement and sometimes override the formal roles and obligations of market participants. Baker concludes by outlining four types of trading crowds and their interactional dynamics, showing how their different composition and characteristics influence the direction of price fluctuation and the magnitude of its volatility.

Chapter 7's focus takes on a more generalized perspective, as Mitchel Abolafia applies the insights of organizational theory to the social dynamics of commodities futures trading. Economists, he contends, have traditionally viewed the action in the trading pits as something closely akin to anarchy. He contests this view through a description of the formal and informal organization which surrounds and buffers the market. He begins by looking at the path of money and information as they flow through the exchange, into and out of the trading pits and through the various market mechanisms and components which comprise the market structure. He then addresses the systems of managerial and institutional control found in the market, showing how both inner discipline and boundary maintenance are effected by the formal and informal mechanisms which flourish within the market's structure. He concludes that all markets exhibit more social organization than economic theory would allow, without which the optimal level of competition would diminish and market participation would decrease.

Institutional Dimensions of the Market

In Chapter 8, David Snow and Robert Parker examine the often taken-for-granted relationship between the news (as disseminated via the mass media) and the market. Both economic theory and commonsense wisdom have traditionally assumed that the two exhibit a linear relationship, that news of unfolding developments is directly responsible for upward or downward movements in the levels of prices. After an empirical test fails to substantiate this thesis, Snow and Parker delve into the process which intermediates between these two objective factors: human beings forming perceptions and interpretations of the news which endows that news with relevant meaning. One of the reasons people will often act differently in the market in response to a single piece of news is the often confusing overabundance of conflicting interpretive schemes which grow out of the various market participation strategies. This ambiguity of how to interpret and act on news exacerbates the problem of investor uncertainty, causing market participants to rely on influential opinion leaders (from popular gurus to brokerage firms).

Snow and Parker next address the relation between the market and the way news of it is handled by the various mass media. Delving into several dimensions through which these media present a distorted image of the market, Snow and Parker note that these misrepresentations function to stimulate investor confidence and activity. They conclude that the market's viability is partly contingent on the way it is portrayed by the media.

Deviance in the market is the subject of Chapter 9. Robert Lejeune reviews the various forms of fraud, deception and outright criminality which exist in the market, from the "cheating" patterns of broker-dealers (violating the fiduciary relationship through churning accounts and misadvising customers in order to enrich themselves) to those of corporate management (acting on inside information and releasing false information to the public). The market offers a structure rife with opportunity for deviance because of the relative ease with which it can be accomplished, the lucrative gains available, the prevailing atmosphere of greed combined with lesser concern for high moral standards of behavior, and the limited risk of punishment. Lejeune also considers the role of the market's self-regulatory system. He argues that although the market is an arena of greed and deception, it is characterized by the appearance of fairness and rationality. The primary function of the self-regulatory system, he concludes, is therefore not the deterrence of deviance; rather, it is to lull the public into a false sense of security and thereby stimulate investor confidence and participation in the market.

NOTES

1. Nearly universal indirect involvement in the market is ensured through peoples' affiliation with company retirement plans or their ownership of insurance policies.

2. For a more detailed explanation of the assumptions underlying the concept of "economic man," see Edwards (1954, p. 380).

3. Sociological interest in financial markets may be on the rise, however, for in addition to this volume two young scholars have recently completed Ph.D. theses in this area (see Abolafia, 1981; Baker, 1981) and offer us a glimpse of their works in Chapters 6 and 7.

4. Much of the material in this section has appeared elsewhere in a slightly different format (see Adler, 1981).

5. This is not to suggest a community of chartists that speak with unanimity regarding the

significance of particular market movements. What chartists share, however, is a common belief that the study of prior price fluctuations is paramount for predicting future price fluctuations.

REFERENCES

Abolafia, M. Y. *Taming the market: Self-regulation in the commodity futures industry*. Unpublished doctoral dissertation, State University of New York, Stony Brook, 1981.

Adler, P. *Momentum: A theory of social action*. Beverly Hills: Sage, 1981.

Alexander, S. S. Price movements in speculative markets: Trends or random walks. *International Management Review*, 1961, *2*, 7–26.

Bachelier, L. Theory of speculation. In P. H. Cootner (Ed.), *The random character of stock market prices*. Cambridge: MIT Press, 1964.

Baker, W. E. *Markets as networks: A multimethod study of trading networks in a securities market*. Unpublished doctoral dissertation, Northwestern University, 1981.

Baumol, W. J. *The stock market and economic efficiency*. New York: Fordham University Press, 1965.

Blotnick, S. *Winning: The psychology of successful investing*. New York: McGraw-Hill, 1978.

Bond, F.D. *Stock movements and speculation*. New York: Appleton, 1930.

Boulding, K. E. *Economic analysis*. New York: Harper & Brothers, 1941.

Bruyn, S. *The social economy*. New York: Wiley, 1977.

Cootner, P. Stock prices: Random vs. systematic changes. *Industrial Management Review*, 1962, *3*, 24–45.

Cootner, P. (Ed.). The random character of stock market prices. Cambridge; MIT Press, 1964.

Douglas, J. D. *American social order*. New York: Fress Press, 1971.

Dreman, D. N. *Psychology and the stock market*. New York: Amacom, 1977.

Edwards, W. The theory of decision making. *Psychological Bulletin*, 1954, *4*, 380–417.

Freud, S. *Group psychology and the analysis of ego*. New York: Liveright, 1922.

Glick, I. O. *A social psychological study of futures trading*. Unpublished doctoral dissertation, University of Chicago, 1957.

Granger, C. W. J., & Morgenstern, O. Spectral analysis of stock market prices. *Kyklos*, 1963, *17*, 1–30.

Granger, C. W. J., & Morgenstern, O. *Predictability of stock market prices*. Lexington, Mass.: Heath, 1970.

Gup, B. E. *The economics of the security options market*. Unpublished doctoral dissertation, University of Cincinnati, 1962.

Hayes, S. P. Some psychological problems of economics. *Psychological Bulletin*, 1950, *4*, 289–330.

Hutchinson, T. W. *The significance and basic postulates of economic theory*. London: MacMillan, 1938.

Katona, G. *Psychological analysis of economic behavior*. New York: McGraw-Hill, 1951. (a)

Katona, G. Expectations and decisions in economic behavior. In D. Lerner & H. D. Lasswell (Eds.), *The policy sciences*. Stanford: Stanford University Press, 1951. (b)

LeBon, G. *The crowd*. New York: MacMillan, 1897.

MacKay, C. *Extraordinary popular delusions*. New York: Noonday, 1932.

Maital, S. *Minds, markets and money*. New York: Basic, 1982.

Malkiel, B. G. *A random walk down Wall Street* (2nd ed.). New York: Norton, 1981.

McDougall, W. *Introduction to social psychology*. Boston: Luce, 1910.

Neill, H. B. *Art of contrary opinion*. New York: Caxton, 1963.

Rose, A. M. Rumor in the stock market. *Public Opinion Quarterly*, 1951, *15*, 461–486.

Rose, A. M. A social psychological approach to the stock market. *Kyklos*, 1966, *19*, 267–287.

Samuelson, P. A. Proof that properly anticipated prices fluctuate randomly. *Industrial Management Review,* Spring 1965, *6,* 41–49.
Smelser, N. *Theory of collective behavior.* New York: Free Press, 1962.
Smith, C. W. *The mind of the market.* Totowa, N.J.: Rowman & Littlefield, 1981.
Thurlow, B. K. Contrary opinion theory: The psychological approach. In C. J. Rolo & G. J. Nelson (Eds.), *The anatomy of Wall Street.* Philadelphia: Lippincott, 1967.

PART I

HISTORICAL PERSPECTIVE

STRUCTURAL CHANGES IN THE MARKET:

THE RISE OF PROFESSIONAL INVESTING

Ritchie P. Lowry

HAS THE MARKET GONE MAD?

Some observers wonder whether or not the stock markets and investing have really changed over the last fifty years. Most Americans know about the crash of 1929, but not everyone remembers the ''October Massacre,'' which took place on the market's 50th anniversary of that event (Arenson, 1979). In October of 1979, the Federal Reserve Board announced steps to raise the interest rate on borrowing money and limit its availability in an attempt to control inflation. While the banks were on a Columbus Day holiday, investors rushed to their brokers to sell as soon as the stock markets opened. Within two days, a selling panic engulfed both small and large investors, volume of shares traded soared, and stock price averages plunged. During one frantic week, the Dow Industrial Average lost a total of 58.62 points, about 7% of its value, representing billions of dollars of worth in the stock shares of major American corporations. Bonds suffered even more. Wall Street set a number of unenviable records to that date: the highest volume of shares ever traded, the largest number of net declines in stock prices, the biggest one-day drop on the American Stock Exchange, and the largest number of downside gaps in a single day. Foreign markets were also influenced as prices fell on the bourses in Amsterdam, Brussels, Frankfurt, London, Milan, Paris, Toronto, and Zurich. Fortunately for the Japanese, the Tokyo Exchange was closed on October 10th for a national Physical Education Day holiday.

This was not the only time in recent history the stock market has been subjected to large volumes in trading and sudden, substantial swings in prices and averages, especially on the downside. From January to March 1980, the Hunt brothers of Texas quietly bought silver on margin through the brokerage firm of Bache Halsey Stuart Shields (Lenzner, 1980). That is, they purchased silver on credit, speculating that the price would soon go higher. However, when silver closed at $20.20 per ounce on the Commodity Exchange on March 25th, this was far below the record of $48.70 on the previous January 17th.

Bache executives informed the Hunt brothers they owed $135-million on their account, and the brothers responded that they could not pay. A Bache executive commented that being told by one of America's richest families that it was unable to pay its bills was ''like walking into a closet and going to turn on a light that was always there and suddenly it was gone.'' Although they had billions of dollars in assets, the Hunts owed creditors about $2-billion and they had little available cash. When the public heard the Hunts, like so many Americans of far more modest means, had been living on credit, silver dropped from $17.50 per ounce to $10.80. On Thursday, March 27, 1980, the Dow Jones Industrial Average fell 32.17 points to a year's low of 727.95 before rebounding to 759.98 by the close of the trading day—a record, breathtaking roundtrip of 62 points in one day. Some financial leaders felt panic had been narrowly averted.

A similar panic occurred on Tuesday, January 6, 1981, while the stock market was surging to its highest level in more than four years, closing above the 1,000 level. That evening and early the next morning, Joseph Granville, a flamboyant Florida investment adviser, telephoned the 3,000 subscribers to his *Granville Market Letter* and told them to ''sell everything,'' since a severe decline in the market and a serious economic recession were coming soon (''As a Seismologist,'' 1981). The following day, Granville's readers apparently had enough faith in his advice to trigger a Dow Jones Industrial Average loss of 23.80 points on a record of 92.9 million shares traded. Total paper losses for this single day came to about $40-billion and were reminiscent of the losses on the day in October 1980 when the market dropped on the news that Aleksei N. Kosygin had resigned as Soviet Prime Minister, though that resignation had been expected for weeks.

Wild market swings and hysterical trading have not been confined to the downside. Starting in August of 1982, the Dow Jones Industrial Average shot up over 250 points in some six weeks. The astounding thing about this gain was that there appeared to be no rational reason for investor confidence, since most economic indicators were bad, with the exception of declining interest rates. On October 7, 1982, a staggering 147.1 million shares were traded on the New York

> History shows . . . that one of the worst times to unload securities is a day on which there's news of a dramatic, uncertain development. In fact, it could have been a time for the history-conscious to buy.

On November 22, 1963, when President John F. Kennedy was assassinated, the Dow Jones Industrial tumbled more than 21 points. When the markets reopened after a suspension of several trading days, the Dow rose more than 30 points. As the Arab-Israeli War broke out on June 5, 1967, the Dow again fell, this time more than 15 points. However, the following session it rose nearly 13 points. Dorfman cites a study by market analyst Edson Gould of 15 unsettling world events over a 22-year period including the Korean War, President Eisenhower's heart attack, the shooting down of the American U-2 spy plane, the Cuban Missile Crisis, and the seizure of the U.S.S. Pueblo by North Koreans. In 12 of these 15 events, the market, from the close of the market on the day of the event to the market close three trading sessions later, was higher. Twenty-one days after the event, the market was up in 9 cases, down in 5, and relatively unchanged in one. What accounts for this is the important structural change in the market since the 1920 and 30s:

> Gould says it's the little guy who's generally the first to panic when uncertain about the impact of a dramatic development. And he's generally a big loser because of it. The big winners: You guessed it; the traders and the institutional biggies who buy during the widespread dumping of stocks (Dorfman, 1981, p. 39).

RISE OF INSTITUTIONAL INVESTORS

Solomon (1974) indicates that, since World War II, individuals have tended to be primarily sellers of common stocks while institutions such as pension funds (usually managed by banks), bank trust departments, and mutual investment funds have tended to be primarily buyers. This tendency accelerated in the 1960s. Before the trend began, the market was about one-third institutional and two-thirds individual as far as trading volume was concerned. By the 1980s, the market was about two-thirds institutional and one-third individual.

The emergence of institutions as the dominant participants in securities trading had a profound effect on a number of traditional market structures and operations. Trading became characterized by large-block sales and purchases, reflected by the rapidity with which new records for volume of shares traded have been set. Minimum, fixed commission rates charged by brokers were replaced by negotiable rates for large-scale traders and most individuals found themselves paying considerably higher commissions than institutional traders (with the exception of those using the new discount brokers). The traditional market became more fragmented as institutional investors sought ways of going around specialists, whose job it is to control wide stock price swings, in order to minimize trading costs and find those who could accept on their accounts the extremely large orders to buy or sell stock. Perhaps most important, the rise of institutional funds signaled a redistribution of wealth in American society in so far as the ownership of stock in major corporations is concerned.

Miller (1979) reports that, by some estimates, there was a defection of at least 7 million shareholders from the U.S. stock markets from 1970 to 1979. A major factor was inflation, which led investors to seek greater security in real estate, commodities, art, foreign securities, futures contracts, and high-yielding money market funds. At the same time, institutional investors stepped into the stock market to fill the void which had been created. Individuals also left the market during the 1970s since, if not a period of depression as Lorie suggested, it was at least a period of severe recession together with inflation which necessitated the use of income to meet daily needs rather than for saving. Table 1 summarizes this historic flight of individuals and families from the marketplace.

So rapid was the entrance of the funds into the marketplace that by the last quarter of 1978, institutional managers reported equity assets of nearly $250 billion, about one-third of the $845 billion market value of all stocks listed on the New York and American stock exchanges (Elia, 1979b). The 100 leading reporting institutions, by total assets, held more than 50% of the shares outstanding of

Table 1
Forms of Investment for the Typical American Family, 1929 to 1978*

Year	*Investment In Stocks*	*Investment In Small Business*	*Investment In Real Estate*	*Historical Factors*
1929	50%	13%		Stock market mania.
1933	30			Market crash and depression.
1939	33	12		"Mom–and–Pop" stores formed.
1945	30	25		War years of hard work with little interest in speculation.
1950	14	30	18%	Cash savings and home buying become popular after World War II.
1968	28	18		Some individual investors return to the market. Mutual funds become popular.
1978	10		30	Small and individual investors leave the stock market. Recession with inflation encourage investments in tangibles such as real estate.

*Percentages for each year do not total 100% since all forms of investment (cash savings, gold, art, etc.) are not included in this analysis.

Source: Adapted from Deborah Rankin's, "The Cycle of Investor Strategies," *The New York Times* (Friday, November 2, 1979), DI & D4.

Table 2
Institutional Stock Holdings in Major Corporations, For Reporting Period Ending December 1978*

Corporation Shares Held in Institutional Portfolios	*Percent of Corporation's Outstanding Shares Held*	*Number of Institutions Holding Shares*
Digital Equipment	71.2	153
Minnesota Mining & Manufacturing	54.4	265
Atlantic Richfield	48.6	274
International Business Machines	43.9	363
Schlumberger	39.2	253
General Electric	37.6	309
Exxon	36.5	344
Standard Oil of California	36.0	264
Eastman Kodak	35.6	303
General Motors	21.3	288
American Telephone & Telegraph	18.7	342

*Over 400 institutions reported for this period. Data was supplied by Computer Directions Advisors, Inc., Silver Spring, Maryland, and the Securities and Exchange Commission.
Source: Adapted from Charles J. Elia's, ''Broader Disclosure of Institutional Holdings Likely to Rekindle Concern Over Dominance,'' *The Wall Street Journal* (Tuesday, March 27, 1979), 47.

29 companies (including Alcoa, American Broadcasting, American Express, Anheuser-Busch, Avon Products, Burroughs, Deere & Co., Eli Lilly, General Mills, General Reinsurance, Halliburton, K-Mart, McDonald's, Motorola, Philip Morris, Raytheon, Revlon, Schering-Plough, Smithkline, Texas Instruments, Travelers Insurance, and Upjohn). Table 2 gives examples of the major American corporations in which institutional investors held shares at the end of 1978. It would appear that at this time the only major corporations still owned primarily by individuals were General Motors and ''Ma Bell.''

THE GROWTH OF QUASI-PUBLIC WEALTH

Americans have traditionally been fascinated by the studies of wealthy individuals and families. For example, a recent analysis of individuals owning more than 5% of a corporation's stock disclosed that William Baron Hilton, founder and chairman of Hilton Hotels Corporation, not surprisingly owned $345 million of that corporations's stock which generated a yearly dividend income for him of $13 million (Metz, 1981). Gordon P. and J. Ronald Getty, descendants of the late Jean Paul Getty who founded the oil company which bears his family name, owned $4.7 billion of Getty Oil Stock, generating $101 million in income. The study indicated there were more individuals with $100 million investments in McDonnell Douglas Corporation than in any other company analyzed. The problem with this fascination about private wealth is that it obscures the major stock market change towards quasi-public wealth.

With the diminished representation of influential families in the market and their replacement by institutional investors, there has been a redistribution of wealth in American society. Institutions not only dominate the markets, their assets also dwarf individual and family wealth in most cases. Furthermore, many of these are quasi-public funds (pension, mutual, and retirement vehicles), which means that though individuals have left the market as individuals, they have returned as group members of participating funds. Table 3 illustrates the manner in which funds assets, both private and public, have surpassed family wealth and worth. The assets of these funds are primarily in the form of equity investments, municipal bonds, and government paper.

In addition, the quasi-public funds, particularly pension plans, are the largest and fastest-growing source of capital in the United States. Rifkin and Barber (1978, p. 10) summarize this change in the following way:

> Pension funds are a new form of wealth that has emerged over the past thirty years to become the largest single pool of private capital in the world. They are now worth over $500 billion and represent the deferred savings of millions and millions of American workers. Pension funds at present own 20 to 25 percent of the equity in American corporations and hold 40 percent of the bonds. Pension funds are now the largest source of investment capital for the American capitalist system. And most importantly, pension-fund capital is neither privately owned nor publicly owned. It is a unique new form of wealth to which three major parties have potentially competing claims: the private financial community, the unions, and the state and local government.

There are presently over 500,000 pension plans in the United States, many with assets as great or greater than some of those listed as a sampling in Table 3, and their rate of growth is estimated to be 10% per year. One example illustrates the potential importance of these funds in the stock market. In 1978, the Senator Metcalf Report showed TIAA-CREF (Teachers Insurance and Annuity Association–College Retirement Equities Fund) was the third largest institutional investor in the country with assets of about $10 billion.

An even more startling conclusion emerges when one compares the asset value and income of some of the largest pension funds with the largest U.S. corporations (e.g., American Telephone & Telegraph and Exxon), moderate-size corporations (e.g., Sears Roebuck), and small but rapidly growing corporations (e.g., Federal Express). Table 4 shows this comparison. In asset value, the largest pension funds are rapidly approaching the value of America's largest corporations, and they have surpassed or are approaching the value of medium-size and small corporations. This finding is particularly important when one remembers that growth of the largest corporations in the depressed economy of the early 1980s is typically below the 10% per year estimated for pension funds. Not only has wealth been redistributed in terms of stock ownership, but the wealth of

Table 3
Estimated Concentration of Wealth in American Society, 1979

Family or Institution	*Estimated Wealth and Worth in Billions of $*
California State Public Employees & Teachers Retirement System	13.3
TIAA-CREF (Private College & University Retirement Plan)	9.4
New York Life Insurance Company Investments	9.1
New York State Common Retirement Fund	6.8
New York City Employees Retirement System	6.7
New York State Teachers Retirement System	5.8
United States Steel Employees Pension Plan	4.1
du Pont Family Investments	4.0
Mellon Family Investments	4.0
General Motors Retirement Program for Salaried Employees	4.0
New Jersey State Common Pension Funds	4.0
Wisconsin State Board of Investment	3.8
General Motors Hourly-Rate Employees Pension Plan	3.7
General Electric Pension Plan	3.6
Ohio State Teachers Retirement System	3.4
Texas Teachers Retirement System	3.4
New York City Teachers Retirement System	3.3
Ford Motor General Retirement Plan	1.8
Harvard University Portfolio	1.5
Ford Family Investments	1.5
Getty Family Investments	1.5
Hunt Family Investments	1.5
Rockefeller Family Investments	1.5
ATT Bell System Savings Plan for Salaried Employees	1.5
Eastman Kodak Retirement Income Plan	1.4
Bethlehem Steel and Subsidiary Companies Pension Plan	1.1
Union Carbide Retirement Program for Employees	1.0
Pennsylvania Bell Telephone Plan for Employees Pension Benefits	.6
Tennessee Valley Authority Retirement System	.5
Yale University Portfolio	.4
Grumman Corporation Employees Retirement System	.4
Kennedy Family Investments	.4
International Paper Company Employee Retirement Plan	.3
Goodrich (B. F.) Pension Plan	.3
Sears Roebuck Employees Savings and Profit Sharing Plan	.2
Delta Pilots Retirement Plan	.2
United Mine Workers 1974 Pension Plan	.2
Sheet Metal Workers National Pension Plan	.1
Carpenters Pension Plan of Ohio	.1

Primary Source: *Pension Investments: A Social Audit* (New York: Corporate Data Exchange, 1979).

Table 4
Comparison of Corporations and Pension Funds, 1979
(all figures in millions of $)

Corporation or Pension Fund	*Estimated Corporate Book Value*[1]	*Estimated Fund Worth*	*Corporate Sales or Revenues*	*Estimated Fund Income*[2]
American Telephone & Telegraph	43,043		45,408	
Exxon	21,309		79,106	
State of California Public Employees and Teachers		13,300		1,197
TIAA-CREF		9,400		846
Sears Roebuck	7,451		17,514	
New York City Employees		6,675		601
Ohio State Teachers		3,424		308
Federal Express	77		259	

[1]Tangible book value per share times common shares outstanding.
[2]Estimated at about 9% of worth; 5% return for equities and 14% return for bonds, certificates of deposit, etc.
Primary Sources: *Pension Investments: A Social Audit* (New York: Corporate Data Exchange, 1979) and *Value Line Investment Survey*, Part 3: Ratings & Reports (New York: Arnold Bernhard & Co., 1981).

public funds may soon surpass the wealth of most of the country's large companies.[1]

One additional trend has contributed to the public redistribution of stock ownership. Over 3,000 American companies offer programs of employee stock ownership through a variety of organizational forms (O'Toole, 1979). For example, cooperatives are businesses in which ideally each worker owns equal shares, is paid equally, and has an equal voice in the governance of the company. Companies successfully utilizing this form of organization have included garbage collection firms in San Francisco, California, and plywood companies in Oregon and Washington. In contrast, joint partnerships include companies in which a founder shares ownership with employees or employees own a large block of shares, and the remainder is owned by the local community or is traded on the stock market. Examples have included International Group Plans (insurance) of Washington, D.C., Vermont Asbestos Company, Saratoga Knitting Mill, the *Kansas City Star,* and Mohawk Valley Community Corporation of New York (manufacturers of library furniture).

Finally ESOPs (Employee Stock Ownership Plans) have been used by some of America's largest and most prominent corporations, including American Telephone & Telegraph,[2] Atlantic Richfield, Mobil Oil, and Sears Roebuck. ESOPs have also been used by the Ralph M. Parsons Co. (engineering) in California, Hallmark (greeting cards), and South Bend Lathe Company. There are many setups for these plans, but typically, a fixed amount of stock is placed in trust as collateral for a loan drawn upon a bank. As the loan is paid off, the stock held in trust is transferred to employees.

All of these plans combine various goals—democratization of the workplace, increasing worker motivation, reform of capitalism through authentic worker ownership—in varying degrees. Obviously, there is an important difference between workers owning a small portion of shares in Mobil Oil and true worker ownership plus control of a South Bend Lathe. There is also continuing disagreement about the success of these various programs in meeting the desired goals. Nevertheless, it is likely that the trend toward worker ownership of stock shares will continue in the future.

All of these trends have also meant the rise of professional and expert fund management. However, the performance of professional fund managers has been disappointing at best and catastrophic at worst. This is also related to structural changes in the market and investment behavior.

THE PROBLEM OF EXPERT FUND MANAGERS

Almost all financial observers, with the possible exception of fund managers themselves, seem to agree that the performance of most managed funds has ranged from disappointing to terrible. Rifkin and Barber (1978, p. 122) point out that, from the end of 1966 to the end of 1976, the annual return on investment for pension fund equity was 33% below the average annual return of the Standard & Poors 500 index stocks (a representative cross-section of stocks listed on the New York Exchange). During that time, the S&P average annual return was 6.6% while banks averaged 4.4% and insurance companies 4% on the funds they managed. On the whole, pension members would have been better off putting their money into straight compounded savings for that decade.

In 1979, a study of a representative sample of 571 pension and profit sharing funds containing both equity and bond portfolios analyzed performance for varying periods of time ranging up to 15 years (Elia, 1979a). This study found the average performance for these 571 funds fell well short of matching both the average inflation rate and the average rate of return on cash equivalents such as Treasury bills. This poor average return held true whether the period investigated was 3, 5, 10, or 15 years. In addition, the average performance for those funds committed primarily to stocks failed to keep up with the Standard & Poors index:

> Other data provided . . . show that over the past 15 years, only 22 of every 100 funds matched or exceeded the average annual return of the S&P 500. The number of overachievers was even smaller over the past 10 years—16 out of every 100. Thus a very large majority of the funds achieved poorer results for their clients than the showing made, by the [average for the 571 funds] (Elia, 1979a, p. 32).

These findings were particularly distressing since the S&P performance for this period was also poor as the stock market experienced frequent declines.

From 1973 to 1974, the assets of some pension funds decreased by 30 to 40% (Rifkin & Barber, 1978, p. 122). In addition, good or bad fund performance in the study seemed to be unrelated to the type of management (banks, insurance companies, or investment counsellors). At the same time, funds managed by smaller institutions tended to be more conservative in investments and to outperform the giants (Elia, 1979b).

Ineffective management of a pension fund can also harm workers in other ways (Nader & Blackwell, 1973). In 1980, a bipartisan Northeast-Northwest Congressional Coalition, consisting of 213 congressmen from 18 states, announced that the manner in which pension funds were invested actually accelerated unemployment and plant closings in economically troubled areas of the country. In effect, the contributions of workers were assisting their own future unemployment and loss of pension rights as capital was diverted from areas needing development to create new jobs. Fund managers, seeking the highest possible rate of return and favoring boom-town regions (the American sunbelt and Southwest), avoided firms and corporations in the North and Middle West. Senator John H. Chafee, Republican of Rhode Island, stated:

> The workers in our part of the country who participate in pension plans could receive substantial long-term benefits, including greater job security, if more of their pension funds were directed to local investments (''Pension-Fund Investing,'' 1980).

Pensions are not the only funds which have performed badly because of ineffective management. The National Association of College and University Business Officers (NACUBO) ranks the performance of college and university funds after factoring out new donations and withdrawals of principal but including dividend and interest income. NACUBO announced that for the 10-year period ending June 30, 1978, the University of Pennsylvania portfolio ranked 94th out of 94 funds analyzed (Pappas, 1980). Like many other universities, Penn pools most of its endowment money and invests the pool in a portfolio of stocks and bonds. Between the end of 1972 and the fall of 1974, the value of Penn's fund dropped about 40%. As of June 30, 1979, the pool was about $127 million out of a total endowment of about $196 million. The bad performance of Penn's fund was of particular concern to both parents and students because yearly tuition increases are needed to cover operating expenses. Most colleges and universities would benefit greatly if their funds could take over the burden of some of these expenses.

Finally, in the fall of 1980, *Forbes* magazine (see ''How *Forbes* Rates,'' 1980) studied 109 mutual funds from November 29, 1968 to June 30, 1980. The funds were generally rated for performance against one another on a scale of A, B, C, D, or F. *Forbes* found that for periods when the market was advancing, the funds averaged a C rating. For periods of market decline, the funds averaged D. From 1968 to 1980, while the average annual total return for the S&P 500 average was 4.5 percent, the funds returned 3.5%. From June 29, 1979 to June 30, 1980, the S&P returned 5.2% from dividend income, while the funds were returning an average of 4.2%.

These examples of poor to awful fund performance can be multiplied almost without end. What has been happening to the management of the ''largest pool of social capital'' in American history? Fund managers have been operating in a changing structural context which encourages them to be too conservative, too willing to trade continuously, and too likely to engage in a form of unwise speculation.

CONSERVATIVE FUND MANAGEMENT

Conservatism is reflected by the avoidance of higher risk investments and the favoring of investments which have historically paid high returns and have not been subject to severe fluctuations. The problem with extreme conservatism is that it may guarantee a performance no better than the market and, in some cases, much worse. The changing contemporary economy no longer clearly signals what is necessarily a reasonable risk, as evidenced by the 1970s collapse of the American automobile industry. Yesterday's blue chip may not be tomorrow's, as many fund managers learned with the sudden decline of the government and corporate bond market in the early 1980s. Extreme conservatism may also lead to excessive trading in order to stay even with the changing market and to enhance fund performance. Often such trading is reflected in a willingness to follow the crowd and buy or sell when other managers are doing the same thing. However, the crowd, influenced by expert opinion, can often be wrong in the short-term, as Granville's advice to his clients showed.

Fund managers are conservative because they operate legally and morally under ''the prudent man'' rule while often utilizing a theory of efficient markets. In 1830, the Massachusetts Supreme Judicial Court ruled that:

> All that can be required of a trustee is that he shall conduct himself faithfully and exercise a sound discretion. He is to observe how men of prudence, discretion and intelligence manage their own affairs, not in regard to speculation, but in regard to permanent disposition of their funds, considering the probable income as well as the probable safety of the capital investment (Porterfield, 1980).

This ruling was modified and expanded a number of times from 1869 on, but the net effect has been to make fund managers extremely cautious. For some managers, the prudent approach in today's economy could be to do nothing differently and avoid risky investment. One of the problems with prudence is that it may be fairly successful in the very long-run, but it can result in unsatisfactory short-term performance (Bulkeley, 1979).

The Efficient Market Hypothesis, discussed in more detail in chapter 3, argues that there is really no reason to try to beat the market since markets already operate in the most efficient manner possible (Langbein & Posner, 1976). The price of a security represents the value of its future earnings, and if there were consensus that a particular stock was too high or too low, no one would want to buy or sell. Therefore, any stock is appropriately priced at its current level, and all an investor can do is try to predict future earnings better than others. However, most large investors have fairly equivalent research sources for obtaining information about a corporation, and modern communications are so effective that all important information is theoretically available to all such investors at the same time. Therefore, don't try to outdo the market; simply be content to stay with it.

A number of studies have attempted to prove the validity of this theory. In 1967, three executives of *Forbes* magazine (''Dart It All,'' 1979) threw darts at the stock page from *The New York Times*. They came up with a list of 28 stocks in which they invested $1,000 each. From 1967 to 1979, the dart board fund grew from $28,000 to $43,279, a gain of 55%. For the same period, the S&P 500 gained 8.2% while the Dow Jones Industrial average lost 4 percent. So far there is no evidence that fund managers have started using darts to make investment choices, though some admit they feel like flipping coins. However, fund managers do utilize indexing which attempts to copy the performance of leading averages. An indexed fund using the S&P 500 would have increased about 8% from 1967 to 1979, not the 55% of the dart board fund. It is also important to note that indexing, darting and coin flips fail to take into account any major social, political or other changes taking place in the economy which might influence future performance of specific industries or corporations. This may be why, when the stock market suffered its major decline from 1973 to 1974, pension funds were saddled with substantial equity investment (Tepper, 1977).

Though the Efficient Market Hypothesis claims that plentiful information cancels out the attempt of large investors to best one another, some contemporary information is so complex that even the experts do not know what to make of it. A brokerage house executive commented on his attempts to advise clients about oil and gas stocks:

> I don't know what to tell them. Heck, I can't tell whether a discovery in the Overthrust Belt is more important than one in Louisiana. We try to go after [fundamental information], but still it's like flipping a coin (Paul, 1981, p. 50).

If technical information is difficult for professional investors to understand, social and political information is almost unintelligible to them.

In reality, fund managers have to pick not only the stocks they feel are good candidates, but they also have to pick the stocks they think will be favored by others. It doesn't do much good to hold an investment which you think is good but no one else knows about, since demand for the investment is what results in capital appreciation. Therefore, trying to guess how the crowd will move has become a reflexive response among fund investors. When Granville recommended to his clients that they sell immediately, many fund managers responded not because they necessarily agreed with his advice, but because they thought others would sell and they wanted to take their profits while they could.

Such a concern for market or investor psychology leads to frequent buying and selling panics as fund managers copy the behavior of one another (Briggs, 1981). Too, the frustration experienced by fund managers who do not meet portfolio performance objectives during a certain period of time creates an increasing emphasis on continuous monitoring of very short-term results. This short-term orientation is enhanced by recent disclosure requirements which obligate managers to publish all holdings at the end of each quarter. As a consequence, markets in the late 1970s and early 80s were characterized by heightened trading toward the end of each quarter (called end-of-quarter "window-dressing") as fund managers cleaned up their holdings for public disclosure. The continuous "churning" of portfolios without regard for long-term consequences incurs heavy commission expenses for investors in addition to the costs of maintaining large research staffs (see Lejeune, Chapter 9, for a more thorough definition of this deviant activity). This practice occurs despite the fact there is some evidence that pension funds with relatively high trading activity do slightly better on the short-term, but they do not do as well as low-turnover pension funds over longer periods (Elia, 1979a). Is there a pattern to changing forms of investing by institutional managers? The concept of professionalism seems to apply.

PROFESSIONALISM AND INVESTMENT GAMBLING

What has happened is that fund managers have become increasingly professionalized, and they and their clients are experiencing the problems associated with this change. Several studies have identified the important characteristics of a profession and the problems associated with these unique occupational forms (Carr-Saunders, 1933; Cogan, 1953), particularly as they apply to traditional professions such as law and medicine. These characteristics and problems appear to be increasingly associated with institutional managers. All professions have in common four major characteristics:

1. personal service by the professional to a client with special needs;
2. use of a technical body of knowledge involving esoteric language and complex theories;
3. licensure and regulation by the state after close consultation with the professionals involved; and
4. peer-group review done by professionals resulting in a strong peer identification.

All professions develop these characteristics allegedly to insure altruistic service of the highest quality to clients and to maintain a professional commitment to upholding societal goals and values. Ironically, each characteristic also creates problems, particularly in the client-professional relationship, which can eventually attentuate the altruistic orientation and high quality of service provided (Lowry & Rankin, 1977).

First, the personal service to a client with special needs tends to encourage the professional to focus only on the particular need, resulting in ignorance or neglect of other needs and problems. In medicine, physicians may argue that they should not be concerned about a patient's ability to pay (the need for national medical insurance), or they may not be aware of the social or psychological aspects of an ailment (the need to treat the patient rather than the disease). Or consider the advice frequently supplied by corporate lawyers to the executives of companies facing serious product safety problems. In crises such as Firestone Tire and Rubber's unsafe 500-radial tires and Hooker Chemical Company's involvement in the pollution of Love Canal, corporations rarely show public sympathy (Hayes, 1980). The executive response typically involves placing the blame on consumers (customers improperly used the tires) or the government (pollution regulations make it impossible to function effectively). In many cases, corporate lawyers counsel against any show of sympathy or voluntary compensation since such gestures could be viewed by juries as admissions of guilt and lead to substantial financial damages. The irony is that this narrowly focused professional advice may be contrary to management's long-run interests. When public outrage increases, consumers start boycotting the corporation's products and government agencies require more stringent controls, the company may experience serious financial and political problems.

Second, the use of technical jargon and complex theories by professional fund managers makes it difficult for clients to understand the full nature and consequences of the services being provided. The more technical their presentations to clients, the more expert these professional managers are assumed to be. The use of such esoteric knowledge and theories can therefore cause professionals to develop a feeling of omniscience, such that their investment decisions may mislead and hence misguide their clients.

A related problem is that fund managers err frequently because the information available on securities is so voluminous and complex that they can get lost in the morass of statistics and figures. While caught up in their self-presentation game, then, they may not be able to see the forest because of so many nonidentifiable trees (Dreman, 1979). For example, a focus on the internal aspects of General Motors Corporation may cloud what is happening to the American and world auto industry as a whole. Or, labor union pension fund managers who worry about short-term dividend and interest return plus capital appreciation while investing in corporations, may overlook, in the long run, that jobs may be destroyed and workers eventually lose their pension rights.

Third, state regulation, only after close consultation with professionals and peer groups, leads to a variety of problems. For instance, investigations into cases of fraud, incompetence and malpractice may be covered up or obscured because professional fund managers may be reluctant to cast aspersions on specific individuals or on their occupation as a whole. The result is that clients and the public find it difficult, if not impossible, to play any active role in this process, or to be able to adequately assess fund managers' performances.

Fourth, fund managers are markedly peer oriented. This colleague orientation may erode their professional commitment to the client. Particularly in periods of economic uncertainty, fund managers look to one another, not to clients or the public, for guidelines on behavior. This peer orientation can result in investment fads or crazes which are neither prudent nor rewarding. Since peers insist on comparative performance as the basic measure of competence, fund managers are enticed to continuously switch investments in order to stay with or ahead of the pack (see Klausner, Chapter 4, for another look at how these fads and fashions affect market functioning).

Professional peer group orientation also mitigates against the notion that public controls developed in conjunction with professional advice provide adequate checks and balances against fraudulent or unwise behavior. A Securities and Exchange Commission special report on the Hunt brothers' 1980 speculation in silver criticized five major brokerage firms. The report stated that the exchange had failed to receive sufficient information from Wall Street houses doing business with the Hunts, that the information received was nonverifiable, and that brokerage firms did not notify the exchange of the potential crisis which was developing (Cole, 1982; Noble, 1982). A professional desire to keep problem information within one's own family and a feeling that professionals could easily handle any difficulties themselves seem to have played a role.

Finally, professionalization can encourage certain kinds of risk taking which may not be prudent or in the interests of a client. Just as physicians are sometimes tempted to perform unnecessary major operations, and lawyers are sometimes tempted to pursue expensive and psychologically distressing court cases, professional money managers may become gamblers, rather than investors.

Hirshleifer (1971) distinguishes between investors and speculators. Investors seek to provide for consumption over time (present and future) in the face of uncertainty. They act essentially as consumers, investing in order to save while minimizing risks. Investors do not attempt to profit from anticipated price revaluations, by holding excess quantities of particular assets against future price increases. An example of the pure investor-as-consumer is the homeowner who purchases a house to live in, not for future profit from eventual resale.

In contrast, speculators believe they are in a position to predict and act upon market revaluations to come. The tendency to speculate is enhanced by the belief in the availability of better information (insider knowledge of what a corporation is doing), low risk aversion (the willingness to take greater risks), and low transactions costs (related to larger amounts of resources available for investment). By placing themselves in a position to act favorably upon future stock prices, speculators act as gamblers. The pure gambler enjoys high risk, can enter the game relatively inexpensively and believes that special knowledge and skill (mathematical chance, understanding of odds, psychological motivation) are crucial. These characteristics describe the social context within which many managers of large funds find themselves.

But are all forms of speculation necessarily gambling and, therefore, destabilizing for the stock market process? Hirshleifer argues that the distinction between intrinsic-value and technical speculators is important. Intrinsic-value speculators try to find undervalued stocks to buy or overvalued stocks to sell. If their judgment is correct, their trading behavior moves stock prices closer to equilibrium values, and they perform a kind of arbitrageur function for the market by keeping prices in line with costs. Once having taken a position in a stock, the intrinsic-value speculator is rewarded by sharing this information with others, in the hopes of encouraging them to make the same move. If an intrinsic-value speculator is consistently wrong in decisions made, that speculator will not be able to keep speculating for long and others will pay no attention to the advice offered. For these reasons, Hirshleifer argues that intrinsic-value speculation is stabilizing for the stock market in the long run.

In contrast, technical speculators do not care about the intrinsic value of an investment. They study market mechanics, psychology and processes, and they act as gamblers. Large scale technical speculation can create a self-validating prophecy, when attempts to rush in and profit from some assumed movement in the market creates the appearance of movement. Since professional technicians (fund managers) can move faster than nonprofessional technicians (individual investors) because they possess greater assets and better access to information channels, the former are more likely to profit while the latter are more likely to fail. This is consistent with the Wall Street myth that "the little people are always wrong." Excessive technical speculation can be responsible for large and sudden market swings that create false valuation signals, misleading investors as well as the corporation requiring capital raised through equity investment.

In Chart 2, the distinctions between investing and speculating are compared to illustrate the impact on market stability. An example of a strategic investor would be the individual who buys 300 shares of American Telephone and Telegraph for later retirement income. This type of investor, when present in the market in large numbers, provides great stability. At the same time, stable market conditions can encourage much strategic investment. Similarly, as Hirshleifer indicates, intrinsic-value speculators can encourage long-run market stability.

Just as technical speculators are destabilizing for the market, the behavior of tactical investors is also a form of gambling. Tactical investors continually shift money, usually in the form of savings and other available cash, from one type of investment resource to another (from savings banks, to money funds, to gold, to art, etc.) in order to achieve the highest yield and security in a period of fluctuat-

Chart 2
Types of Investors and Speculators
and Market Stability

		Condition of the Market	
		Stable	Unstable
Types of Market Participants	Investors:	strategic	tactical
	Speculators:	intrinsic–value	technical

ing rates of return and high uncertainty. Tactical investors worry about immediate return in favor of long-term growth and security, and, like gamblers, they attempt to assess investor motivations and psychology, and the impact of unpredictable events (war, recession, etc.).

When there was a preponderance of small and individual investors in the stock markets, strategic investment and intrinsic-value speculation tended to prevail. In contrast, fund and institutional managers have, in recent years, increasingly acted as tactical investors and technical speculators, both in response to and thereby creating unstable market conditions. This tendency is contrary to the interests of those whose funds they manage (workers contributing to retirement plans, for example), and it makes corporate planning and analysis extremely difficult.

To recapitulate, the financial market has undergone major structural changes in the last sixty years. These changes have given rise to new forms of investment behavior which are often destabilizing to an orderly market process and result in poor performance. Does this mean that we could have another 1929? Probably not, but we could have a 1989 version of a market crisis. Just as the next war never looks exactly like the last war, the next recession, depression, or stock market "crash" will not look like previous financial crises. What is needed are new relationships between fund managers and their clients and new public policies to deal with the changing character of Wall Street.

NOTE

1. Clearly, a comparison of corporate wealth ("real" assets) with fund wealth ("financial" assets) is somewhat problematic. Despite the limitations of these comparisons, however, the purpose of Table 4 is to illustrate the relative strength public funds have attained.
2. All references to American Telephone and Telegraph are before the January 1, 1984, breakup.

REFERENCES

Arenson, K. W. The great crash of '79. *The New York Times,* October 14, 1979, Sec. 3, pp. 1; 18.
As a seismologist, he's a good stock analyst. *The New York Times,* April 11, 1981, p. 16.

Briggs, J. A. What's Japanese for 'herd instinct'? *Forbes,* April 27, 1981, p. 62.
Bulkeley, W. M. Manager of Harvard's endowment finds staid policy stayed effective. *The Wall Street Journal,* October 23, 1979, p. 33.
Carrington, T. Computers, luck help big board handle large increases in volume. *The Wall Street Journal,* October 14, 1982, p. 33.
Carr-Saunders, A. M. *Professions: Their organization and place in society.* Oxford: Clarendon, 1933.
Cogan, M. L. Toward a definition of professions. *Harvard Educational Review,* 1953, *23,* 48–49.
Cole, R. J. Bache firm fined $400,000 for role in '80 silver crises. *The New York Times,* October 21, 1982, pp. 1; D4.
Dart it all! *Forbes,* March 5, 1979, pp. 108–109.
Dorfman, D. The market in crisis. *Boston Globe,* April 1, 1981, p. 39.
Dreman, D. Why the experts are nearly always wrong. *Forbes,* November 26, 1979, pp. 117–121.
Elia, C. J. Pension fund performances are rated as poor regardless of type of manager, study shows. *The Wall Street Journal,* March 26, 1979, p. 32. (a)
Elia, C. J. Broader disclosure of institutional holdings likely to rekindle concern over dominance. *The Wall Street Journal,* March 27, 1979, p. 47. (b)
Hayes, T. C. Corporate reply to social crisis. *The New York Times,* June 7, 1980, pp. D1; D8.
Hirshleifer, J. *Reflections on the role and functioning of the organized exchanges* (Report No. P-4666). Santa Monica: The Rand Corporation, 1971.
How *Forbes* rates the funds. *Forbes,* September 1, 1980, pp. 74; 81–82.
Langbein, J. H., & Posner, R. A. The revolution in trust investment law. *American Bar Association Journal,* June 1976, pp. 764–768.
Lezner, R. Seven days in March. *Boston Globe,* May 27, 1981, pp. 47; 54.
Lohr, S. The puzzling stock market. *The New York Times,* January 13, 1981, pp. D1; D9.
Lorie, J. H. The second great crash. *The Wall Street Journal,* June 2, 1980, p. 23.
Lowry, R. P., & Rankin, R. P. Professionalization. In R. P. Lowry & R. P. Rankin (Eds.), *Sociology: Social science and social concern* (3rd ed.). Lexington, Mass.: D.C. Heath, 1977.
Metz, R. $100 million stockholders. *The New York Times,* April 15, 1981, p. D10.
Miller, J. S.E.C.: Watchdog 1929 lacked. *The New York Times,* October 31, 1979, pp. D1; D19.
Nader, R., & Blackwell, K. *You and your pension.* New York: Grossman, 1973.
Noble, K. B. S.E.C. staff faults brokers in report on '80 silver crisis. *The New York Times,* October 21, 1982, p. D4.
O'Toole, J. The uneven record of employee ownership. *Harvard Business Review,* December 1979, 185–197.
Pappas, V. Penn finds it needs more than friends to run endowment. *The Wall Street Journal,* March 26, 1980, pp. 1; 35.
Paul, B. Puzzling petroleum. *The Wall Street Journal,* January 21, 1981, p. 50.
Pension-fund investing held harmful to workers. *The New York Times,* December 24, 1980, p. 9.
Porterfield, R. A difficult definition: The 'prudent man'. *Boston Globe,* April 29, 1980, pp. 31; 40.
Rifkin, J., & Barber, R. *The North will rise again: Pensions, politics and power in the 1980s.* Boston: Beacon Press, 1978.
Solomon, E. The impact of the emerging system on securities trading and the economy. In H. G. Manne, E. Solomon, K. J. Cohen, & J. Baumol (Eds.), *Wall Street in transition.* New York: New York University Press, 1974.
Tepper, I. Risk vs. return in pension fund investment. *Harvard Business Review,* March–April 1977, p. 103.

PART II

THEORIES OF THE MARKET

ECONOMIC THEORIES OF THE STOCK MARKET:

RANDOM OR NON-RANDOM WALK?

Vincent J. Tarascio

Much of the research conducted in the financial community regarding stock prices falls into two general categories—fundamental and technical analysis. The fundamental approach tends to focus on those factors which influence corporate earnings, since earnings are assumed to have the most important influence on stock prices. Hence if future earnings are known, then the course of stock prices can be predicted. In practice, earnings are difficult to predict because they are influenced by other factors, such as the prices of output and production costs, which depend on many "external" factors such as demand for output, foreign competition, interest rates, wages, price levels, etc., which, in turn, are affected by monetary and fiscal policy, the general state of economic activity, government regulation, both domestic and foreign, and so on. So if earnings are to be predicted accurately, one must know virtually everything going on in the economy—the problem of "infinite regress," as it is known in economics. In spite of such complexities, fundamental analysis accepts the limitations of human capabilities and settles for less than complete knowledge.

On the other hand, technical analysis, recognizing the complexities mentioned above, admits to the futility of predicting earnings, and instead stresses the behavior of stock prices themselves. Underlying technical analysis is the premise that all relevant information is reflected in the prices of stocks, and therefore the behavior of stock prices is a better indicator of future prices. In addition to the analysis of stock prices, other "indicators" internal to the market are presumed to affect stock prices, such as volume of trading, number of advancing stocks and declining stocks, new highs and new lows, and various indexes of stock prices such as the Dow Jones Industrial Average or the Standard and Poor's 500 Index, and so on. Also the behavior of various categories of stock market participants, such as specialists, who make markets in stock on the exchanges, short sellers, and odd-lot (who buy and sell less than 100 shares) traders are studied as to their effect on stock prices. What is important is that technical analysis relies on historical patterns as a basis for predicting future stock prices and/or trend recognition.

What is implied in both the fundamental and technical approach is that stock price changes can be predicted. Brokerage firms, investment advisors, banks, and other institutions devote considerable resources, and their clients, both individual and institutional, pay considerable amounts, either directly or indirectly for advice based on such analyses. It is one thing to forecast, or make recommendations based on forecasts, it is quite another thing to be *consistently* accurate in forecasting. Unfortunately, the financial community has been characterized by an abundance of the former and a dearth of the latter.

In recent years, there have been many studies by academic researchers which account for such a poor performance and which cast doubt on the efficiency of both fundamental and technical approaches to stock price research. Such doubts are reflected in what has become known as the Random Walk Hypothesis. The technical aspects of the hypothesis will be discussed later in this chapter. At this point, it is important to become familiar with the presumed environment in which stock market decisions are made, which is linked to the Random Walk Hypothesis.

In practice, individuals, whether they be private investors or institutional managers, make decisions to buy or sell stocks on the basis of future expectations. Thus, expectations are formed on the basis of very "imperfect" knowledge of the present, to say nothing of the future. Such expectations are modified with new information. It is this very reaction to new information (which alters expectations) which causes fluctuations in stock prices from day to day, week to week, and month to month. Since the arrival of this information cannot be predicted in advance, it takes on the appearance of a random process, and hence resulting stock price reactions convey a similar process at work. The speed by which stock prices adjust to new information is influenced by the efficiency of the stock market as an "information processor." The stock market is viewed as an efficient information processor. What this amounts to saying is that in the absence of "inside" information, it is difficult, if not impossible, for any system deriving from fundamental or technical analysis to outperform the "general market,'' in the *long-run*. This conclusion has attracted wide attention in the financial community for obvious reasons; it questions the basis for its recommendations to the investing public. The implication for the investor is that all one can hope to do is to buy and hold a well diversified portfolio of stocks which is expected to grow with the economy. Short-term trading in the hope of achieving superior results is not profitable to the investor, but only to the brokerage firm whose commissions depend on turnover.

The real issue then is whether or not short-term trading can produce results superior to long-term investing (buy and hold), and this is why much of the literature on the random walk is devoted to the analysis of short-term trading systems. My purpose is to reexamine the issue of the random nature of stock prices within this context, namely, the Efficient Market Hypothesis, and the random versus the nonrandom nature of stock prices in a short-term trading environment.

BACKGROUND

Prior to the 1960s, stock prices were assumed to be determined in the same way as any other price, namely by conditions of supply and demand. Although this statement is true, it is too vague to explain precisely the process of stock price occurrence. What was needed was a theory to explain those factors which influence supply and demand. Academicians in the fields of finance and economics contributed to what eventually evolved as the Efficient Market Hypothesis (EMH), and this hypothesis has become the prevailing doctrine in those fields.

The implications of the EMH are very important for ''applied'' stock market research characteristic of the financial community. Such research generally takes the form of fundamental and technical analysis. The EMH casts doubt on the efficacy of such research. Indeed, with a few exceptions, such research is considered worthless in terms of outperforming the ''market'' or some randomly selected portfolio.

In view of the important implications of the EMH, it is not surprising to find an entire literature devoted to ''testing'' it empirically (some of which were discussed in chapter 2). Since the EMH cannot be tested directly, its various forms have been tested indirectly. The results of these ''tests'' have seemed to be supportive of the EMH, but more recently results seem too mixed so that, at least for the present, the status of the EMH is more tentative. Nevertheless, it still remains the dominant ''explanation'' of stock price determination among academic researchers.

THE EFFICIENT MARKET HYPOTHESIS

The EMH states that the market is an efficient information processor, so that any new information will cause prices to adjust quickly to that new information.

What this means is that it is difficult, if not impossible, to make money on the basis of newly available information, since it is quickly discounted. If the market were ''inefficient'' in its response to new information then the delay in discounting through price adjustments would present the opportunity to profit from such information.

The ''*weak form*'' of the EMH states that stock prices approximate a random walk. The term random walk has both a mathematical and statistical meaning. As applied to stock prices, the term means that stock price changes more or less wander aimlessly over time. Knowledge of past price changes is no predictor of future price changes.

The ''*semi-strong form*'' of EMH states that as soon as information becomes public knowledge, the stock price adjusts usually instantaneously and accurately to such knowledge. Sometimes prices will overreact or underreact so the adjustment is not perfect. Hence recognition is given to an efficient, but not perfect, market. The semi-strong form of the EMH is consistent with the weak form: a continuous stream of information is becoming public knowledge randomly, and, in response, affected stock prices will be walking randomly.

The ''*strong form*'' of the EMH states that the stock market adjusts rapidly not only to public information but to all information, public or not. In other words, it takes account of ''inside'' information as well. Obviously, this is the most difficult form to test, since inside information trading is illegal.

Each form of the EMH has been subjected to empirical investigations, and, as stated above, most have been supportive of the EMH. What is important for our purposes is that those which are supportive recognize some imperfection in the time rate of adjustment, of price changes in response to new information (usually due to under and overreactions). When transaction costs are included, however, these investigations maintain that any apparent advantage over the performance of a ''buy-and-hold'' strategy which could be gained by trading either with or against such ''random shocks'' disappears. This lagged time rate of adjustment (caused by random shocks fluctuation) is acknowledged by both the weak form, in cases where some degree of time dependence is found in the form of serial correlations, and by the semi-strong form, caused by ''unexpected'' new information such as may be found in annual earnings announcements.

The purpose of this chapter is to examine the weak form of the EMH. Specifically, I pose the question of whether the market exhibits random ''walk-arounds'' (a fluctuating price pattern related to the random availability of public information) or ''walk-backs'' (a return to the ''true'' value level from the under or overvalued price range which was caused by the excessive public reaction and, hence, random shock). In the first condition, the market can be said to exhibit true randomness, while the latter condition consists of an alternating time series structure, sometimes exhibiting randomness and sometimes not. A ''test'' using daily data will be described and the results presented. Hopefully, this chapter will clarify some issues related to the EMH controversy.

Weak Form Tests of the EMH

Although a spate of research has been conducted by economists to test the validity of the EMH, the results have been highly inconclusive. Supporting the EMH are tests which were unable to show any recognizable pattern to the fluctuation of price levels. Such studies as Fama (1965; 1970), Hagerman and Richmond (1973) and Solnik (1973) seem to demonstrate no evidence of substantial direct dependence between lagged price changes or returns to common stocks. Alexander (1961), Fama (1965), Fama and Blume (1966), and Van Horne and Parker (1967) found that "runs" (continuous price changes over several days) could not be used as a basis for generating abnormally high returns during subsequent days (even when combined with filter rules, as will be discussed shortly). Finally, Fama and MacBeth (1972) found that monthly returns were indicative of risks, and little else. The time series data used in the above studies involved daily to monthly observations.

Refuting the EMH's weak form, Niederhoffer and Osborne (1966) found evidence of time dependence (patterning) on tickertape transactions. Green and Fielitz (1977) have found evidence of long-time dependency in stock prices, and Osborne (1962) noted some substantial departures from a simple picture of a random walk. Rozeff and Kinney (1976) detected seasonality in the New York Stock Exchange Index, whereas Umstead (1977) found a four-year seasonal structure to the Standard and Poor index of price changes.

While these tests have not yielded unanimous results, the balance seems to lie in favor of the EMH. It might be worthwhile to point out that the semi-strong test results were less clear; in general it is difficult to discern a substantial case for or against the existence of patterned overreactions and walk-backs when the market is presented with unexpected news.

The Ranging Pattern of Stock Prices

It will be recalled that the weak form of the EMH is merely a restatement of the Random Walk Hypothesis. This hypothesis deserves further discussion. One way of expressing the Random Walk Hypothesis is to say that price *changes* are independent in time, or statistically, that there exists no "serial correlation" (patterned fluctuation from one day to the next) between successive price changes.[1] Therefore some empirical studies have focused on serial correlation.

Kendall (1953) and Alexander (1961) found little evidence of statistical dependence using weekly and longer time series data. However, Fama (1965) showed the existence of serial correlation between successive changes in the natural log of price for each of the thirty stocks of the Dow Jones Industrial Average, for the time period 1957 to 1962. The serial correlations of successive changes in $\log_e$ price were shown for differencing intervals 1, 4, 9, and 16 days. The table presented by Fama summarizing his results showed some 19 coefficients for various differencing intervals being twice their computed standard errors. Some of these were positive, some were negative. Other coefficients revealed little evidence of statistically "significant" linear dependence. Later Fama (1971, p. 323) concluded that:

> In particular, it is unlikely that small absolute levels of serial correlation that are always observed can be used as the basis of substantially profitable trading systems.

Fama's research results raises two questions: (1) Why did a few individual stocks exhibit serial correlation while most of the others did not? and (2) Why is it not possible to use cases where serial correlation exists as bases for a profitable trading system?

If one looks at an historical time series chart it is obvious that the "structure" of the time series changes, presumably in unpredictable ways. We see, for instance, stock prices wander aimlessly for a while, then "runs" of varying durations develop, actions and reactions occur, and with time, the discerning of "trends" in price movements. No one denies these characteristics of stock prices. The problem has been not so much the observation of such changes historically, but the apparent lack of predictable patterns in this ranging process. It is not surprising that Fama's research would show differential results among stocks; and it is precisely these differential results which are of interest here.

Now let us turn to the second question. Serial correlation itself cannot be used to develop trading rules because it is difficult to know what the degree of serial correlation must be in order to lead to "substantial" profits. So one must look for indirect evidence to develop trading rules. The first major effort of this kind was Alexander's (1961, 1964).

The most thoroughly examined case by Alexander (1961) is one in which a "filter" system was tested. Under this popular trading system, securities are bought and sold according to their patterns of rising and falling prices. When a stock's price rises a predetermined percentage (say, 5%) above its low point, it is purchased and held. As soon as it turns around and falls for that same percentage (5%) from its new high point, it is sold and a "short" position is taken. The short position is held until the stock once again reverses its direction and rises by that 5% from its "bottom." The percentage change in the price of the security used to initiate a position is called the filter. Alexander used filters of from 1 to 50%, using daily data from 1897 to 1959.[2] To the extent that a filter is able to separate out random movements from nonrandom ones, it should lead to superior performance. Although Alexander was optimistic in this regard in his original study, he later (1964) concluded that after transactions costs, his filters were not a practical way to beat the performance of a "buy and hold" strategy.

Soon afterwards, Fama and Blume (1966) found, as did Alexander, that for very small filters it was possible to devise a trading scheme based on very short-term trading.[3] But such schemes also generated high transactions costs, causing their advantage over buy and hold to disappear. Regarding the matter of serial correlation and filters Fama (1971, pp. 325–26) concludes:

> Thus the filter tests, like serial correlations, produce empirically noticeable departures from the strict implication of the efficient markets model. But in spite of any statistical significance they might have, from an economic viewpoint the departures are so small that it seems hardly justified to use them to declare the market inefficient.

In summary, although the existence of some serial correlation and filter rules may raise questions regarding the random walk character of stock prices, neither produce ''practical'' results to invalidate the EMH.

The filter systems approach is intended to capture profits in cases where the direction of the price change will persist. It also allows for price movement reversals, and they too are presumed to persist beyond the filter. Such an approach, which presumes that past price changes will continue in the same direction in the future without considering the *probability* of a price movement reversal, seems lacking.[4]

A better approach would be to identify cases where the probability of a price movement reversal is high and to confine trading activity to such cases. Profits might be made by taking positions *opposite* to the direction of the price movement (in a contrarian manner). Such an approach is appealing from several points of view. To begin, it reduces the problem of ''whip-saws'' (false signals characteristic of filter rules, where the price movement reverses for just long enough to cause a reversal of one's stock position, only to change direction again shortly thereafter) and the transaction costs associated with them. Secondly, it has the appeal of going against the currently available information which is historical and therefore fully discounted. Thirdly, it separates random versus nonrandom movements in a more systematic manner. Such an approach is presented below.

A STATISTICAL DECISION APPROACH

Bussmann (1975) has noted the existence of both random walk-around and walk-back characteristics of time series, suggesting that the random walk is bounded.[5] Price movements beyond these bounds result in walk-backs to random walks. His major interest lies in how corporate earnings affect stock prices. My interest is in prices themselves.[6]

My hypothesis, in this chapter, is that any price movement beyond the bounds of a random walk will eventually walk back to a random walk. Empirically, such boundaries are not directly observable. The problem is to identify points where price movement reversals are expected to take place. Nothing can be inferred directly from prices themselves. What is needed is an index of changes. By decomposing a time series (such as differencing or percentage change in prices), an index is obtained which fluctuates around a mean of zero. Observation can be made of the fluctuations and extreme points identified, where the probability of a price movement reversal is greatest.

Let us define x as the average daily percent change in the price of a stock, or

$$x_i = \frac{P_t - P_{t-i}}{P_{t-i}} \cdot 100/i$$

where i is the time interval in days and P is the stock price. Then x_4, x_{10}, x_{20} will be the average daily percent change in the stock price for 4, 10, 20 day intervals respectively. Most of the time, the ranging pattern of x will be bounded, but occasionally movements beyond the ''normal'' range will be observed.[7] The hypothesis is that such movements of x will eventually reverse themselves to bring x back to its ''normal'' range. This ''walk back'' should result in a price movement reversal. A price movement will take place, but the extent of this reversal is unknown. Hence it seems appropriate that a position will be closed out arbitrarily, let us say within 4, 10, 20, 30 and 50 days, in the tests.[8]

A Test for Walk-Back

The problem is estimating the ''normal'' range of the random variable x. Initially daily prices of five stocks covering the two-year period 1974–1975 were used as test data. Calculations were made for x_4, x_{20}, x_{50}. In addition, stock prices were adjusted relative to the New York State Stock Exchange Index to determine to what extent ''market'' conditions would influence the results. These are designated x_{R20}, and x_{R30}, where the subscript R indicates relative price data.

The test data were expanded to 60 stocks for the period 1975 to mid 1976, and the various xs were calculated daily for each stock. Each time an important price reversal in the movement of a stock was observed (ex-post) the value of the xs were recorded for the point of reversal. Regressions were used to determine the relationship between the reversal xs and the Beta coefficients of the stocks involved, for each of the 5 time intervals studied.[9] Generally stocks with large Beta values tended to have higher extreme values of x. A General Index applicable to any stock whose Beta coefficient is known was developed, in order to ''predict'' reversal points of stocks not previously used in the test data.

Further analysis involved the construction of a cumulative probability table of ranging limits both for the unadjusted xs and the General Index. These are shown in Table 1. Table 1 gives the probability of a price reversal for a stock price movement for the various values of the xs and General Index. The x_4, x_{20}, x_{50} are labeled very short term (VST), short term (ST) and intermediate term (IT), respectively; whereas x_{R20} and x_{R30} are labeled STR and ITR, respectively.

Obviously, whether or not the information in Table 1 can be used to achieve

Table 1
Cumulative Probability Table of Ranging Limits

		Time Interval				
x (*Absolute*) *Value*	*Index* (*Absolute*) *Value*	*VST Probability* (*n* = *364*)	*ST Probability* (*n* = *166*)	*IT Probability* (*n* = *77*)	*STR Probability* (*n* = *166*)	*ITR Probability* (*n* = *128*)
20	50	.00	.00	.01	.00	.01
40	100	.00	.11	.58	.11	.48
60	150	.03	.58	.87	.58	.85
80	200	.09	.82	.97	.82	.97
100	250	.28	.99	.999	.99	.999
120	300	.47	.999	—	.999	—
160	400	.76	—	—	—	—
200	500	.92	—	—	—	—
240	600	.98	—	—	—	—

VST = very short term
ST = short term
IT = intermediate term
STR = short term relative to the NYSE index
ITR = intermediate term relative to the NYSE index

superior results depends to what extent it remains valid over time. If it does then it should be able to ''predict'' reversals in stock price movements on the average sufficiently enough to make the effort worthwhile. Nevertheless one would not expect the information to be valid too far beyond the data used in the calculations. For this reason the ''test'' period was confined to a period from May 10, 1976 to August 26, 1977. In addition to the 60 stocks originally used, an additional 74 new stocks or a total of 134 stocks were used for the ''predictor'' test. In spite of the relatively short time involved, approximately 167,000 X values and index values were generated.[10]

The trading rules for the period were based on arbitrarily chosen values of xs and General Index. For VST periods, action was taken on those stocks whose x_4 value reached an absolute 160 value or greater, or an Index value of 400. For example if a stock reached $x_4 = 160$, it was shorted, in anticipation of a price movement reversal (fall); if $x_4 = -160$ then it was bought in anticipation of a reversal (rise). For ST periods absolute values were $x_{20} = 80$ and Index value = 200. Finally for IT periods stocks with absolute $x_{50} = 60$ or Index values of 150 were chosen as points where positions were initiated.

When a stock reached any of the above values, appropriate transactions were assumed to be made (bought or shorted), in anticipation of a price movement reversal. The stock price was recorded for arbitrarily selected holding periods of

Table 2
VST Trading Period (117 Transactions)

	Percentage Gain or Loss for Various Holding Periods				
Statistical Parameters	*4 Days*	*10 Days*	*20 Days*	*30 Days*	*50 Days*
Total Percentage Gain for the 10 Month Period	133.82	294.40	315.85	328.43	339.15
Mean Gain Per Transaction	1.14	2.42	2.70	2.81	2.90
Standard Deviation	3.287	5.270	7.442	8.374	11.293
Coefficient of Variation	2.874	2.175	2.757	2.983	3.896
Net Yield after 2% Per Transaction Cost (Round Trip)	—	60.70	81.85	94.43	105.15
Annualized Net Yield		72.84	98.22	113.32	126.18
Success Ratio	1.31	1.93	1.72	1.54	1.44

4, 10, 20, 30 and 50 days. Transactions were assumed to be closed out at the end of each period, and the percentage gain or loss of the stock price was recorded. Again, the reason for the arbitrary holding periods is that there is nothing in the walk-back approach to predict the end of a price movement *towards* the "normal" range. The holding periods chosen are of no particular significance in themselves, empirically, but were chosen merely to reveal the possibility of optimal transaction periods. Because of the additional days required to generate xs at the beginning of the test data and the holding period at the end, the actual *transaction* period covers August 23, 1976 to June 16, 1977.

Table 3
ST Trading Period
(20 Transactions)

	Percentage Gain or Loss for Various Holding Periods				
Statistical Parameters	*4 Days*	*10 Days*	*20 Days*	*30 Days*	*50 Days*
Total Percentage Gain for the 10 Month Period	32.15	81.05	71.61	58.74	71.28
Mean Gain Per Transaction	1.33	4.05	3.58	3.11	3.56
Standard deviation	3.55	7.73	9.09	7.69	12.21
Coefficient of Variation	2.66	1.90	2.54	2.47	3.43
Net Yield after 2% Per Transaction Cost (Round Trip)	—	41.05	31.61	18.74	31.28
Annualized Net Yield		49.25	37.93	22.49	37.54
Success Ratio	3.0	3.0	1.86	1.50	1.50

Table 4
ITR Trading Period
(7 Transactions)

Statistical Parameters	*Percentage Gain or Loss for Various Holding Periods* 4 Days	*10 Days*	*20 Days*	*30 Days*	*50 Days*
Total Percentage Gain for the 10 Month Period	14.01	51.22	44.86	27.66	23.53
Mean Gain Per Transaction	2.00	7.31	6.40	3.95	3.36
Standard Deviation	2.47	10.05	12.51	16.59	12.05
Coefficient of Variation	1.24	1.37	1.95	4.20	3.59
Net Yield after 2% Per Transaction Cost (Round Trip)	.01	37.22	30.86	13.66	9.53
Annualized Net Yield	.012	44.66	37.03	16.39	11.44
Success Ratio	2.5	6.0	.75	1.33	1.33

Analysis of Results

The results of the respective trading periods are summarized in Tables 2, 3, 4 and 5 in tabular form. What is remarkable is that *not one* of the total percentage results for each period VST, ST, ITR and IT (ST and STR were similar so the latter results are not shown in the report) or for each holding period shows a negative value. In general, the cumulative percentage gains were greater in the following order VST > ST > ITR > IT. Holding period results vary for each trading period. *Net* (after transactions costs) results are positive for every period except 4 days for VST and ST. The best results were obtained for the following

Table 5
IT Trading Period
(1 Transaction)

Statistical Parameters	*Percentage Gain or Loss for Various Holding Periods* 4 Days	*10 Days*	*20 Days*	*30 Days*	*50 Days*
Total Percentage Gain for the 10 Month Period	1.42	13.33	20.48	31.43	15.24
Mean Gain Per Transaction	—	—	—	—	—
Standard Deviation	—	—	—	—	—
Coefficient of Variation	—	—	—	—	—
Net Yield after 2% Per Transaction Cost (Round Trip)	0	11.33	18.48	29.43	13.24
Annualized Net Yield		13.60	22.18	35.32	15.89

Table 6
Results of Random Selection
(Sample Size = 117)

	Holding Time Periods				
Statistical Parameters	*4 Days*	*10 Days*	*20 Days*	*30 Days*	*50 Days*
Total Yield (Percent)	−45.43	−34.15	−51.88	−24.38	−34.19
Mean	−.388	−.292	−.443	−.208	−.292
Standard Deviation	3.09	4.75	5.97	6.90	9.02
Coefficient of Variation	−7.96	−16.26	−13.47	−33.12	−30.87

categories: VST, 30 and 50 days; ST, 10 days; ITR, 10 days; IT, inconclusive (because of small sample).

Comparative Analysis with Random Selection and "Buy and Hold" Strategies

In order to test the relative performance of the above results, a purely random selection of stocks for the same population and the same time period for the study was made and the results evaluated for comparable holding periods. The results are as follows:

The results of the random selection process are rather poor, if not puzzling; all total yields, excluding transactions costs are negative (see Table 6). If it is assumed that stock prices are random variables, then one would expect results with a mean of zero. There are three possibilities as to why the sample means are all nonzero (negative): (1) In the short run stock prices are serially correlated, (both positive and negative) and not independent; (2) there is a bias in the random selection process used in this test; (3) the sample size is not sufficiently large. Examination of these possibilities would require a study beyond the scope of this chapter.

If instead, one wishes to use a "buy and hold" comparison, the total return (after transaction costs) for the same period is 17.94%, or 14.35% annualized (including dividends). Neither the random selection nor the buy and hold comparisons consistently outperform the walk-back approach. The results strongly favor the latter.[12]

CONCLUSION

Out of the approximately 50,000 possibilities, the walk-back transactions occurred only 145 times, according to the criteria used for this study. Hence such events are relatively rare and involve large data sets to generate sufficient instances to make them worthwhile. Also, it would seem that the probability table would require updating, all of which suggests large computational costs.[13] Nevertheless, the results suggest the possibility of profitable trading, but only for professional traders.

Theoretically, the idea of a bounded random walk and the walk-back phenomenon suggests the possibility of a reconciliation between the purely random versus nonrandom views of stock prices. Therefore I would view the results as suggestive of a possible modification of the weak form of the EMH, where most of the time stock prices are random walks and the exceptions confirm the rule.

The results are consistent with the idea that capital markets are efficient, but not perfect. Given the relative rarity of walk-backs (as this study demonstrates), the market may be more perfect than often presumed, at least as far as very short-term and short-term trading are concerned.

What, then, are the sociological implications of this conclusion, that is to say, what are the concrete circumstances which cause these results to occur? Since information only affects prices through the indirect mechanism of people buying and selling shares of stock, somebody must be buying on good news and selling on bad news to cause the price to adjust itself properly. One such group of people are corporate insiders, who often act illegally on the basis of privileged knowledge. In the case of corporate mergers, for example, almost half of the market's reaction to a merger proposal occurs before the day it is made public.[14] When corporate insiders do not prediscount price levels, the discounting is usually done by market professionals, those traders who frequent the floor of the exchange daily and react to new information in the first seconds and minutes after it is released. Thus, it is primarily the action of market *insiders* that produces this efficient discounting effect, making speculation unprofitable for *outsiders*.

Yet it is precisely those outsiders who are often encouraged to engage in short-term trading in the hope of taking advantage of the volatility of stock prices. The beneficiaries of short-term trading are those investment advisors who offer advice on the basis of short-term trading "systems" and the brokerage firms, through larger volume of turnover. In such circumstances, the novice is best served by avoiding the temptation of short-term trading and leaving the field to the professionals.

ACKNOWLEDGMENT

This paper would not exist had it not been for the assistance of my wife, Linda S. Tarascio, who over the past seven years, has devoted literally thousands of hours to statistical computations and data processing in this and related research.

NOTES

1. Obviously price levels are not independent. The probability of highly capitalized stocks, such as IBM, doubling in price in one day is rather small.

2. The test data consisted of the closing prices of the Dow-Jones Industrials 1897 to 1929 and the Standard and Poor's Industrials 1929 to 1959. No individual stock prices were used.

3. In this case, 30 individual stocks of the Dow-Jones Industrials were used. In doing so, one basis for criticism raised against Alexander's results by critics (i.e., that one cannot buy and sell the "averages") was eliminated.

4. Later, Alexander (1964) did analyze "swing mortalities," presumably with this purpose in mind.

5. Earlier, Cootner (1964) described the activities of professional speculators which had the effect of producing a random walk with "reflecting barriers." The focus of his study involved random price movements about a moving average. The decision rule was: if the price is greater than the 200 day moving average, buy and if less, sell short; if the prices rise above the moving average, cover short positions and if the price falls below, eliminate the long position. A refinement of this rule was added involving a 5% move above or below the moving average to eliminate the excessive transactions costs when the stock price was confined to a narrow trading range around the moving average. The "reflecting barriers" concept used by Cootner, in the light of his decision rules, is different than "walk-back" used by Bussmann.

6. This study was begun in late 1973 before Bussmann's book was available. Data limitations, budget constraints, and other commitments conspired to delay completion until recently.

7. "Outlyers" are the most interesting example. Whereas "outlyers" are viewed statistically as data distortions which should be adjusted for, in stock market analysis they are indications of unusual activity often preceding a price movement reversal. Examples are "blow-offs," extraordinary volume accompanying a sustained price rise or fall, price gaps, etc.

8. What this means is that, contrary to the filter approaches of Alexander (1961) and Fama and Blume (1966), funds are committed to stocks only a part of the time.

9. The Beta Coefficient defines the stock's sensitivity to the movement of the general market.

10. These calculations are made on a day by day basis in "real time." This allowed us to generate the data for the test period at the same time "transactions" were made on paper, a "true" ex-ante approach, by necessity not choice.

11. The success ratio shown in the tables is the ratio of profitable transactions to unprofitable ones.

12. In the case of the walk-back, uncommitted funds were assumed to be held in cash and *not* in interest bearing assets. Therefore the results understate the "yield" since they include only transactions.

13. It is difficult to estimate the rate of decay of the reliability of the probability table. Caution would be on the side of frequent updates to see what extent the probabilities change over time.

14. As found by Keown (cited in Quinn, 1983, p. 11E), Louis (1981, pp. 72–82) and Merjos (1981, p. 11).

REFERENCES

Alexander, S. S. Price movements in speculative markets: Trends or random walks. *International Management Review*, 1961, *2*, 7–26.

Alexander, S. S. Price movements in speculative markets: Trends or random walks. In P. Cootner (Ed.), *The random character of stock market prices*. Cambridge: MIT Press, 1964.

Bussmann, R. L. *The statistical game theory of speculation*. Deerfield Beach, Fla.: Bussman Press, 1975.

Cootner, P. (Ed.). *The random character of stock market prices*. Cambridge: MIT Press, 1964.

Fama, E. F. The behavior of stock market prices. *Journal of Business*, 1965, *39*, 34–105.

Fama, E. F. Efficient capital markets: A review of theory and empirical work. *Journal of Finance*, 1970, *25*, 383–417.

Fama, E. F. Efficient capital markets: A review of theory and empirical work. In M. D. Intriligator (Ed.), *Frontiers of quantitative economics.* Amsterdam: North-Holland, 1971.

Fama, E. F., & Blume, M. E. Filter rules and stock market trading. *Journal of Business,* 1966, *39,* 226–241.

Fama, E. F., & MacBeth, J. D. Risk, return, and equilibrium. *Journal of Political Economy,* 1972, *81,* 607–636.

Green, M. T., & Fielitz, B. D. Long term dependence in common stock returns. *Journal of Financial Economics,* 1977, *4,* 339–349.

Hagerman, R. L., & Richmond, R. D. Random walks, Martingales and the OTC. *Journal of Finance,* 1973, *28,* 897–909.

Kendall, M. G. The analysis of economic time-series. *Journal of the Royal Statistical Society,* 1953, *116*(Part I), 11–25.

Louis, A. M. The unwinnable war on insider trading. *Fortune,* July 1981, pp. 72–82.

Merjos, A. Clear crystal ball? Many stocks show handsome gains in advance of takeovers. *Barron's,* January 2, 1981, pp. 11; 23–24; 105.

Niederhoffer, V., & Osborne, M.F. M. Market making and reversal of the stock exchange. *Journal of the American Statistical Association,* 1966, *61,* 897–916.

Osborne, M. F. M. Periodic structures in the Brownian motion of stock prices. *Operations Research,* 1962, *10,* 345–379.

Quinn, J. B. The inside story. *Newsweek,* February 7, 1983, pp. 11E–11G.

Rozeff, M. S., & Kinney, W. R., Jr. Capital market seasonality: The case of stock returns. *Journal of Financial Economics,* 1976, *3,* 379–402.

Solnik, B. H. Note on the validity of the random walk for European stock prices. *Journal of Finance,* 1973, *28,* 1151–1159.

Umstead, D. A. Forecasting stock market prices. *Journal of Finance,* 1977, *32,* 427–441.

Van Horne, J. C., & Parker, G. G. C. The random-walk theory: An empirical test. *Financial Analysts Journal,* 1967, *23,* 88–94.

SOCIOLOGICAL THEORY AND THE BEHAVIOR OF FINANCIAL MARKETS

Michael Klausner

The behavior of financial markets is very much a social phenomenon. People's decisions to buy, hold or sell securities are greatly influenced by what others are saying and doing with respect to the financial markets. The emotions of fear and greed, coupled with people's perceptions of the economic scene and their own psychological predispositions, are some of the major elements that affect market behavior. Thus the movement of markets is not so much a function of "objective" economic realities as much as it is dependent on investors' emotions, personality, predispositions, and subjective perceptions and evaluations of economic conditions. As a result, theories of human behavior that stress the way in which individuals perceive and interpret situations, as well as those that underscore the dynamics of the social influence process, should be helpful in accounting for the human factors that affect price movements. Moreover, since the action of the markets can be viewed as a form of mass or collective behavior, sociological theories that attempt to account for such phenomena may be of particular value.

My contention is that the actions of financial markets, to a great extent, can be analyzed and understood in terms of the concepts and theories that are part of the existing corpus of sociological and social psychological knowledge. Human beings' financial market decision behavior should be seen as a manifestation or subset of general social behavior and therefore amenable to explanation through the use of theories that have been developed to account for social phenomena. Thus, a new or special theory specifically designed to explain market decision making behavior is not necessary. What is required is for current behavioral science theories to be *applied* to financial market phenomena.

Before this can be done, however, we need to familiarize ourselves with those theories from the sociological and social psychological literature which are the most germane to market behavior. Toward this end, I will present and discuss the following perspectives and their basic assumptions about human nature, human behavior and human social organization: sociological views of mass behavior; contagion theory; value added theory; fashions, fads and financial markets; convergence theory; cognitive dissonance theory; social comparison theory, and contextual analysis. I will then draw out the implications of these perspectives for financial market behavior to some degree, but mostly leave this to be further addressed by later chapters.

SOCIAL PERSPECTIVES ON MASS BEHAVIOR

The sociological concept of the ''mass'' is an appropriate and useful unit of analysis for studying market movement. Sociologically, a mass refers to a plurality of individuals who are usually physically dispersed, unknown to one another and who focus their thoughts and actions on the same object. They also desire to attain similar goals (Lang & Lang, 1961, p. 38). People who watch television, vote for political candidates and trade securities belong to particular masses. According to Blumer (1969, p. 77), a mass possesses the following characteristics:

1. *A mass consists of people from all walks of life.* Of course those most apt to be involved with the financial markets are likely to belong to the middle and upper socioeconomic classes. However, since a person can directly participate in the stock market with as little as one hundred dollars, those in the lower middle class can also be participants.

2. *The mass consists of anonymous individuals who do not directly interact with one another.* In most instances an investor does not directly interact with or even know the person from whom he either bought or sold shares. Investors deal with brokers who serve as mediators between people wanting to buy or sell stock. Even though the overwhelming majority of stock market participants are physically dispersed and are strangers to each other, the ticker tape, desk top quotation machines and data communicated via the media enable members of the stock trading mass to learn about and be affected by one anothers' market behavior.

3. *The mass is not organized to any appreciable degree*. Those participating in securities transactions are not organized as such, but the effects of their joint actions on price movements may give the *appearance* that they are organized and acting in concert. This is because investors tend to react in a similar manner to news that is relevant to the market in general and to specific stocks. For example, when it is reported that a major bank has raised the prime rate, many investors will sell their stocks because they believe that high interest rates will have an adverse affect on corporate earnings. Whenever the majority of market participants interpret a news event in the same manner and translate their interpretation into buy and sell orders, it may seem that they are working in concert, even though they are not.

Two theorists of mass behavior have observed that, ''In its pure form [the mass] would consist of a number of separate individuals, each responding independently to the same stimulus in the same way'' (Turner & Killian, 1972, p. 112). Of course, the mass very seldom, if ever, behaves in terms of its ''pure form.'' Blumer has made a similar point and has also indicated the powerful and significant effect the mass may produce when its members' actions converge independently.

> The form of mass behavior, paradoxically, is laid down by individual lines of activity and not by concerted action. These individual activities are primarily in the form of selections—such as the selection of a new dentrifice, a book, a play, a party platform . . .—selections which are made in response to the vague impulses and feelings which are awakened by the object of mass interest. Mass behavior, even through a congeries of individual lines of action, may become of momentous significance. *If these lines converge, the influence of the mass may be enormous. . . .*'' (Blumer, 1969:78, emphasis added).

Blumer goes on to note that especially under conditions of excitement, anxiety or tension, the behavior of the mass comes close to being like that of a crowd. ''At such times it is likely to be influenced by excited appeals such as appear in the press or over the radio—appeals that may play upon primitive impulses'' (Blumer, 1969, p. 79). Stock market participants are continuously subjected to such appeals via the media. Credentialed as well as self-proclaimed experts have easy access to the media and spout views that, on the one hand, claim that ''the end is near and we should take to the hills,'' and on the other hand, argue that ''the greatest buying opportunity now exists and that people should be a hundred per cent in stocks since the Dow will reach five thousand soon.'' Such pronouncements serve to stir the primitive emotions of fear and greed.

An individual becomes a participant in a particular mass when his/her choice and subsequent behavior coincides with the choices and behaviors of many others (Lang & Lang, 1961, pp. 344–345). Within the general mass of market participants, we can differentiate submasses based upon such criteria as whether they are buying or selling, which issues they are buying or selling and whether or not they are selling short. The nature, degree and direction of mass action can be ascertained by the use of summary indices which are able to indicate the sum of a multitude of individual market decisions and actions. This is precisely the function of the various stock, bond and commodity indices.

Even though members of a mass are physically separated and do not engage in much direct communication, they tend to form a conception of the feelings and views of other members of the mass (Lang & Lang, 1961). This perception of the prevailing climate of opinion affects their own feelings, perceptions and behavior. Market participants, for example, usually find it exceedingly difficult to buy stocks when the prevailing climate of opinion is bearish or to sell when it is bullish. Lang and Lang (1961, p. 347) make the important point that, "this mass perspective explains the cumulative and contagionlike spread of mass behavior over and above what it would be if individuals acted autonomously without any image of what nameless others were doing." This and related points will now be discussed in detail as we examine the contagion theory of collective behavior.

CONTAGION THEORY

The contemporary version of contagion theory has its roots in the observations made by LeBon (1897) who attempted to analyze and explain crowd behavior. While the mass does not have all of the attributes of crowds, the mechanisms and dynamics of the social contagion process are similar for both.

The basic assumption of contagion theory is that increased degrees of suggestibility, emotionality and emotional diffusion lead members of a mass to behave in similar ways (Turner, 1964). Fundamental to contagion theory is the notion of "circular reaction." Circular reaction refers to a form of interstimulation where the behavior of individuals serves to stimulate other individuals to produce the same behavior which is then reflected back to those who initiated the behavior (Blumer, 1969, p. 65). As a result, there is an escalating degree of emotionality and similar behavior, each one reinforcing and intensifying the other.

It is often implied that people must be in close physical proximity in order for the circular reaction and social contagion processes to occur. However, this is not a necessary condition for social contagion to develop. King (1973, p. 123) put it well when he observed that, "modern technology has redefined a crowd, though crowds still act in ways known to tradition. Persons no longer need to be in physical contact (e.g., ghetto riot; religious revival meeting) to get the 'crowd feel' or to act with a sense of oneness in decision-making." The widespread, immediate and ready availability of news about the financial markets and the economy enable the circular reaction and social contagion processes to occur even if people are not in close proximity. The observation of just completed stock transactions and volume data as reported on the tape and quote machines can have a potent stimulatory effect on the recipients of such information. This arousal effect is most likely to occur when stocks are moving sharply up or down, volume is heavy, the tape is "late" and large blocks of stock are crossing the tape. Market watchers are especially vulnerable to the circular reaction process when stocks that they hold or contemplate buying or selling are active and exhibiting volatile price movements. Tape watchers who observe a relatively inactive stock begin to rise on heavy volume may conclude that "something is brewing," that "insiders are accumulating the stock," or that "it may be a takeover attempt," and hence are apt to buy the stock. This produces further volume and price increases which are observed by others who then reach similar conclusions and act accordingly by translating their conclusions into buy orders. Thus, we have a circular reaction process even though the participants are not physically proximate. The circular reaction effect is further intensified as other investors learn of the volume and price increases from their newspapers. The emotional arousal and stimulation generated by such observations is likely to result in a temporary suspension of critical judgment and thinking.

While there have not been many carefully controlled empirical studies to test aspects of contagion theory as it applies to market behavior, a recent one has been made by Schachter (cited in Blustein, 1982). He hypothesized that market participants are most likely to become highly emotional and subject to social contagion when prices of stocks are rising or falling sharply. He contended that during raging bull markets people become very euphoric and unduly optimistic about stocks, feeling that prices will continue to rise indefinitely. Conversely, during bear markets, they feel and act as though stocks will never stop falling in price. Emotional feelings of any extreme, euphoric or depressive, tend to interfere with rational, critical thinking processes. According to Schachter, peoples' market behavior is most likely to be rationally based when the market is relatively stable and not fluctuating much in any direction. He found that "during a bull or bear market a strong buy recommendation would, on the average, send a stock up more than one and a half percent the day that the recommendation appeared . . . and a strong sell recommendation would spark an average drop of our percent" (Blustein, 1982, pp. 1;17). However, during a relatively stable market climate he found that a positive recommendation would increase the stock's price an average of only a half a percent and a negative one would push it down by only one and a half percent. Schachter accounts for these results by maintaining that during both bull and bear markets people are highly aroused emotionally. At these times, they are most apt to "grasp at straws" which will provide for them a feeling of psychological security and satisfaction that they are doing the "correct" thing. One such "straw" is a stock recommendation given by an analyst that, for example, is published in the *Wall Street Journal's* "Heard on the Street" column. During periods of hyperemotional arousal people are most vulnerable to suggestions and rumors and are very likely to act on the basis of them (see Rose, 1951). In addition, during bull or bear markets, analysts are apt to disagree as to whether the "top" or "bottom" has been reached and if people should sell, or whether there is still a long way to go before the market peaks and they therefore should buy. One student of both sociology and the market has noted the following relevant point:

> While mass behavior most commonly occurs as a result of a breakdown in social organization—when accepted beliefs are breaking down—it is also likely to occur in situations where there is a lack of accepted beliefs to begin with, or when there is no overall order to any beliefs. It is specifically this latter condition which characterizes the market. The very number of different market theories creates what is basically an ambiguous, unordered situation (C. W. Smith, 1981, p. 135).

Thus the very nature of the state of market prognostication, a state that is presently more an art than a science, tends to generate conditions which are particularly conducive to circular reaction and social contagion.

Wheeler (1970) has further elucidated some of the mechanisms involved in social contagion by distinguishing between social facilitation and behavioral contagion. For any of these two mechanisms to operate, the behavior of interest must first be part of a person's behavioral repertoire. Social facilitation occurs when an individual observes someone perform a particular behavior which serves to remind him that he can also perform it. It is probably not necessary for the person to directly observe the other person engage in the behavior. The viewing of symbols of the behavior can generate the social facilitation effect. When a market participant views the reports of stock transactions via the tape or the media, the social facilitation effect may be sparked. Behavioral contagion takes place, according to Wheeler, when a person's inhibition to act becomes reduced after observing someone else perform a similar act. Thus, someone who may have been contemplating buying a stock, but whose feelings of fear have restrained him from doing so, may buy the stock when he sees others buying it, either directly or indirectly.

Contagion theory is useful because it underscores the importance of both the spread of emotions and the effect of others' behavior on price movements. It reminds us that price fluctuations are, to a large extent, dependent on peoples' mood swings as their perception and interpretation of events makes them oscillate between rampant optimism and deep pessimism. This is not always the result, as fundamentalists believe, of significant changes in a company's worth. This is especially apt to be true for short-term fluctuations. The actual value of a company's stock based on such factors as assets, earnings, yield and future prospects does not vary from day to day or month to month as much as its stock's gyrations would seem to suggest.[2] In the short run, value and price movements may not correlate with one another. People tend to overreact emotionally to both the fluctuations of stocks and news items pertaining to them. Feelings about the general market, specific industry groups and individual stocks can quickly take a complete turnabout. In many cases the turn from gloom and doom to unbridled optimism can occur without there being any clear indication that fundamentals have changed for the better. Contagion theory helps us to understand some of the processes and dynamics responsible for such changes in investor sentiment. It sensitizes us to some of the ways in which investors become swept up in the prevailing market climate, act in terms of it, and by so doing, intensify the existing sentiment. The part that the social contagion process plays in the production of financial panics and crazes will be examined as we discuss these phenomena in terms of value added theory.

VALUE ADDED THEORY

Value added theory, developed by Smelser (1962), is quite useful in helping to account for financial market behavior. It is especially valuable in specifying the necessary and sufficient conditions that must prevail for market busts and booms to occur. The theory provides a framework for the categorization and organization of the determinants of extreme forms of mass behavior. Our focus will be on how the theory can be applied to financial panics and crazes.

Central to Smelser's theory is the "value added" concept. This notion is borrowed from economics and refers to the idea that value is added to a material as it completes successive stages of processing. Smelser uses the example of iron ore being transformed into an automobile through a series of steps. Such sequential steps would include mining, smelting, shaping, combining it with other parts and painting. The completion of each successive step brings us closer to the desired end result. Moreover, each step must combine in a precise manner with previous steps before the next stage of processing can take place. As Smelser (1962, p. 14) puts it, "earlier stages must combine *according to a certain pattern* before the next stage can contribute its particular value to the finished product." It would be counterproductive, for instance, to paint the steel before it is molded into the desired shape. Every step represents a necessary but not a sufficient contribution to the completion of the desired end product. As the value added process proceeds, the nature and probability of the final outcome becomes increasingly specific and likely.

Smelser has applied the logic of the value added notion to a wide range of mass phenomena. He postulated six conditions or determinants that must be present before a particular type of mass behavior can occur. Each successive one is more specific than preceding ones and, if present, increases the likelihood of a unique outcome. The six determinants are:

1. *Structural conduciveness*. This refers to basic and general circumstances which must exist if a particular type of mass phenomenon is to emerge. Thus for a financial panic or boom to be possible, a society's economic institutions must allow people's assets to be exchanged within the framework of an institutionalized market structure. If this were not possible to begin with, then the

potential for financial panics and crazes would not exist. The mere existence of structural conduciveness, however, does not necessarily indicate that a panic or boom will occur; it only means that the *potential* for such phenomena exist.

2. *Structural strain.* This determinant denotes feelings of stress, fear, uncertainty and anxiety that people experience. It is characterized by a state of hyperarousal existing within people.

3. *Growth and spread of a generalized belief.* When individuals begin to attribute their feelings of frustration, anxiety and uncertainty to a specific situation or state of affairs, they have begun to form generalized beliefs. These beliefs do not have to be objectively true for them to contribute to the emergence of a form of mass behavior. The main requirement is that they are *thought* to be true by a significant number of people. When this occurs the generalized belief serves to predispose people to some type of mass behavior. The two major types of generalized beliefs that we will be concerned with are hysterical and wish-fulfillment ones. The former belief leads to panics and the latter one to crazes.

4. *Precipitating factors.* These are events which serve to trigger the episode of mass behavior. The nature of the event may be relatively trivial in and of itself. However, when it is combined with the three previous determinants, it greatly increases the probability of some form of mass activity occurring. Examples of precipitating factors that may lead to a panic would be the failure of a bank or the bankruptcy of a brokerage firm.

5. *Mobilization for action.* Once the preceding conditions exist the only necessary condition remaining for some form of mass behavior to take place is action by individuals. Examples would be the actual riot, panic or craze.

6. *Mechanisms of social control.* While all of the preceding conditions function to successively increase the chances of an episode of mass action occurring, social control measures are those that serve to prevent or reduce any of the conditions. Some of them can be initiated prior to the outbreak of mass behavior. Efforts on the part of authorities to quell rumors or to show that they are without substance would be examples. Social control measures can also be implemented after the mass action has taken place. The closing of banks or the use of the state police to put down a riot are examples.

Smelser applies his value added theory to two financial conditions which are relevant to us here: panics and crazes. He defines the former as a "collective flight based on a hysterical belief" (1962, p. 131). This conception of panic is broad enough to cover situations where physical danger is present (people trapped in a burning theater) as well as cases where the danger is to people's financial assets. Included in the notion of panic are such elements as a sense of threat, psychological strain, increased vulnerability to suggestion and to the social contagion process. Financial panics are thus brought about through the progression of conditions described in value added theory.

Craze behavior can be viewed as the extreme opposite of panic behavior. When people panic, they have an intense desire to flee from or avoid something that is perceived as harmful. When they are caught up in a craze, people want to rush toward or obtain something that they feel will greatly benefit them. The essence of craze behavior has been captured by Wallace (1968, p. 57) in his observations:

> In the craze, the members of the group seem to be driven by both a hope for some desirable thing and a fear of being left behind while others enjoy themselves. In a sense the craze is a 'positive' panic: the urgency of the situation lies not in the imminence of danger, escape from which becomes less likely with each passing moment, but in the availability of a benefit, access to which may be reduced in the near future.

This description is particularly relevant to financial crazes. A craze is fueled by a "positive wish-fulfillment belief" (Smelser, 1962, p. 171). People involved in crazes have an obsessive belief that unless they take certain actions they will lose out on some fabulous opportunity. The genesis and life-cycle of a craze can be analyzed in terms of the same set of determinants that were used to study a panic.

Empirical Test of Value Added Theory

Value added theory, as it applies to financial panics, was tested by three social scientists who studied a "run" that occurred on an Australian bank (Mann, Nagel & Dowling, 1976). The authors interviewed people waiting outside of the bank who were attempting to make withdrawals or deposits. Those who withdrew money were systematically compared with those who deposited money. Little evidence was found for the existence of a panic in the traditional sense. "Most withdrawers were very anxious, but they waited patiently in well-ordered, self-regulated queues" (Mann et al., 1976, p. 229). There were no cases of pushing, shoving or queue jumping. The "run" on the bank did, however, conform to Smelser's conception of a panic. Large numbers of very "anxious individuals converged urgently and rapidly to demand payment, in response to either a premonition of disaster or a bogey rumor about a threat to their savings" (Mann et al., 1976, p. 229). Having established that the run on the bank met Smelser's notion of panic, the authors then set out to determine whether Smelser's postulated conditions for mass behavior were present.

Circumstances existed which were quite conducive to the emergence of panic behavior. In addition to the existence of a system that enabled people to withdraw their money at will, the bank credited interest to accounts on the day of the panic. As a consequence, there were an above average number of people outside of the bank. The image created by lines of waiting customers during a period of economic uncertainty gave the impression that something was amiss. The authors note that, "it is our assumption that beyond a critical mass or number a threshold is reached where participants and observers alike define what is happening as a cause for alarm" (Mann et al., 1976, p. 229). In addition, in the year that the run occurred, there existed record inflation, high unemployment, industrial unrest and a government-imposed credit squeeze which affected all segments of industry. Thus, the condition of structural strain seemed evident as well.

Two questions were used to measure the growth and spread of generalized beliefs: (1) Do you believe the rumors that have been circulating concerning the bank's problems?; and (2) Do you believe that the bank will fail? Seventy percent of the withdrawals but only twelve percent of the depositors said that they believed the rumors. Forty-eight percent of withdrawers but only five percent of depositors felt that there was a good chance that the bank would fail. Thus the withdrawers were much more likely to hold panicky beliefs than were the depositors.

The prominent publicity given to the long queues by the media seemed to be the precipitating event that triggered the majority of the withdrawals. Sixty percent of withdrawers said that they had been influenced by the actions of others versus only twenty-six percent of the depositors. This shows that the precipitating event for the bank run itself was not the same one that caused panic among those who withdrew their money the day after the run. Most of the withdrawers said that they heard about the run the previous day. Many of the withdrawers came in groups of two or more as if to give emotional support to each other. Often, husbands and wives came together. The majority of depositors, however, came alone.

The Premier tried to reassure these citizens, but without much success. Most of the withdrawers claimed that they had not been reassured by the Premier's statements. In contrast, every depositor who had heard the Premier's exhortations said that they had been reassured by his words.

The investigators found that differences did exist between those who withdrew their money from the bank and those who deposited money. The withdrawers were older than the depositors, poorer in appearance and were likely to come from foreign countries with a history of political and economic instability. Also, withdrawers were less knowledgeable about the actual situation concerning the bank. Most of them used their account for a specific purpose (to save for a car, vacation) while the majority of depositors used the bank for daily transactions. The authors observe that "the people caught up in the run tended to be those whose anxieties, lack of information and vulnerable position would render them highly suggestible under conditions of uncertainty and tension" (Mann et al., 1976, p. 231).

The authors concluded that their study supported value added theory. When panic behavior did occur, all of the determinants specified by the theory were present. When they were not present, as was the case with the depositors, panic behavior did not take place. As value added theory predicted, economic panics occur in two major phases. The "real" phase, where participants are motivated by the hysterical beliefs they hold and the precipitating event, and the "derived" phase, where they are impelled to engage in panic behavior because they learn of others doing so.

Smelser's value added theory of mass behavior takes into account both social structural and situational factors as well as the subjective psychological states of people, showing the relationships and interdependencies among broad classes of factors.

FADS, FASHIONS AND FINANCIAL MARKETS

The concepts of fad and fashion are useful in helping us understand certain aspects of financial behavior. A fad can be defined as an ardent but relatively short-lived interest in some idea, object or behavior. Fads may arise within a diverse range of arenas. The realms of dress, food and recreation are fertile ones for the emergence of fads. The intense but brief obsession with hula hoops, Nehru suits and disco music are examples of fads that have seen their day. Faddish behavior may involve new activities or the resurgence of fascination with old ones. Thus there may be a cyclical dimension to fads. Another feature of faddish behavior is that it appears to be irrational to those not caught up in it (Turner & Killian, 1972, p. 129). During the period that faddish behavior occurs "the attention of the faddist is severely restricted—to the point that alternatives pass unnoticed. Consequently, money may be invested in highly improbable schemes or exaggerated fears may be maintained when the evidence against both is clear to the nonfaddish" (Turner & Killian, 1972, p. 130).

Examples of investors becoming obsessed with particular industry groups abound. The investing publics' passionate affair with companies involved in the gambling industry is a prime one. During the peak and latter stage of the gambling stock fad, after first and second tier gambling companies' shares had risen sharply, investors then bid up the shares of low and questionable quality companies. Indeed, all a company would have to do to see a sharp rise in its shares would be to issue a press release indicating any of the following: they were in the process of negotiating a deal for land in a state that had legalized gambling; they were thinking of building a gambling casino; they were negotiating for a loan in order to buy an interest in a casino or they were contemplating starting an airline that would exclusively be used to transport people to Atlantic City. Buyers of the shares of such companies did not seem to realize or care that the negotiations may fall through, that once a casino was completed the competition for gamblers would be greater than it was at present or that as other states legalized gambling the profit margins of the gambling companies would decrease.

As the enthusiasm and interest in the fad industry gains momentum, propelled by the publicity given to it by the media and the upward price movements of stocks in the industry, it develops a "mystique" or "charisma" in the eyes of present and potential market participants. This functions to further increase their appeal. Blotnick (1980b, pp. 198–99) has observed that, "less than three investors in one hundred will say—'this group has gone far enough—let's take profits and get into another'."

During the course of an industry stock fad, investors' obsession with stocks of the fad industry is so great that they become oblivious to stocks in other industries which may be extremely undervalued. Such stocks are ignored because they are not in the spotlight and are vastly overshadowed by the stocks of companies involved in the fad industry. Blotnick (1979b, pp. 116–17) has concluded from his study of the responses of a sample of investors that, "investor behavior is similar in many ways to consumer behavior generally. When people go into a bookstore they usually buy bestsellers." This principle clearly applies to the stock selection tendencies of the unsophisticated investor. Most of these people are attracted to stocks that are rising on heavy volume and being ballyhooed by the media rather than to those that are languishing from inattention, even though they may be great bargains. Many of those investors in Blotnick's sample would not even think of buying a stock unless the industry it represented was receiving favorable attention and whose companies' stocks had already begun to rise sharply. This is probably due to the fact that after people buy a stock they like to have it show an immediate profit for them. Most likely, this will occur when the stock bought is in the limelight and has been advancing, even though the immediate gain may be the only profit they will extract from that stock.

Fashion, as is the case with fad, denotes a collective change in choice regarding some idea, thing or behavior. However, while the notion of fad refers to a rapid, abrupt and relatively brief change in preference, fashion denotes a slower, continuing pattern of change. Also, changes in fashion are more likely to be of a cyclical nature. Blumer (1968, pp. 341–45) observes that while the concept of fashion has been primarily applied to dress, it can be germane to many other realms. He states that ". . . any area of social life that is caught in continuing change is open to the intrusion of fashion." Clearly, the notion of fashion can be profitably applied to the behavior of financial markets. Indeed, some students of the market speak of industry or stock group rotation. Fashion can thus strike the very essence of speculative behavior itself, conferring temporarily irresistible popularity on first one and then another type of market participation. The "go-go-years" of the late 1950s through the early 1970s provide an example of a dynamic market boom and hysteria based on large scale participation and extended endurance. The relatively quiet stock market succeeding World War II was followed by a period in the mid-1950s when people started buying securities once again. Soon there was not enough of the traditional "blue chip" stock to go around as more money and purchasers became available. One securities analyst described how a new phenomenon arose on Wall Street to fill this need—the "growth stock":

> It's patently absurd when you think about it to call any group of stocks growth stocks, like they're supposed to grow by guarantee and the others aren't, but the phrase caught on and new stocks appeared that started at $5 and went to $200; $10 stocks went to $1000. People were literally waiting around and calling their brokers to get in on a new stock as soon as it was issued. (Adler, 1981, pp. 124–125).

Active leaders appeared in the market to seek out new "high-quality growth stocks," commanding massive followings that pushed prices up by the sheer force of their self-fulfilling certainty. Stock prices soared from twenty and thirty times earnings to fifty times and above, being expected to continue rising forever. These were thought to be "one-decision stocks:" ones only bought and never sold, since they escalated infinitely. But suddenly it became unfashionable to own growth stocks, and a new breed of "two-tier securities" were discovered that were considered quality issues of a lower echelon. The dynamic escalation of the growth stocks shifted into reverse while the new group gained in popularity. These remained popular for a couple of years until their prices rose to unaffordable levels, only to be replaced anew by the next wave of mass interest. One stockbroker describes the transfer of momentum:

> Once the second tier had equalized itself with the blue chip stocks, suddenly a new slogan emerged from nowhere: 'smokestack companies.' Boom! That's what everybody wanted to buy. They were only selling at 3 or 4 times earnings while the others were at 40 times earnings. Then all the 40 times earnings stocks were sold. (Adler, 1981, p. 125).

But smokestack companies were replaced a year or so later as the pendulum swung again. In 1975 with the country in an illiquid situation and heavily printing money, the illogical decision to demand high dividend payoff emerged. A new group of companies promising "total return" and paying 11%–12% yields plus capital gains began an upward surge, collapsing the growth stocks. A securities analyst explained the changeover: "The new title gave total return stocks an identity with momentum. There was new confidence in one group and a lack of confidence in the other."

But total stocks have also faded, replaced with the most recently fashionable "sound approach:" market timing on the technical side, and trying to formulate all analyses with a computer. Disdaining fundamentalism, these "fashionists" are now busily trying to get in on the bottom of a narrow cycle and turn a quick profit without looking at the growth, dividend payoff, or even the fiscal solubility of the companies they buy and sell.

Yet even for those who stick with fundamentals, the swings of investment fashion can be volatile. Shifts in sentiment can be dependent on a variety of factors: changes occurring within industries, economic trends, and advice conveyed by securities analysts. Blumer (1968, p. 342) has noted that "prestigeful personages . . . through their advocacy of a model give social endorsement or legitimacy to changes in fashion." For financial markets this function is performed by economists and market analysts via the mass media (see chapter 8).

CONVERGENCE THEORY

Convergence theory explains mass behavior in terms of the "simultaneous release of already existing predispositions, which a number of people share as latent tendencies" (Turner & Killian, 1972, p. 18). The theory claims that under the right circumstances these latent predispositions will be translated into behavior. People possessing the same personality tendencies will behave in similar ways when they are set off by particular conditions and environmental events. Unlike contagion theory, which does not focus on the part that personality traits play in the generation of mass behavior, convergence theory views such behavior as the manifestation of *converging personality traits* which impel people to act in specific ways.

Convergence theory can be used to account for various types of market behavior. The financial markets, together with the numerous moves that they enable investors to make, provide an arena for the expression of peoples' personality dispositions. Investors possessing similar personality tendencies will be apt to make similar decisions when they experience specific market conditions and circumstances. For example, those who have "conformist" tendencies would be likely to sell when the majority of others are doing so and buy when that is what the majority is doing. Conversely, market participants who have a strong streak of "independence" within their personalities are most apt to subscribe to the contrarian theory of investment strategy. They will buy when everyone else is extremely bearish; they will sell when everyone else is euphoric about the stock market causing it to make new highs daily. People who are confident and self-assured would not be likely to be influenced by what the "big name" advisors and economists are saying about the market and the economy. Investors who have inflated egos and who have a difficult time admitting that they are wrong can be expected to hold on to a declining issue and refuse to sell.[3]

Personality dispositions are also apt to influence the types of stocks that people will buy. The person who thrives on excitement and enjoys risk taking will be attracted to highly volatile and speculative stocks. The timid, fearful individual who has a low threshold for anxiety and risk taking will be inclined to purchase stocks that have both low downside and upside potential for appreciation.[4]

The relevance of personality characteristics to investors' market decisions has been demonstrated by two studies. Blotnick (1979a, p. 124) has classified a segment of his survey sample of investors as "high rollers." He observes that the stock market for such people is "not a place to invest but a game against which to test their luck and skill." Those belonging to this category crave fast-paced action with stocks that are highly volatile; they lack the patience needed to wait for situations to pan out. They tend to buy stocks that are very active and moving up sharply. As a result they would not be interested in issues that are out of favor even though they may be very much undervalued. The significance of personality factors in affecting people's market behavior is brought out in Blotnick's (1979a, pp. 124–125) point that, "to know how far a stock will go, it is more important to know what *sort* of person is buying it than it is to know how *many* people are buying it." He goes on to note that "at some time after a reasonable profit the average investor will say—enough—and take his profits. But high rollers don't sell on the way up, but hold on to buy more. Their expectations become more and more inflated as their stock goes up."

Another study conducted to determine if personality differences existed between successful and unsuccessful investors and brokers was done by Baker (1971). He reported that, "psychological tests showed that the successful investors—those who did substantially better than the Dow Jones Industrial average—had definite personality patterns. They also were more likely to be women" (Baker, 1971, pp. 59–60). In rank order of their ability to differentiate successful from unsuccessful investors, the personality characteristics correlated with successful investing were: (1) dominance; (2) social presence; (3) capacity for status; (4) flexibility; (5) tolerance; (6) psychological mindedness; (7) self-acceptance; (8) sense of well-being and (9) intellectual efficiency.

Using the same psychological tests previously used, Baker studied sixty stockbrokers associated with major firms. Statistically significant differences were found to exist between the successful and unsuccessful stockbrokers. Summarizing the personality profile of the successful broker, Baker (1971, pp. 85–86) asserts:

> The successful broker can most likely be characterized as aggressive, ambitious, outgoing, enterprising and competitive. He is extremely confident in his social interactions, with a high sense of personal worth. Self-doubt and disillusionment do not plague him. . . . While he places a high value on cognitive matters, he is flexible and adaptable in his thinking and social behavior.

In addition, the successful stockbrokers scored high on tests measuring efficiency, perserverence and resourcefulness.

Convergence and contagion theories should be seen as being complementary rather than as mutually exclusive or incompatible. The main advantage of convergence theory is that it sensitizes us to the part that people's personality tendencies play in the action of financial markets. It reminds us that the same set of market circumstances and stimuli can and do produce different market behaviors by people. These variations are the result of the existence of different personality predispositions.

COGNITIVE DISSONANCE THEORY

Cognitive dissonance theory is useful in helping us understand the behavior of investors *after* they have bought or sold a stock. The theory contends that a person will experience feelings of psychological stress when he holds two or more cognitions that are inconsistent with each other (Festinger, 1957). Cognitions refer to ideas, thoughts, beliefs and opinions. Since the holding of incompatible cognitions produces feelings of unease and tension, the person becomes motivated to reduce or eliminate these emotions. This can be done through the use of two major strategies. The person can change one of the cognitions so that it will be consistent with the other one, or he can add additional cognitions (new ideas or information) that will serve to make the initially inconsistent cognitions compatible. This theory has generated a vast amount of research and has been used to account for a wide range of behaviors. Our aim will be to show how the theory can be used to account for some of the behaviors (or lack thereof) that people enact after they buy or sell a stock.

People who desire to become involved in the stock market face a difficult decision. They have literally thousands of stocks from which to choose. The decision is fraught with much tension for two major reasons. First, the possibility always exists that their decision will result in a financial loss. Second, if they lose money in the market they are likely to experience feelings of self-deprecation, inferiority and embarrassment.

Prior to making a stock purchase decision, individuals are likely to collect much relevant information and put a good deal of time and energy into the decision making process.[5] After research and careful deliberations, they may narrow down their choices to companies X and Y. Both stocks may seem attractive for purchase, but for different reasons. Both possess certain desirable as well as undesirable features. For example, company X may have a low price-earnings ratio, be selling below book value, and have little debt. On the other hand, it may not be in a ''glamour'' industry and may be currently out of the spotlight as evidenced by the low volume of shares traded. Company Y, however, may be in a glamour industry (high technology, for example), be trading at a high volume and be in an industry that is a current favorite of investors. However, it may have a high price-earnings ratio, be trading near its all-time high and have much debt outstanding.

After weighing the pros and cons, let us presume that these individuals buy shares in company X. Then, according to the principles of cognitive dissonance theory, they will refrain from seeking data about company Y—the company whose stock they were considering purchasing, but did not. They are apt to begin to discuss their purchase of company X's stock with friends, telling them enthusiastically the reasons for their decision to purchase it and perhaps even urging them to do likewise. They may cite studies indicating the advantages of buying stocks that have the features of company X. Our hypothetical stock purchasers are also likely to proclaim that the only way to make money in the market is to discover undervalued stocks and buy them before others discover them. In addition to extolling the virtues of the stock that they bought, they are apt to disvalue the stock that they decided not to buy. For example, they will argue that people who buy stocks selling at their all-time highs are taking a big chance because there is much downside risk. They may contend that stocks in glamour industries are usually bid up to unrealistic prices—prices that bear little relation to their "true" value. They may also argue that competition is fierce in glamour industries and that a competing company could develop a product that would make the one produced by another company obsolete.

How can such behavior be explained? Cognitive dissonance theory claims that after a person makes a difficult decision—one that involved the expenditure of much time and energy and whose consequences are important to the person—dissonance is experienced. It emerges because the final selection is usually never totally perfect and the alternatives that were considered, but eventually rejected, are never entirely without some merit. This was clearly the case in our hypothetical illustration. Specifically, the stock purchasers' cognition that they bought shares in company X is incompatible with the cognition that there are certain negative features about company X. Similarly, their cognition that there are several positive features about company Y—the one they decided against buying—is incompatible with the cognition that they did not purchase its shares. These dissonant cognitions create feelings of strain and unease. The people's behavior after they bought company X can be explained in terms of their dissonance reduction properties or consequences. By proclaiming the merits of the chosen stock and either ignoring or belittling the problems with the rejected alternative stock, dissonance is reduced. The people are thereby cognitively widening the distance that they perceive to exist between the selection actually made and the one that was rejected. They highlight the advantages of the selection chosen and ignore or downplay its negative qualities. At the same time, the disadvantages of the stock not chosen are emphasized while its positive features are ignored.

Support for this phenomenon comes from a number of studies done in a variety of contexts. In a classic study by Brehm (1956), women were asked to rate the desirability of owning different appliances (toaster, coffee maker, etc.) and were told that they would be allowed to have one as a reward for cooperating in the study. In the condition that was hypothesized to produce much dissonance, subjects were asked to select an item from two that were rated very highly. In the condition hypothesized to create low dissonance, subjects were asked to choose an item from two that were rated far apart. In the control condition, an item was selected by the researcher and given to the subject. The women were asked to read some brochures put out by the manufacturers of the products and, after having done so, to re-rate the items. The results confirmed the hypothesis and supported dissonance theory. In the high dissonance condition, the items the women chose as gifts were rated higher than the gift they could have selected but did not. The nonchosen gift was rated lower in value and desirability than it had been the first time they rated it. Women in the low dissonance condition did not reevaluate more positively the items they chose as gifts for themselves, nor did they disvalue or downgrade the items that they rejected more than they had during the first evaluation.

There are several significant implications of cognitive dissonance theory for investor behavior. Since, in order to reduce dissonance, investors will selectively perceive and focus on events that serve to justify their decision and ignore those that indicate that they made an unwise decision, they are not likely to sell the stock even if it begins to decline in price.[6] In addition, they are not likely to sell the stock if it falls in price because doing so would create additional dissonance. The cognition "I am a smart investor" is incompatible with the cognition "I sold a stock at a loss." If the stock falls the person is likely to create new cognitions which will serve to reduce the dissonance caused by the cognitions "I am a smart investor" or "the stock I bought is falling in price and I have a paper loss." Examples of such new cognitions would be: "The stock is undergoing a temporary correction before it resumes its upward advance;" "profit-taking is taking place in the stock, it will rise when the profit-taking is over;" or "my loss is only on paper and paper losses do not count." Moreover, studies have shown that people tend to become more confident that a decision was the right one *after* they make it and translate it into action as compared to before they do so. In another study, for example, horse race bettors en route to placing their bets were asked by researchers how sure they were that the horses they selected would win. Other bettors were asked the same question after they had placed their bets. Those who had already bet on their selections were more certain that their horses would win than were those who had made their selections but had not yet actually placed the bets (Knox & Inkster, 1968). This phenomenon serves to reinforce the post-decisional behavior that arises for the purpose of reducing dissonance.

Blotnick's (1980c, p. 135) following observations based on the responses of his sample of 1500 investors lends further support to the relevance of cognitive dissonance theory for explaining investor behavior.

> When speculation was high and the market was going up investors become more involved with the market's daily fluctuations. When it began to go down they became less involved saying that they weren't 'gamblers' and didn't want to be involved 'each and every day.' They soon began reclassifying themselves as 'conservative investors.' The more fully invested they were the more that was the case.

The reclassification of the type of investor they see themselves as being functions to reduce the dissonance created by holding the incompatible cognitions: "I am a speculator;" "I am not following the market everyday." By seeing themselves as conservative investors who are in for the long pull, they mitigate the dissonance brought about by perceiving themselves as speculators, while also asserting that they are not monitoring the market as frequently as they did when it was rising. This behavior, according to Blotnick, is counterproductive to the objective of making money by buying low and selling high.

ful of an important psychological
they make a choice between two
dissonance effect and its conse-
d and to occur within a variety of
estor behavior is obvious.[7]

N THEORY

nans have a relentless desire to
Festinger, 1954). When "objec-
ble for the purpose of determining
behaviors, people compare their
0, p. 272) claims that, "an opin-
nd 'proper' to the degree that it is
liefs, opinions and attitudes." He
compare their evaluations about
are similar to them in significant

d usefulness of social comparison
r comes from several observations
data collected from a sample of
s' judgment of what is sensible is
ate their stock market expertise by
erienced with those made by their
ket savvy by comparing the perfor-
re doing the best at any given time.
g they feel that the stocks they hold
should be doing as well," writes Blotnick. He states that, "Investors tend to measure the performance of their entire portfolio against the performance of the hottest market group at the time."

Interestingly, then, it appears that while investors do select similar investors with whom to compare their performance (which is predicted by social comparison theory), they also evaluate their market acumen by comparing their stocks' performance with those that are doing the best at a given time. Thus, unless they also hold those stocks, they are likely to feel that their market expertise is inadequate. This mode of comparison is unwise since, as Blotnick observes, it results in people selling stocks that would be apt to rise in the future and in purchasing issues that most likely had already made their major upward moves.

Comparisons of all kinds are rampant on Wall Street by professionals and amateurs alike. In addition to investors comparing the performance of their portfolios with those of others, the performance of mutual funds are contrasted with each other and with the various stock indices. This encourages the managers of those funds to make moves that will make them look good (or at least not bad) in the short run, but not necessarily in the medium or long range time frame. Indeed (as Lowry shows in Chapter 2), the term "window-dressing" has been created to refer to the changes money managers make in the portfolios they manage so that the funds' quarterly statements will show that they have positions in the current favorites. For example, in the summer of 1982, the 130 point surge in the Dow Jones Industrial Average (on record volume) was fueled, in part, by money managers' desire not to be caught holding much cash while stocks were soaring. This helps to explain why no major correction occurred even after the Dow rose nearly two hundred points in only two months. Those money managers who had not committed money to the market during the early stages of the advance because they wanted to wait for the correction, did so upon seeing that no substantial correction developed. Thus the awareness that the performance of their fund would be compared with other funds and with the Dow affects managers' decision making. This awareness on the part of the money managers can also be used to account for sudden and sharp declines in a stock's price. As A. Smith (1982, p. 26) has observed:

> Corporations generally divide their pension fund management among several banks and investment managers. The treasurer of the corporation keeps track of the investment performance; he compares each manager quarter by quarter to the market as a whole and of course to each other, and he reports to the board. In a down market, some director will say, 'We are paying these fellows to *lose* money?' So the treasurer lops off the two worst performing funds and gets two others. . . . So the procedure is, once a stock starts to collapse, it collapses completely, because no institutional manager can afford to show it in his portfolio at the end of the quarter. . . . At some point in the slide, the managers sell the stock because they know that other managers are selling the stock because nobody wants to show it in the portfolio at the end of the quarter.

Social comparison theory makes us aware of some of the undesirable consequences that result from the continual comparisons that investors—professional and amateurs—make between the performance of their portfolios. It shows us how their behavior is, in part, affected by those to whom they compare their market record.

CONTEXTUAL ANALYSIS AND MARKET BEHAVIOR

Fundamental to the sociological perspective is the assumption that the cultural, situational and group contexts within which people interact affect their behavior. Several sociological studies which have become classics illustrate this point very well. One is Durkheim's (1951) study of suicide rates. He showed that a country's divorce laws, among other factors, affect the rates of suicide among single and married individuals. Another study (Lipset, Trow & Coleman, 1962) which nicely illustrates the potency of contextual variables, indicated that whether or not a union member votes in line with his political predispositions is dependent upon the nature of the political sentiment prevailing in the printing shop where he works. Finally, Davis' (1966) investigation showed that when students' high school grades and SAT scores are controlled for, they will obtain higher grades if they attend less competitive colleges. Their choice of careers will also be influenced by the degree of competitiveness that characterizes the college they attend. Thus, for these studies, the contextual variables are: a country's divorce laws; the political sentiment prevailing in a printing shop, and the degree of competitiveness characterizing a college. All of these studies show that the nature of the context within which people interact may either facilitate or inhibit the expression of their individual tendencies.

Contextual analysis, while not a theory in the strict sense of the term, can be useful in illuminating the relationships that exist between individual stocks and the industries to which they belong, the market on which they are traded, the national economy, and the international financial situation as a whole.

The stock of a corporation can be viewed as analogous to an individual, its price fluctuations analogous to the behavior of that individual. Each corporation's price movements may thus be seen as dependent upon the characteristics of the several different contexts within which it is situated: (1) the industry to which the company belongs; (2) the market on which its stock is traded; (3) the national economy, especially with respect to conditions which impact on the industry of which the company is a part; and (4) the international economy more generally. We will briefly discuss these four contexts and show how they may affect the price movement of a company's shares.

Industry Context

Most companies are part of particular industries. The price action of the company's shares will be affected by the demand for the products it produces or the services it provides. Internal political decisions, such as the amount of money the government will allocate for defense, health care and mass transportation, will also influence an industry's fortunes. Similarly, laws which either increase or decrease the regulation of industries will have an effect on the companies that are part of these industries. In addition, demographic and lifestyle changes may affect the health of particular industries. The postwar baby boom, for example, had a positive effect on industries that produced baby food, toys and crayons, to cite just a few. Similarly, the recent trend toward dual-career households has been a boom to the daycare industry. Also, the recent nearly obsessive concern on the part of the public with developing and living a health-generating lifestyle has had a favorable impact on the athletic equipment, health food and vitamin industries. Demand for an industry's products can also be influenced by the emergence of consumer fads. For example, items which have come into vogue over the past several years include food processors, video casette recorders, home computers and video computer games. The stocks of companies manufacturing these items ride the roller coaster of their products' popularity.

Context of the Stock Market

The state of the stock market also serves as an environment for the stocks that are traded on it. While the market as a whole is, of course, affected by the contexts just discussed, it also generates its own context. Such technical variables as volume, market averages in relation to their historic highs and lows, number of issues making new highs and lows, short interest, margin debt and the advance-decline ratio, affect the action of individual stocks. While there is considerable disagreement among market analysts as to the predictive power of technical analysis, the fact that an increasing number of investment professionals and amateurs alike believe it has some validity adds to its importance.

National Economic Context

The state of the national economy will clearly have an impact on various industries and the corporations comprising them. In many cases the impact is varied depending on the type of industry. For example, during times of high interest rates, high unemployment and low inflation, industries involved in the production of basic essentials such as food, pharmaceuticals and discount department stores are apt to do well. During times of low interest rates, low unemployment and moderate to high inflation, natural resource, housing and automobile industries will be robust.

International Economic Context

The economies of the world constitute yet another environment for corporations. Generally, however, when the United States economy is strong the economies of other nations will benefit. The pervasive interdependence among the world economies has recently been underscored by the possibility that several countries, Argentina, Mexico, Poland and Cuba, may default on billions of dollars of loans that were made to them by United States and Western European banks. If one or several such defaults were to occur, the repercussions would be enormous.

Contextual analysis, as applied to the behavior of stocks, directs us to see their fluctuations as a function of a variety of interconnected contexts and the specific stocks under consideration. It underscores the notion that corporations do not operate within a vacuum but, on the contrary, engage in a continuous series of interchanges with their environments. This is important because there is a tendency among investors (especially the unsophisticated ones) to overemphasize the attributes of specific stocks at the expense of considering the present and possible future states of the stocks' environments. This tendency is analogous to the fact that people usually attribute the cause of human behavior primarily to factors that reside within the individual, in contrast to cultural, social and situational contexts within which the individual exists.

In this chapter I have attempted to lay a theoretical foundation to enhance the reader's understanding of how financial market behavior can be viewed from a sociological perspective. To some extent I have drawn out the implications of these theories for analyzing specific instances and forms of action. Let us now focus on some more specialized dimensions of our financial markets, where these theories will be used and applied to particular arenas and their characteristics.

NOTES

1. One stock market participant, reflecting on the many exceptions that can be found to apply to any type of strategy designed to ''beat the market'' observed, ''The only rule is that there are no rules.''

2. This is not always the case, of course. Dramatic positive or negative developments can occur abruptly and have a major impact on a company's future earnings and prospects. Examples of such positive events would be the discovery of a major oil field or a gold mine; the acquisition of another company or, conversely, the purchase of the company's shares by another corporation; the awarding of a major contract, or the hiring of a person who has a proven record of success. These types of events may and can have a justifiably sharp upward affect on the price of the company's stock.

3. These examples assume that there is at least some empirical validity to the traditional notion of personality as a set of interrelated traits which are relatively trans-situational, enduring through the life cycle and predisposing people to behave in particular ways. This traditional concept of personality has been criticized by several psychologists who argue that the correlation between personality traits and behavior is not significant and that situational types of variables are adequate to explain most behaviors (Mischel, 1968). Both the traditional trait theorists and the situational theorists have in many cases overstated their positions. As Bowers (1973, p. 307) has remarked, ''Although it is undoubtedly true that behavior is more situation specific than trait theory acknowledged, it is herein argued that situations are more person specific than is commonly recognized.'' An approach which focuses on the *interaction* between traits and situations appears to be the one that is most acceptable, both theoretically and empirically. This approach attempts to ''assess the relative variance contributed by situations and persons to behavior, and examines how situations and persons *interact* in evoking behavior'' (Endler, 1973).

4. It can also be plausibly argued that the opposite may also be true. A person who thrives on excitement and enjoys risk-taking in one realm (sports, dangerous occupations) may be timid and fearful when it comes to risking his money. Similarly, the individual who is shy and fearful in matters involving physical danger or social interaction may be an aggressive market participant, one who seeks out risky situations and highly speculative stocks. Indeed, he may behave this way with respect to financial matters *because* of his timidity in other realms. Which possibility actually is most likely to be the case can only be determined through empirical investigations.

5. There are, of course, many exceptions to this statement. Some people are most apt to follow the advice of a broker or market adviser who has done the research. Others may purchase a stock merely upon hearing it mentioned by a friend or casual acquaintance.

6. Astute market students and participants are aware of the strong temptation to hold on to declining issues even though they may not be cognizant of the underlying psychological dynamics

that are responsible for it. That is why many of them advocate the use of mechanical type formulas. The use of a stop loss order where the broker is instructed to sell the stock once it declines a certain amount from the price at which it was bought is an example of such a strategy. Indeed, some brokers advise clients to put in a stop-loss order at the same time they have received confirmation of their buy order.

7. Cognitive dissonance theory and its implications are also applicable to investment decisions made by a group or committee. Many institutions use this approach to investment decision making. Also, it is probable that dissonance reduction behavior is reinforced by the "groupthink" phenomenon, defined by Janis as ". . . a mode of thinking that people engage in when they are deeply involved in a cohesive in-group, when the members' strivings for unanimity override their motivation to realistically appraise alternative courses of action" (Janis, 1972, p. 9).

REFERENCES

Adler, P. Momentum: a theory of social action. Beverly Hills: Sage, 1981.

Baker, W. The successful investor. *Psychology Today,* November 1971, pp. 59; 84–86.

Blotnick, S. In search of a story. *Forbes,* April 2, 1979, pp. 124–125. (a)

Blotnick, S. Stocks are like books. *Forbes,* May 28, 1979, pp. 116–117. (b)

Blotnick, S. Small lies, big losses. *Forbes,* January 7, 1980, p. 266. (a)

Blotnick, S. Don't sit on it, it rotates. *Forbes,* March 17, 1980, pp. 198–219. (b)

Blotnick, S. The bear and the ostrich. *Forbes,* March 31, 1980, pp. 134–135. (c)

Blumer, H. Fashion. In D. Sills (Ed.), *International encyclopedia of social sciences* (Vol. 5). New York: Macmillan, 1968.

Blumer, H. Outline of collective behavior. In R. R. Evans (Ed.), *Readings in collective behavior.* Chicago: Rand-McNally, 1969.

Blustein, P. Is the stock market really efficient? Go ask a bubba. *The Wall Street Journal,* March 15, 1969, pp. 1; 17.

Bowers, K. S. Situationism in psychology: An analysis and a critique. *Psychological Review,* 1973, *80*(5), 307–335.

Brehm, J. Post-decision changes in desirability of alternatives. *Journal of Abnormal and Social Psychology,* 1956, *52,* 384–389.

Davis, J. The campus as a frog pond: An application of the theory of relative deprivation to career decisions of college men. *American Journal of Sociology,* 1966, *72,* 17–31.

Durkheim, E. *Suicide.* New York: Free Press, 1951.

Endler, N. S. The case of person-situation interactions. *Proceedings of the 81st Annual Convention of the American Psychological Association,* 1973.

Festinger, L. Informal social communication. *Psychological Review,* 1950, *57,* 271–282.

Festinger, L. A theory of social comparison process. *Human Relations,* 1954, *7,* 117–140.

Festinger, L. *A theory of cognitive dissonance.* Stanford, Cal.: Stanford University Press, 1957.

Janis, I. L. *Victims of groupthink.* Boston: Houghton-Mifflin, 1972.

King, J. *Human behavior and Wall Street.* Athens, Ohio: Swallow, 1973.

Knox, R., & Inkster, J. Post-decision dissonance at post-time. *Journal of Personality and Social Psychology,* 1968, *8,* 319–323.

Lang, K., & Lang, G. *Collective dynamics.* New York: Crowell, 1961.

LeBon, G. *The crowd.* New York: MacMillan, 1897.

Lipset, S. M., Trow, M. A., & Coleman, J. S. *Union democracy.* Garden City, N.Y.: Anchor, 1962.

Mann, L., Nagel, T., & Dowling, P. A study of an economic panic: The 'run' on the Hindmarsh building society. *Sociometry,* 1976, *39*(3), 223–235.

Mischel, W. *Personality and assessment.* New York: Wiley, 1968.

Rose, A. M. Rumor in the stock market. *Public Opinion Quarterly,* 1951, *15,* 461–486.

Smelser, N. *Theory of collective behavior*. New York: Free Press, 1962.

Smith, A. Stock values: Notes on the lemming syndrome. *The Wall Street Journal,* March 26, 1982, p. 26.

Smith, C. W. *The mind of the market*. Totowa, N.J.: Rowman & Littlefield, 1981.

Turner, R. H. Collective behavior. In R. Faris (Ed.), *Handbook of modern sociology*. Chicago: Rand McRally, 1964.

Turner, R. H., & Killian, L. *Collective behavior* (2nd ed.). Englewood Cliffs, N.J.: Prentice-Hall, 1972.

Wallace, A. Mass phenomena. In D. Sills (Ed.), *International encyclopedia of social sciences* (Vol. 10). New York: Macmillan, 1968.

Wheeler, L. *Interpersonal behavior*. Boston: Allyn & Bacon, 1970.

PART III

INDIVIDUALS, GROUPS AND ORGANIZATIONS

THE MARKET AS COLLECTIVE BEHAVIOR

Patricia A. Adler and Peter Adler

Chapter 1 outlined the various perspectives which have been applied to financial markets. As noted there, markets have been construed as either a perfectly rational allocator of funds (almost devoid of human qualities) or as an irrational mass arena that is unpredictable and therefore incomprehensible. From a sociological point of view such extreme evaluations appear to be unwarranted. In this chapter we will show how and why the stock market operates in a very understandable, albeit unpredictable, manner.

First, we suggest that instead of the stock market reacting directly to trends and events in society, that macro social, economic, political and business forces can only affect stock price values through their influence on the thoughts and deeds of people engaged in buying and selling shares of stock. These social beings are subject to the whimsies and complex motivations uniquely characteristic of human behavior. It is their social psychological reaction, organization and selection processes (Mead, 1934) which transform the inert, supportive machinery of the market into the vibrant social institution we all know. Taking stock price values as the dependent variable, then, we recognize human investor behavior, rather than some abstract, external force, as the independent causative variable.

Second, in contrast to the economists who view human market behavior as so overly-rational as to be machine-like and the crowd psychologists who view the participating public as so irrational that they consider them subhuman, we take the actions and reactions of people involved in the stock market as quite representative of the ordinary behavior patterns witnessed in other spheres of life. We intend to show that the collective behavior of market participants is a series of understandable responses to the social structure, social organization, perceptions, communications and mobilization occurring within this setting. Finally, extrapolating from insights gleaned from Blumer (1951), Smelser (1962), and Adler (1981), we draw out the social psychological, symbolic and collective characteristics of stock market behavior, presenting and analyzing the effects of the social interaction patterns we find there on market pricing.

SOCIAL PSYCHOLOGICAL CHARACTERISTICS

As we have noted, abstract political, economic, social and business trends are able to become translated into expression only through the concrete realities of stock market functioning: through human beings buying and selling. As contrarians clearly recognize, it is human volition which fuels the dips and recoveries of Wall Street, motivated by individuals' attitudes about opportunities for gain and caution (rooted in their feelings of fear, greed, optimism, etc.). Social psychological traits provide a crucial framework, then, because all other influences must be filtered through these human actors.

Interaction Patterns Within and Between Groups

The responsibility for making judgments about the validity and timing of buying and selling is always hazardous, confusing the bold and terrifying the indecisive. One result of this situation is the prevailing "*sheep mentality*," the dominant stock market pattern of following others' thoughts and initiatives, thereby obviating the financial and self-esteem risk of personal decision making. Although popular sentiment often resembles a confused rumbling of ideas and emotions, indistinguishable in origin or path of diffusion, two discrete models of such mirroring can be discerned.

Following "like" others occurs on all levels and among all groups of market participants. This anxious conformity to the analyses and behavior of peers represents a clear manifestation of the human herd instinct.[1] In this pattern, the ideas being frenetically and emphatically passed around the group have no clear point of initiation; they somehow arise through the hesitant offerings and compounding certainty of the interactive process, through "groupthink" (Janis, 1972). Stock market outsiders, because of their general uncertainty and ignorance, are understandably prey to jumping aboard these "latest notions." The corporate mailings they receive are predominantly incomprehensible to laymen and access to real business knowledge about firms is unavailable. Thus, they watch each other closely to ensure remaining abreast of any new information received. One broker describes the scene created by these "board watchers" or "brokerage sitters" at his place of business:

> They all know each other and they stir up a great deal of momentum amongst themselves. When one guy gets an idea to buy 1000 shares of ABC stock, either because he's heard a rumor, tip or "hot" story from someone else, he'll run up to the rail and yell his order across to his broker. Then the guy in the next chair will immediately run over to his broker and order 2000 shares of the same stock.

Stock market insiders are no more impervious to this suggestibility than those on the outside; in fact, they may be even more subject to its influence. People considered experts in the field are constantly interacting with each other to seek out opinions, and because market movement is tied to the volatile whims of human nature, they are often as unsure about trends and directions as their less informed compatriots. Thus, as one investment banker remarked, they, too, hug the flow of the fold:

> People base their opinions on the prevalent attitude of others like themselves, being affected by group psychology and the momentum of the market. They're nothing but a bunch of sheep trampling after each other. If the market is weak for one week you'll find the overwhelming attitude among these "professionals" a pessimistic one. Similarly, the most bearish individual won't stick his neck out when everybody is thinking bull.

Professional managers of institutional funds are especially prone to this fear motivation, panicking into the market and out of it as soon as they detect the slightest indication of this tendency among their colleagues; their concern is not overall profit, but establishing a performance record that compares favorably with other money managers.

> Relative performance is all that matters to me. If the market collapses and my funds collapse less that's okay with me. I've done my job (Dreman, 1977:110).

Thus, by circularly shadowing the beliefs and actions of like others, market participants create and foster the type of groupthink or sheep mentality that will push an originally sound investment judgment past the limits of its value.

The second observable pattern of interaction involves *copying opinion leaders,* where information and imitation diffuses from an inside central core toward the outer fringes. The center of this behavioral chain is a nebulously defined "They," who supposedly control the market with their inside information and immense purchasing power (see Bond, 1930; Smith, 1967). Different theories hold that "They" have the power to move stocks and that "They" always get the information first, or maybe even create the information. Although ascribed membership in this group varies with each opinion consulted, inside speculators and floor traders are carefully observed by others because of their propinquity to the actual base of price fluctuation, giving them the power to whip up a spiraling momentum through a frenzy of interstimulated trading. Securities analysts are also prime candidates to be "Them," since they create the fundamental analyses which form the foundations of conventional wisdom. And recently, with the rise in power and influence of the institutional funds, professional money managers have been accused of being "Them" (Smith, 1967, pp. 208–215; Lowry, Chapter 2). These opinion leaders are all market insiders, working in the exchanges daily as a profession. From among their midst comes a continual stream of evaluations and pronouncements which are then transmitted outward toward the buying public.

Large brokerage houses are prime carriers of this information, publishing the opinions and "buy lists" of their resident analysts, and distributing them to each affiliated customer's representative around the country. These individuals then dispense advice to their clients on market conditions, theories and the management of portfolios. Active and knowledgeable clients in turn distribute their information and opinions to friends not as abreast of the current market situation. Thus, copying opinion leaders includes following the opinions and actions of both specific others (analysts, brokers or trusted friends) and the generalized other (They).

Implications of These Behavioral Patterns

The communication patterns we have just noted affect the character and dynamics of the market greatly, creating a series of effects on its price fluctuations. Following "like" others leads to the development and perpetuation of a cyclical buying and selling rationale, where people seek to follow the momentum of what is happening, and in so doing, give thrust to its legitimacy anew. As increasing numbers of people are drawn to this burgeoning collective belief, a *bandwagon effect* begins to develop, accentuating any existing market trend and pushing it further along in a given direction.

The outward diffusion created by following opinion leaders yields another market dynamic: the *lag effect*. Here, the ideology and excitement pass from group to group, affecting those on the outer fringes later than those in the central core. Once a belief in some idea has solidified, it can develop the self-generating and escalating force of "momentum" (Adler, 1981), so that withdrawing the initial source of drive does not halt the idea's progress; rather, motion continues, spurred by the acceptance it has gained, until it eventually coasts to a stop. Thus, when insiders stop buying and begin selling, outsiders continue their purchasing, as yet unaware that their leaders have switched tracks. Out of ignorance, outsiders are still propelled by the preceding but now moribund bullish attitude.

Conversely, an *anticipatory effect* is also highly evident in the market because of the "*discounting*" practice, where future performance potential is incorporated into the value level of existing securities. Highly subjective in nature, prices thus go beyond reflecting a corporation's current worth to yielding an assessment of how people evaluate the firm's upcoming growth, earnings and dividend potential. Any new information concerning either one particular company or the general political, economic, social and business context which surrounds it, will immediately cause a reconsideration of the former expression and, through a flurry of buying and selling, be included in the new measure of the company's stock value.

What we have, then, is a highly excitable arena where multiple groups and philosophies constantly interact in a complex and ultimately unpredictable manner. And, because of the volatile nature of public sentiment, the prevalence of sudden shifts in collective attitude adds the *pendulum swing* to the overall pattern of price fluctuation caused by group social psychological characteristics.

BOOMS AND BUSTS AS COLLECTIVE BEHAVIOR

> Born in a boom and cradled in a panic, the history of the stock market has been that of an alternation of booms and panics (Pratt, 1912, p. 349).

Indeed a volatile arena, the stock market swings back and forth between the extremes of high and low with a far greater frequency and intensity than does the surrounding business economy. This very fact is testimonial once again to our assertion concerning the role of human group behavior in causing prices to fluctuate. We now consider the dramatic extremes of high and low that occur within the market, using them to *illustrate* both the social psychological patterns we have just sketched out and the role of collective attitudes and actions in causing these booms and busts. When carried to its fullest, this perspective suggests that booms and busts can be conceptually defined as a certain progression of collective behavior which is then reflected in stock market prices. Thus, the market is seen as more than an institutional superstructure composed of roles and mechanisms which permit the fluid exchange of capital and business goods; as Blumer (1969) proposes, macro forces and structures are in fact no more than people interacting with people, no more than an interlinkage of action which can be concretely studied and described.

In the following discussion we will explore the progression of market price fluctuations and the collective behavior underlying and fueling them. Beginning with structural preconditions and following through the initiation, intensification and termination of market swings, we will examine crazes and panics leading to booms and busts, pointing out both their basic similarities and their modes of divergence.

Preconditions

As noted in Chapter 4, Smelser posits a range of conditions which he describes as necessary to the eruption of panic or craze behavior.

Structural conduciveness. There must be a degree of structural conduciveness inherent in the arena. The first dimension of this is rooted in the financial liquidity of the market. Under normal conditions, people can readily acquire or dispose of securities or commodities through institutionalized channels with great ease; a phone call to one's broker is generally all that is necessary to effect the purchase or sale of stocks. Thus the market offers maneuverability, flexibility, and a differentiated system for the ready trading of assets.

A second dimension of the market's structural conduciveness to extreme forms of collective behavior is rooted in the rapid and facile dissemination of relevant information. People are subject to being highly influenced by the mass media and each other, especially with regard to financial market behavior. The ease with which rumors, news, opinions, beliefs and emotional states can be communicated and acted upon makes this a highly volatile sphere.

Strain. A second precondition Smelser attributes to the development of financial panics and crazes is the element of strain. People who participate in financial market transactions are vulnerable to a variety of strains caused by their myriad feelings of uncertainty. They are subjected to conflicting opinions given by friends, associates, economists and market analysts. Further compounding the strain is the fact that investors have no control over the variables that affect both the market as a whole and the specific stocks which they own. They cannot influence what the GNP, prime interest rate or consumer price index will be. Nor do they have the power to control the sales, earnings or profit margins of companies whose stock they own. Feelings of psychological strain and uncertainty are most likely to occur when there is a significant change in economic policy and when there is no consensus regarding the effects of the policy changes on the economy and financial markets. Strain which can lead to panics is apt to be especially pronounced when some negative event occurs such as the assassination of a president, the cutoff of a necessary commodity or the outbreak of war.

In contrast, strain which leads to craze behavior and financial booms is most likely to occur under the following conditions (Smelser, 1962, pp. 188–189): (1) uncertainty as to the amount of return to be expected from current modes of investing money; (2) ambiguity concerning the level of profit that may accrue from alternative forms of investment; and (3) ready availability of money to invest in new forms of speculation. Thus, craze behavior becomes increasingly likely when people experience a sense of dissatisfaction with the return that they are receiving from their present investments and when they have the idea that they may receive a greater return on their money if they engage in financial experimentation. When these individuals are relatively unsophisticated about financial matters, the chances of a craze occurring increases.

Spread of generalized beliefs. Smelser's third prerequisite to the development of panics and crazes is the spread of generalized beliefs. All types of mass phenomena are based on collective orientations which ready people for action. Hysterical beliefs are the type which predispose people to engage in panic behavior. They are characterized by ambiguity, anxiety and a redefinition of the situation. Feelings of threat and disaster which were initially ambiguous and uncertain become certain and clear-cut when people accept a particular belief as true. During periods of uncertainty and strain, rumors are likely to be spread and believed. If market participants believe that an international banking crisis is imminent or that a major brokerage firm will file for bankruptcy, for example, they become predisposed to panic behavior.

Collective assumptions which move people toward crazes usually take the form of wish-fulfillment beliefs. Such fantasies are present in at least latent form among people living in most western countries, especially the United States. "The 'get-rich-quick' mentality . . . is an established cultural belief that does not have to be 'created' for every new speculative outburst. It is always present and needs only to be excited by the presence of other conditions" (Smelser, 1962, p. 201). The prevalence of the get-rich-quick ethos can be noted by the frequency with which books advising their purchasers on how to make a fortune in either stocks, real estate or the mail order business, etc. appear and become bestsellers. Such tale, lore and illustrations function to keep this element of our American cultural belief system embedded in people's consciousness.

When individuals learn that others are receiving a much greater return on money than they have been obtaining, they become predisposed to reallocate their financial resources. They develop the belief that if they only knew where to invest their money they, too, could realize this higher return. Such attitudes make them vulnerable to the allure of each successive investment fad. And, as Chapter 4 notes, collective inclinations toward accepting new beliefs are highly influenced by the vacillations of fad and fashion. As one securities analyst advised:

> Never underestimate the importance of fashion in any sphere of life, especially the stock market. It's what sets the attitudes of all the sheep on Wall Street who are busy running around trying to catch up with the latest trend.

Slogans and catchwords that represent new ideas can be vitally important in gaining initial attention, securing recurring recognition and ultimately obtaining positive acceptance for a new market ideology. The germ of a fad can come from a new product—catching the public eye and boosting confidence in its manufacturer. Or, fashion can strike an entire industry as Mackay (1932) describes tulips did in seventeenth century Holland or the South Sea bubble of eighteenth century England, possessing people with the unquenchable drive to invest in a particular commodity. This phenomenon can even strike at the very essence of investment behavior itself, causing people to jump on the bandwagon of one investment strategy after another as the credibility of different analysts waxes and wanes, and perceptions of situational market conditions shift (as the section on investment fads in Chapter 4 discusses). Thus, through the various processes outlined here, the ordinary ambiguity and diversity of ideas among market participants becomes replaced by a shared belief that the market as a whole or one specific part of it is becoming either "hot" or dangerously weak.

Initiation

Stock market booms and busts can take a variety of forms, being launched, developed and concluded in either a leisurely or abrupt manner.

Spark starts. Given the background just described, the occurrence of what Smelser terms a "precipitating factor" will most likely throw the market into a sudden motion. Spark starts are characterized by "quick trigger reactions," a flurry of trades that quickly move a stock price higher or lower. A spark start can originate from a number of distinct causes. Charismatic events, singly or in a series, can send people scrambling to adjust their holdings so that they will reflect the latest in a series of continuously evolving expectations. Public news detailing developments of a less dramatic nature can also provide an impetus, creating a wave of optimistic or pessimistic anticipation to ruffle market prices. Both of these precipitating factors yield what Smelser calls "mobilization to action," where people act by buying and selling on the basis of their collective interpretations of the future effects an event will produce.

Collective behavior arising from the dispersal of private news (i.e., inside information, tips, rumors) results in a somewhat different pattern of initiation. Here, the unequal and selective dissemination of information forms a contrast to the instantaneous and universal availability of public news. Secret knowledge finds its way to the surface through complex leakage mechanisms based on interactional patterns that can be both inadvertent and purposeful, moving from the inner core outwards. The predominant type of private news is inside information about upcoming social, economic, political or business developments. Corporate directors and executives usually have advance knowledge of such plans as stock splits, mergers, or dividend cancellations, and although technically they are legally prohibited from taking a position in the market or passing this information on to friends, such occurrences are fairly common.

Tips are another form occasionally taken by inside information, but these pieces of news, furtively passed from one individual to another (especially among brokerage sitters and other outsiders) are as likely to be groundless in fact as they are to be valuable. Nevertheless they excite a flurry of emotion and prompt rapid buying and selling. Rumor is the most nebulous type of private news, mysterious in origin and variable in accuracy. Passed from one aggregate of people to another, it can turn out to be advance public news, inside information, deliberately misleading information, or innocent falsity (Rose, 1951).

In contrast to public news, where the "startle effect" hits everybody simultaneously and creates a market surge that expends itself in one period of great intensity, private news seeps out in an alluring way that slowly begins to gain attention. As people begin to wonder why a stock price is moving unusually rapidly, they may hesitate at first but often try to follow the trend before it is announced publicly. The fascination of secret information can thus seduce people into exaggerated collective reactions, causing a greater collective thrust than had it been revealed instantaneously.

The result of this initial impetus on generalized attitudes is to transform previous vague suspicions into a more certain specific belief by confirming ideas which had already begun to form. Any type of communication, whether face-to-face or via the mass media, can help to establish this common definition of the situation, solidifying what had previously been an uneasy and unorganized glimmer of ideas. For the unfolding market bust, the unfocused anxiety is replaced by concrete fear of collapse, while in the case of developing boom, the fantasy of unlimited financial gain becomes attached to definite goals and means. Good news, though, never seems to produce as strong an effect as its inverse. The strength behind a burgeoning bear plummet is hence always more forceful than that underlying a bull rally, although the spread and concentration of movement is less noticeable during this initial impetus than during succeeding phases of the swing.

Gradual starts. A different type of boom or bust inception is represented by the gradual onset. Market swings which take shape over a longer time period can be rooted in a variety of sources. These more protracted instances of market price fluctuation are influenced by slowly unfolding fundamental business developments, as well as by the shifting pressure of collective attitudes.

Various factors can contribute to the gradual onset of a collective stock movement, in contrast to those precipitating a spark start. Pieces of undramatic news that slowly fit together into a developing picture can quietly but steadily give rise to a collective opinion that fosters the gradual origin of a market swing. From business, emerging labor troubles, overproduction, growing wage costs, increasing competition, government controls, and unforeseen accidents can contribute to a downturn. A turnover of personnel encourages increasing confidence in a company's stock, bringing new vigor, spirit, and ideas; the steady growth of earnings and dividend issuances; products that show promise of mass appeal and profitability; and international promotion of the firm through personal appearances by the directors, stockholder literature, and advertisements in the mass media.

A second class of influences on slowly emerging market movements arises from the social, economic, and political realm. Favoring the growth of collective negative opinion and actions is an ever-tightening money situation, increasing unemployment, a further drain on gold, the nearing possibility of world war, and the gradual decline of the United States as an international power. Conversely, soaring personal incomes with accompanying consumer spending, growth of total census figures, and powerful funding for defense and aerospace programs brings a relaxation of budgetary controls and an optimistic effect on upward price expansion. International as well as domestic trends can thus provide impetus to a boom or bust's gradual onset.

Although reactions to the stock market are usually highly emotional, the form of gradually developing momentum we witness over longer-term periods is more reassuring to most participants. Slow upward movements are somewhat expected, especially in periods of high inflation, thus arousing little response. Weak daily drops, even when they combine to produce an evolving pattern, also pass generally unremarked, particularly when contrasted with their sharper, more unexpected counterparts. This relative withholding of social psychological response can be traced partly to the ambiguity of gradual market motions and the overall hesitancy to pronounce a trend as developing until hindsight has made it clear. Emotional involvement is thus restricted to the dreams people have of wild and unfounded growth, and the very beginnings of more seriously based greed or malaise.

Manipulation. A third type of boom or bust's initiation, different in both form and character from both spark and gradual starts, can be found in cases of securities or commodities market manipulation. This term has two often conflicting connotations: It can refer to highly skilled and diplomatic speculators who use adroitness to conceal the intent of their trading so that others remain unaware of their plans, or it can denote the fraudulent or deceptive operator who illegally or immorally influences price changes (Pratt, 1912, pp. 364–366). Stock market manipulation of the first type has always been practiced by individuals and represents the ideal of entrepreneurial acumen in a competitive setting. Groups have also engaged in the latter procedures, combining their resources to force prices to respond in a desired way.

In the past, associations known as "pools" were created for the purpose of controlling stock prices. Legal arrangements were drawn up specifying the members, their intents, and the procedures to be followed. Usually pools went "long" on stocks, secretly purchasing all the available shares in order eventually to create an "oligopoly," the market condition where there are few sellers (demand exceeds supply). Various techniques would be employed to acquire a saturation amount of stock. First the "floating supply," or quantity of shares not held in long-term investment by individuals or corporate executives, would be gradually bought over several months by different pool members seeking to conceal their accumulation. Then "shake-out" techniques, ranging from the spread of malicious rumors to temporarily flooding the market to drive prices down, would be effected in the plan to jar more stock loose from investors. With the scarcity of salable stock thus achieved, one member of the pool would begin offering purchase bids, confident that few sellers remained. This would cause a tremendous boom to steadily develop, driving the price to indefinitely high levels, where the pool then dispersed of their holdings, as was previously determined. On rare occasions a pool would be formed to go short and seek an "oligopsony," or scarcity of demand. By discreetly borrowing massive shares of a leading stock to sell and then driving the price down with false reports, the pool members could repurchase their obligations at wholesale prices, before the misinformation was discovered.[2]

Unfortunately, the unified efforts of a few were so often successful in totally controlling market prices, stopping them or driving them at will to the detriment of all outsiders, that the SEC was forced to provide regulations outlawing such banding together. Due to the profitability in pooling funds to make vast purchases and "corner the market" in a given security or commodity, however, this behavior still surfaces illegally on a smaller scale.

The recent publicity surrounding the Hunt brothers' case offers a small glimpse into what may happen today with greater frequency than is suspected. In this situation, the heirs of billionaire H. L. Hunt attempted (and succeeded in the silver market) to illegally corner the market in soybeans and silver on the Chicago Board of Trade and New York's Commodities Exchange. Allied with family members and a pool of Arab investors, the Hunt brothers succeeded in acquiring more than 22 million bushels of soybeans in early 1977 (nearly one third of the market) and over 200 ounces of silver by early 1980. This caused the Commodity Futures Trading Commission to impose such restrictions that the silver market broke and threatened to topple the entire commodities exchange.[3] Usually affecting only one security or commodity at a time, manipulation is the power to dominate price fluctuation at will; once control has been acquired the individual or group can create a gradual movement, sudden rush, or total freeze.

Intensification

A general proclivity toward panic or craze behavior coupled with an initial thrust is not adequate to ensuring the advent of a complete bust or boom. In addition, there must be some secondary or "derivative" (Adler, 1981) reaction that builds upon the primary impetus and carries the behavioral and, hence, price movement beyond it. The perception, generalized belief and mobilization for action must spread to include an increasingly large group of people, through the contagion of either joint "interstimulation" (Blumer, 1951) or individual telescoping of the value added process (Smelser, 1962). Only once this reactive procedure has occurred can the collective behavior be considered to have developed an internally self-generating force which will sustain its ascension to even greater levels of intensity and momentum. Let us first consider the intensification process which succeeds and anchors the strength of the spark start and then examine the intensification growing out of the more gradual onset.

Carry through. For all its drama the panic or craze's spark start cannot develop into a boom or bust without subsequent "carry through" to intensify its initial potency. During the spark start's carry through phase we note the difference between bull (upward) and bear (downward) movements: upward surges generally take longer to cultivate and instill, while downward plunges can escalate rapidly with greater ease. Thus price swings growing out of spark starts are generally of the bear, bust or panic variety. In this situation, the precipitating factor has created a negative atmosphere where optimism about the market's future stability is cast into doubt. Avid bears who chronically seek to profit by selling short can exploit an initiated spark and heighten it through speculation. Their active role of selling borrowed shares in order to drive the value down for later repurchasing thrives on the chaos and misfortune they create, fostering a general confusion, especially among outsiders, who are usually ignorant about such manipulative practices. As these investors become paralyzed by uncertainty and worry, the downward momentum builds.

The spark start to panic behavior does not always develop into a full-fledged bust. As Smelser notes, a variety of "mechanisms for social control" exist which can catch and contain a runaway market slide before it gets out of hand. An arrest to a burgeoning panic can be purposefully orchestrated by an immediate suspension of trading: most exchanges' boards of governors have the authority to suspend trading in a particular issue or to close the entire exchange whenever they deem such action necessary to salvage stability and prevent excessive downward price motion. Such actions occur regularly for individual stocks when inside rumors set off runaway prices that threaten investor security at the hands of wily speculators. Wide-ranging traumatic events capable of plunging the entire market into pandemonium, such as a presidential assassination, require dramatic action to restore calm. In the case of Kennedy, it took two hours for the governors to assemble the suspension and vote it into effect, but the market remained closed from that Friday until the following Tuesday. By that time Johnson had been sworn in, the transition was accomplished in orderly fashion, and the entire decline was immediately recovered. Thus, the length of trading interruption judged necessary depends on the rapidity with which the underlying maelstrom or uncertainty dissipates.

Other stabilizing influences derive from the role of Wall Street clearing-houses and investment (merchant) banks that do heavy volume transacting with stock market participants and businesses in need of short-term loans. When adequately warned of an impending panic, these institutions possess the power to cut a potential panic short:

> Nothing could have been more unexpected and terrifying than the shooting of McKinley. . . . The next morning, before the stock market opened, a meeting was held at the Clearing-House, attended by the leading bankers, at which a pool of $30,000,000 was formed, and the announcement made that this sum would be loaned in the Exchange at market rates. Not a

> dollar of the money was used . . . the very assurance that the banks were ready and able to protect the market was sufficient to prevent any panics (Pratt, 1912, p. 366).

Further stabilization can come from parties sponsoring a particular stock. When major individuals, pools of people, institutions, or corporations themselves hold sufficient shares in a security, they cannot afford to let fluctuations develop that will gravely affect the worth of the company. Therefore, when the price starts to drop they will intercede to buy more shares and create a bottom limit. Similarly, when an upward sweep begins to burgeon, sponsors will offer part of their own holdings for sale to force a ceiling.

Turning from structural to active factors, the incident that sparked the panic can be effectively nullified by an opposing incident, as an experienced broker illustrated:

> Just yesterday, to cite a case, the President's Commission came out with a new report citing the extreme dangers of cigarette smoking. Naturally all the tobacco companies started falling right away. But then a tobacco industry spokesman held a press conference and accused the presidential aide of being an ex-smoker on a personal vendetta, and the stock bounced back up.

Occasionally, even the preventive measures undertaken are inadequate to contain a fledgling burst of panic, and the precautionary actions taken are swept aside by the force of the raging tide. In October 1929, after the initial tremor of shock and horror had shaken the New York Stock Exchange, a leading group of bankers under the direction of J. P. Morgan formed a pool, or "consortium," with $2.4 million available to render the fall more "orderly" and minimize the extent of the disaster. These funds proved to be insufficient, however, as the accumulated loss at the end of three weeks totalled close to $50 million (Bond, 1930, pp. 196–201).

Emotional reactions to such rapidly born negative swings grip participants more acutely because of the surprise element accompanying the sudden shift. Initially, people respond with a loss of confidence, although they are likely to hold their feelings in abeyance pending continuingly similar performance along the same trend. With tenacity, a dynamic market panic can bring mounting feelings of fright and anxiety. Sudden and massive downward explosions, which leave little time for emotions and rational strategies to adjust, produce the most extreme trauma, in which suicidal despair can occur.

Intensification of the gradual start. Both bull and bear markets can be characterized by the gradual modes of onset and acceleration. Here, as the collective buying or selling behavior begins to build from its moderate launch, it gains in potency and surety. In this situation time is the main judge of the transformation from the inception stage to that where a boom or bust can be considered established; the gradually intensifying collective movement shifts phases so subtly and smoothly that the transition can go unnoticed. One indication of advancement past the impetus is that external stimuli are no longer the only contributors to the growing price swing: It has become a self-generating force that feeds off itself. Social psychological patterns of collective behavior are triggered in an almost chain reaction, as the generated fear or greed further supports the evolving trend. This applies especially to indecisive or insecure individuals who follow a burgeoning boom or bust in a sheeplike fashion, hoping that its force will carry them.

Both bull and bear markets have their own intensification styles, complete with characteristic reactors that heighten the mushrooming momentum. In the bearish mode, the banks and credit institutions are the major swing factor, as they control the loans to people who buy on credit. They must keep their finger on the pulse of the market to determine when their own financial security is threatened by the growing down trend. Their role, although decisive, is thus reactive to a boom or bust already in progress (as contrasted with the short sellers, who are active initiators). Calling in loans, which forces calling margins, results in the sale of more stock, exacerbating the falling market. Once wiped out financially by this procedure, individuals are unable to gain a new foothold in the structure, which might slow the process.

Here, the bland passivity of the "wait-and-see" attitude is abandoned and stronger feelings begin to emerge. Fear, insecurity, and loss of confidence intensify as people react with developing signs of individual and mass hysteria. Still, because of the gradual onset of this condition, they usually have time to recognize and accept the results of these financial developments without being uncontrollably overwhelmed by them.

In the flourishing bull market there is no corresponding institutional or structural element playing the part served by banks. Smelser emphasizes the importance of key individuals who manipulatively promote certain investment issues, describing their role in leading the public to the widespread purchasing of a single stock or commodity as a major contributor to the intensification of stock market crazes. Whether charismatically manipulated by an outside individual or collectively generated through a groupthink process, the collective opinion of active market participants must gel with certainty into a favorable stance toward one investment strategy for a major market swing to become firmly established. At moments when this collective belief wavers or threatens to turn, a charismatic reification of its value can be provided by an unexpected stock split and extra dividend issuance, or by the flamboyant example of someone who has struck it rich via this investment means.

What really transforms a cautiously optimistic market into a raging upward rush is the entry of the mass public into stock buying. People's suspicions and resistance to involvement in the capricious market are only overcome, though, as they observe opinion leaders climbing aboard the bandwagon and effortlessly earning paper profits. Hence, unaffiliated persons become involved in stock purchasing in waves, as the collective behavior sweeps concentrically outward, encompassing greater numbers and types. Tempted by hope, greed, and the desire to "get in on a good thing," they add their money to the gluttonously expanding system, which becomes bloated by success and confidence. Then the fringe element, through their ignorance and gullibility, become infected with "speculator's fever" and bid prices beyond skyscraper limits. Indefinitely repeating technical formulas, they artificially inflate stock prices beyond what even psychological expectations can support. At the heights of the boom we see what Smelser calls the "speculative" phase, where investment for the purpose of high return becomes replaced by repeated buying and selling to capitalize on the skyrocketing appreciation. The practice of "pyramiding," or borrowing against the increment in a stock's value to purchase more stock, abounds and this clinches the departure from reality that pushes prices near the "natural ceiling" level.

Termination

The termination of a boom or bust, like its start and intensification, can occur either abruptly or more slowly.

Sudden breaks and turnabouts. A sharp conclusion to a dramatic market trend can be caused either by a turnabout, by that trend's replacement with its antithesis, or by an abrupt break. Quick breaks and turnabouts are most characteristic of boom terminations, where the runaway bubble receives a sharp puncture and deflates. In some cases this may be caused by an interruption to the stimulus which fueled the craze. For example, should something happen to remove a boom's chief promoter from the fore, the impetus he or she has generated could shatter and result in a collapse. More recently, the technical predictions of chartists have also been responsible for sudden terminations. When certain formations or breakpoints can be recognized (i.e., "head and shoulders" breakpoints), chartists often act individually, *en masse,* to halt a movement underway. For sudden market turnarounds, though, structural and collective preconditions favoring a new market swing have usually begun to build far in advance of the reversal's occurrence. As Smelser notes, only then can the antithetical collective behavior receive a true impetus from one thruster. One investor underscores this relationship: "Whenever you have a single event triggering a large number of events, that signifies that the trend was already set to go off without the precipitating factor." Thus, what differentiates this terminating phase from the simple spark start is the collective movement-within-a-movement—the preparatory build-up of elements (often passing largely unnoticed) that will eventually contribute to a sudden, great readjustment.

The crash of 1929, Wall Street's most famous reversal, illustrates this point.

This turnaround was preceded by spiraling investment trusts, holding companies, the reinvestment of paper profits, very high interest rates, and all the classical indicators of a "runaway boom." Under these circumstances many people, particularly the inexperienced public, lost sight of the demands and restrictions of real value in their expectation that prices would continue to soar increasingly upward. Virtually all the people in the country were drawn into investing in the stock market as they saw their equally amateurish friends and colleagues becoming "paper rich" effortlessly. This group constituted what insiders call the "fringe element," that marginal component of ignorance and ineptitude that creates the final overblown peaks and valleys in the price fluctuation curve. Unaware of the rational laws that usually moderate stock market swings, holding them within reasonable bounds, these nonparticipants continued investing indefinitely, based on their collective assumption that the market had no limit. Here the stage was set for the market to fall "of its own weight."

The transitionary phase serving as harbinger to the upcoming, short-term plummet is known as the "nervous" market. An active agitation prevails, causing securities prices to rise and fall with abnormal frequency, the gaps between trades often exceeding the one-eighth-point norm. New highs are again set, only to fall dramatically between each one. No clear collective movement toward any goal exists, but excitement runs rampant.

Finally, the break comes, sometimes induced by a specific impetus, although this is not requisite. There was no such charismatic external event on "Black Tuesday"; the insiders of Wall Street reacted, seemingly instinctively, to the overblown situation. Sensing the nervous market, many professionals had begun liquidating their portfolios to the wildly buying public. The overextension of bank loans for margin purchases and the skittish price pattern convinced insiders to turn bearish and begin selling short. Always the last to recognize and follow any new trends, the public was caught in the ensuing squeeze. The manifest cause of Wall Street's single busiest day to that point (8 million shares were traded) was the widespread calling of loans by banks, investment trusts, and credit companies. This set off a chain reaction that instantly intensified the collective behavior as brokers had to put out margin calls to their customers. Before people had time to realize what was happening they had lost their profits and investments, flooding the market with even more "forced-sell" shares. With the departure of many professionals, an overabundance of amateur speculators were left to uphold the market, thus creating a situation where few knowledgeable sponsors remained who could have alleviated the crash. Spanning from October 29 to November 13, 1929, the fall lasted barely over two weeks but covered approximately 174 points in the decline.

Here we see how the conclusion of one market momentum can fertilize the roots of the next: when one collective belief and behavior pattern has pushed itself too far in a given direction (as greed encourages), the pendulum swing is apt to occur, replacing it suddenly with a mass flight toward the opposing inclination.

Gradual ends and reversals. Gradual finales signifying the end of collective movements frequently occur as a bust is terminating. These less precipitous abatements often overlap in character with a market swing's leisurely incipience, especially in the final phases of the reversal, where the motion begins anew. The market thus revolves cyclically, never escalating indefinitely or collapsing in bankruptcy at the bottom.

The bear market's slow finale sees the collective selling easing as prices continue to fall, although at a lingering rate. As heavy liquidation runs its course, people become aware that the market may be reaching its bottom. This discourages selling, since many now hope they will soon see a rise. Naturally, the insiders are the first to become aware of this trend and they may slowly begin to repurchase shares being released by the last outsiders. When the price level finally does reach the nadir, the complete halt to the drop is often accompanied by extremely low-volume trading, as one Wall Street broker described: "At that point the most pervasive emotion in the market is boredom: confidence has reached an all-time low, no one has a compulsion to buy or sell, and there is a general loss of interest."

The rebound from bear to bull is typically a slow, painstaking process. People who have incurred losses on the way down may be reluctant or financially unable to reenter the market and start the upward swing. Here the fabled "bargain hunters" emerge to purchase valuable stocks cheaply, but their numbers are few and they are generally stock exchange professionals.

Bull markets finish sedately a smaller percentage of the time because the forces that pull the public in breed an excitement and irrationality not easily contained. If the upward price movement has a chance to subside due to the influence of pessimistically portending external events that put a damper on general enthusiasm, price rises may be curtailed, permitting a gradual decline in fluctuation intensity. The reverse thrusters that slow a boom's climbing force can also stem from within:

> The best professionals who earn their living on Wall Street must develop a "sixth sense" of when irrationality has run its course and when a sense of reason must return and make its presence felt. They cannot afford to be professional gamblers, throwing themselves against the tide to gain the long-odds winner. A sure and steady income comes from being aware of how external and internal influences come together; that's how they're able to feel when the bull market has played out its strength.

Therefore a counterforce to the runaway greed of the public can emerge from the insiders who unobtrusively but steadfastly relax the excited craze with the unruffling hand of calm selling pressure.[4] The intensity of upward movement thus brought to an end, the market will most often start into a pattern of gradual deescalation.

Terminations, whether taking the gradual or sharp form, are hence often linked to the appearance of market "ceilings" or "bottoms," largely caused by shifts in the collective perception and evaluation of surrounding factors and by the subsequent belief system and mobilization for action forming in response to them.

CONCLUSIONS

Contrasting the overall nature of the collective behavior and price fluctuations found in booms and busts, we note that downward stock movements plummet about twice as fast as upward movements climb, doing so in far greater concentration:

> A bear market, in other words, goes down by successive plunges in contrast to the steady, even when swift, ascent of prices in a general bull market. (Bond, 1930, p. 39)

Here, a single bearish week may wipe out the gains so excruciatingly wrought over a year's time.

What are some of the social and psychological elements underlying and contributing to this disparity? The first causative factor can be attributed to differences in *structural control* between the boom and the bust. Amounts and types of built-in controls inherent in their associated collective behavior, market mechanisms and the greater society, represent one dimension where an obvious disparity can be traced. For busts, the means of effecting control are primarily lodged in the early stages of its rise, through preventing its occurrence (by circulating calming information or redefining precipitating factors as harmless). Once the hysterical behavior has taken hold of the group there is little that can be done to diminish its force. Those seeking to moderate a boom have a greater chance of success, however, because structural controls can be utilized both prior to its rise and once it is underway to help abate its intensity (i.e., any normative regulation designed to ensure the honesty of stock market procedures, such as regulations on credit extension, margin purchasing and financial policies; laws against fraud, misrepresentation and inadequate information distribution) and control through leadership by officially discouraging excessive speculation. Booms are thus liable to greater external pressure and restriction (Smelser, 1962).

The *organization* of collective behavior is another area of diversity which can help to explain the difference in boom and bust price movements. Busts, as we have seen, are often sparked by professional insiders who regularly engage in short selling, and are exacerbated by the banks and brokerage houses who heighten the downward momentum by calling loans and margins. Booms, although occasionally orchestrated by a few individuals, are dependent for their full strength on the entry of the mass into the buying ranks. These two groups are clearly differentiated by their degree of organization: the insiders and major credit institutions operate with established lines of communication and known procedures for swiftly responding to familiar turns in the market, while the unconnected hordes of outsiders move haltingly and individually, unsure of which source of advice to follow. The tightly organized action of the bearish group thus enables them to bring their market results to fruition much faster and more surely than the uncertain disarray of those fostering rising prices.

A third contributor to this disparity is rooted in the human *emotions* which characterize market investment. Hope, the feeling propelling price ascensions, is a weaker and more fragile sensation than fear, the reaction driving values down. Confidence thus builds and intensifies more gradually and hesitantly than the gripping terror linked to potentially losing all. Therefore, the foreboding certainty of pessimism, which sets in more quickly than budding, cautious optimism, causes the collective beliefs and actions fueling busts to produce a greater concentration, intensity and velocity than those forging booms.

This study of the market suggests that human behavior patterns found there are neither totally rational as economists think, nor totally emotional and irrational as crowd psychologists think. Both views are fundamentally askew, the former based on statistical analyses and absolutist assumptions, the latter on overly hysterical and mystical models, both of which fail to understand the complex motivations underlying people's day-to-day social psychological characteristics and behavior. From the preceding discussion we see that people's actions concerning the market, although occasionally irrational, are predominantly understandable responses to the social structure, social organization, perceptions and collective beliefs of this complex arena, where they come to rely on certain patterns of information diffusion, advising and following the lead of seemingly knowledgeable others. The enormous masses of individuals who participate in market speculation or investment are thus highly influenced by the various groups, ideologies, actions and behavioral patterns we have discussed. The result of these ingrained social psychological features is that if enough people adopt a certain belief (no matter how financially baseless it may be), its ramifications will soon become realized in the market. The mass mood can thus vacillate between hugging fundamental economic realities closely, and departing from them through short-term fits and starts of optimism and fear. Further, even greater cycles of boom and bust can be social psychologically rooted and/or exacerbated, making the cognitive interpretations and actions of real people in concrete situations the ultimate determinant of financial market functioning.

The observations of this chapter thus stand in direct contrast to some of the implications of the Efficient Market Hypothesis, especially in its weak (Random Walk) form. Random Walk hypothesists argue that there is no *momentum* in the market (cf. Malkiel, 1981, pp. 129–130), none of what Tarascio (in chapter 3) has referred to as "serial correlation." This is because economists view price fluctuation as dependent on the public release of news (i.e., a new mineral vein strike, a corporate director's death), which they believe occurs in a random fashion. Economists argue that the market has no memory and that the direction of each day's price movement can be no more accurately predicted by looking at past movements than by randomly flipping a coin (Malkiel, 1981, pp. 130–134).

We argue, in contrast, that *there is momentum in the market*. The market is, in fact, one of the greatest arenas where momentum can be witnessed, precisely because of the dynamics of collective human behavior which occur there. People are uncertain about how the market will act due to the multitude of business, worldwide and social psychological influences which affect the fluctuation of prices. They are risking either their or someone else's money (a valuable commodity in our society) when they act. As the performance of the influential professional fund managers illustrates (especially with regard to their "window-dressing" tendencies), market participants often act out of fear motivation, following the crowd because they are afraid to get caught out of a collective trend. This herd instinct and bandwagoning effect dominates the character of price fluctuations in the short run, causing small swings in a stock's price to build into larger ones and small trends for the market as a whole to grow into a group fever. This tendency for people's behavior to influence each other also affects the development of many business and political events as well, so that the economists' idealized hypothesis that news occurs in a random fashion is false as well. Thus the events which surround the market and the collective dynamics of participating individuals who comprise the market are not independent (random), but serially correlated (both positively and negatively), causing momentum swings to occur in the ebb and flow of prices.

ACKNOWLEDGMENT

A portion of this chapter is reprinted with permission from Peter Adler, *Momentum: A Theory of Social Action,* © 1981 Sage Publications, Inc.

NOTES

1. Many theorists liken the nonreflective contagion of ideas and emotions to the conduct of animal herds. Writing of the emotionality of the mass, Simmel (Wolff, 1950:35) notes how "the softest wing beat, the slightest jump of a single animal often degenerate into a panic of the whole herd." And Blumer (1951, p. 170), too, cites the example of cattle building up to the intense fear and excitement of a stampede as illustrating a basic form of the circular reaction humans display.

2. This type of practice was obviously more feasible in the days before instantaneous mass communication became widespread.

3. For further details see the *Wall Street Journal,* January 10, 1979, and *Newsweek,* April 7, 1980, as well as *passim,* this volume.

4. However, as noted, although it does occur, this type of gradual end to a boom is rare, precisely because of the greed and exploitation possibilities that are ripe for insiders once the public is

drawn into the market. As just described under sudden turnabouts, the more likely end to an inflated condition is the nervous market, where insiders rapidly make the turn from bull to bear and profit from the cupidity and ignorance of outsiders.

REFERENCES

Adler, P. *Momentum: A theory of social action.* Beverly Hills: Sage, 1981.

Blumer, H. Collective behavior. In A. M. Lee (Ed.), *New outline of the principles of sociology.* New York: Barnes & Noble, 1951.

Blumer, H. *Symbolic interactionism: Perspective and method.* Englewood Cliffs, N.J.: Prentice-Hall, 1969.

Bond, F. D. *Stock movements and speculation.* New York: Appleton, 1930.

Dreman, D. N. *Psychology and the stock market.* New York: Amacom, 1977.

Janis, I. L. *Victims of groupthink.* Boston: Houghton-Mifflin, 1972.

Mackay, C. *Extraordinary popular delusions.* New York: Noonday, 1932.

Malkiel, B. G. *A random walk down Wall Street* (2nd ed.). New York: Norton, 1981. (Originally published, 1973.)

Mead, G. H. *Mind, self and society.* Chicago: University of Chicago Press, 1934.

Pratt, S. S. *The work of Wall Street.* New York: Appleton, 1912.

Rose, A. M. Rumor in the stock market. *Public Opinion Quarterly,* 1951, *15,* 461–486.

Smelser, N. *Theory of collective behavior.* New York: Free Press, 1962.

Smith, A. *The money game.* New York: Random House, 1967.

Wolff, K. H. (Ed.). *The sociology of Georg Simmel.* New York: Free Press, 1950.

FLOOR TRADING AND CROWD DYNAMICS

Wayne E. Baker

What happens when an order to buy or sell a security reaches the floor of a securities exchange? The typical investor's attention is focused solely on two points in the trading process: when an order is placed and when confirmation of execution is received. What transpires between these two points is a mystery; other than vaguely understanding the rudiments of floor trading (such as presented in Engel, 1977), the typical investor knows little about what actually happens on the floor. And the typical investor probably cares little about what happens there, since it is generally believed that prices are determined solely by the forces of supply and demand. But the argument made in this chapter is that the ways in which actors on the floor interact with one another also influence prices. Prudent investors, as well as policy makers, need to understand the social dynamics of floor trading in order to more fully comprehend how prices are determined in the securities market.

The goal of this chapter is to present an "insider's view" of the securities market, explaining how securities are actually traded and how prices are influenced by floor trading. To accomplish this, I have divided the chapter into two main sections. The first section provides a general orientation to the market, beginning with a wide-angle view of market organization, and then progressively narrows the focus to describe the floor trading environment, extant market mechanisms, and the formal group context of trading. The second section continues the progression, refocusing on "crowds"—the groups of actors who congregate on the floor to trade securities. The four main types of crowds are described, including their characteristic effects on price determination. Two predominant types—the competitive market and the fragmented market—are analyzed in detail. A brief conclusion discusses some of the public policy implications of the analysis.

This chapter is based on extensive sociological research conducted over the past few years. Multiple research methods were used: participant-observation at two national exchanges; informal interviews with brokers, traders, exchange managers, trading-floor designers, and staff members of federal regulatory agencies; and mathematical modeling of floor trading and its effects on price determination. The data and information gained through the use of these methods, along with the use of archival and literature sources, provided the basis of the "insider's view" presented here and elsewhere (Baker, 1981, 1982, 1983, 1984).

MARKET ORGANIZATION AND FLOOR TRADING

Market and Marketplace

Empirical markets take a variety of forms. Throughout most of economic history, when the market was a peripheral and minor mode of economic exchange, markets were typically bounded, local affairs: buyers and sellers met face-to-face at a designated area and haggled out the exchange of goods (see, e.g., Bohannon & Dalton, 1962; Polanyi, Arensberg, & Pearson, 1957). In such settings, market and marketplace are nearly coterminous. In contrast, modern capitalist economies are dominated by national market systems, vast and decentralized networks of buyers and sellers who conduct exchanges at a multitude of dispersed locations. In these settings, the marketplace is only an abstract concept; it's a place where no one has ever been.

Unlike most modern markets, the securities market is a combination of old and new market forms—a remarkable hybrid of market and marketplace. On the one hand, the financial community that trades securities is worldwide; on the other hand, all transactions take place in centralized marketplaces, the floors of formally organized securities exchanges ("Exchanges"). Each Exchange is a visible market nexus where the forces of supply and demand are brought together, embodied, and played out. As such, the organization of the securities market into centralized marketplaces creates unique opportunities to observe and study the workings of a major modern market.

In addition to the role of an Exchange as a marketplace, an Exchange is a bureaucracy charged with the administration, management, and general support of trading and trading-related activities. For example, every Exchange employs a large professional staff that performs the functions of market regulation and surveillance, the management of floor operations, research and planning, and so forth. While these aspects of an Exchange are important and deserve study (in fact, the bureaucracy is as under-studied as the marketplace itself), this chapter focuses primarily on the trading activities of actors on the floor of the Exchange (see Abolafia, Chapter 7, for an excellent discussion of the formal bureaucratic regulation of the market).

Trading environments. The formal trading environment includes the trading floor and the physical structures used as trading arenas. While each Exchange's trading floor is somewhat unique, all trading floors have some common characteristics. The perimeter of a trading floor contains rows of telephone booths, usually rented by member firms, and staffed with firm employees. Orders are received by clerks at the booths, who write the orders on forms. Runners pick up the orders, and carry them to the firm's floor brokers in the trading arenas. After a floor broker has executed the order, runners collect the forms, returning them to the clerks at the telephone booths. The customer can then be notified that the order was "filled" (executed).

In the inner area of the trading floor are the physical structures used as trading arenas. These structures are the heart of the marketplace: the locations at which buyers and sellers meet face-to-face and negotiate the exchange of securities. Each security is assigned a unique location in a trading arena; thus, a designated physical marketplace exists for each security. All participants who desire to trade a particular security must do so at its designated locale.

A great variety of physical structures are used by the Exchanges. A common physical structure is known as a "post." Posts on the New York Stock Exchange, for example, are horseshoe-shaped counters occupying about 100 square feet of floor space. Clerks and Exchange employees stand inside the horseshoe; all trading takes place on the outside of the horseshoe, along the counter's perimeter. About 90 stocks are traded around each post (Engel, 1977, pp. 76–79). Other Exchanges combine the traditional post configuration with the typical physical structure used in the commodity Exchanges—the "pit." (A pit is a large raised platform consisting of a series of concentric octagonal steps ascending from floor level to the top of the platform and descending in toward the center, forming the "pit" area.) In the post-pit combination, the trading area is constructed like a pit adjacent to a counter. The trading structure itself may either be a raised platform abutting a counter, or a series of steps forming a depression in front of the counter.

Exchanges experiment with an amazing number of fantastically-shaped physical trading structures. Exchanges prefer to use custom-designed structures rather than utilize designs used at other Exchanges. While part of this preference stems from the desire to design a structure well suited to the unique needs of an Exchange, it also appears that Exchanges prefer custom designs in an effort to symbolically differentiate their "products" (i.e., the securities and the unique market environment in which they are traded) in the eyes of the investment community, especially the large institutional buyers. By proferring a unique "product" to large investors, the Exchange management hopes to attract a large flow of orders to its marketplace.

The configuration of a trading structure, its dimensions and general design, shapes the environment in which trading takes place. Each configuration differentially constrains patterns of communication and trading among floor participants. For example, a small structure can only accommodate a limited number of actors. This physical constraint is not problematic if the security traded at the small structure is relatively inactive, attracting a small number of brokers and traders. But if the security suddenly became very active, as a result, for example, of an unexpected news report, a large number of actors would migrate to the trading arena and quickly overcrowd it. Such overcrowding would hamper traders' ability to communicate and trade effectively. A large physical structure, of course, would better accommodate large numbers of participants, facilitating the communication of offers to buy and sell, and enhancing the efficiency of the market.

Market mechanisms: Variations on a theme. The market mechanism is the formal organization and process of trading employed by an Exchange to bring buyers and sellers together and enable them to negotiate the exchange of securities. The market mechanism includes the formal roles in which participants may trade, the bundle of obligations and privileges incumbent in each role, and the set of rules and regulations governing trading conduct. In addition, the formal market mechanism is enmeshed in a social organization—the patterns of informal roles and relationships, group dynamics, norms, rules, and the like—that emerge from the recurrent interactions of people in the marketplace. Some of the major characteristics of the social organization of trading are presented in the second section of this chapter.

Although the Exchanges employ somewhat different market mechanisms, they are all variations on a theme: each mechanism is a conscious attempt to enact an ideal of how markets should work. This ideal is the theoretical model of markets found in neoclassical microeconomics: the model of the perfectly competitive market (e.g., Malinvaud, 1972). "Ideal" in this context has two meanings: first, it means that the perfectly competitive market is an intellectual model, residing in theoreticians' heads, of how a market ought to work; second, and more important, it means that the perfectly competitive market is a model of what is desirable in practice, a blueprint that should be followed in designing, regulating, and making markets. Thus, extant securities market mechanisms may be understood as attempts to implement perfectly competitive markets in real life. But of course, the implementation of the perfectly competitive market ideal falls short of the theoretical model. The main reason it does is that the market is not populated by members of the mythical race known as "economic man," those hyperrational, superanalytic, maximizing creatures of the economist's imagination. Instead, the market is populated by real people, actors who possess humanly limited cognitive powers and capacities, who operate in an environment of complexity and uncertainty, and who live in a social world (see Baker, 1984; Williamson, 1981). Human actors create a market that is much different than the theoretical model; the goal of this chapter is to describe the ways in which the market is created by human actors.

Three Empirical Market Mechanisms

Three different market mechanisms are employed by Exchanges: the specialist system, the competing market-maker system, and electronic trading. The first two systems are human-mediated forms of trading; in these systems, all orders are transacted on Exchange floors through face-to-face negotiations. Electronic trading replaces human-mediation with a computer algorithm used to match offers to buy and to sell. Although the human-mediated market mechanisms are nearly ubiquitous in the securities market, electronic trading is especially important to consider for two reasons—first, by removing the "human element" from the market mechanism, proponents claim that the securities market would much more closely approximate the perfectly competitive market ideal; second, some Exchanges have begun experimenting with electronic trading, and some futurists predict that electronic trading will eventually supplant all human-mediated forms of securities trading.

The specialist system. The specialist system is the traditional way to organize trading, used primarily by the old and well established stock exchanges—the New York Stock Exchange and the American Stock Exchange. This system is also used by the Philadelphia Stock Exchange. There are two main formal roles in the specialist system: floor broker and specialist. The floor broker acts as an agent, buying and selling securities for other individuals. For example, an order received by a brokerage firm (e.g., Merrill Lynch) would be executed on the floor of the Exchange by a broker employed by the firm for this purpose. In busy times, a firm may also use one of the independent floor brokers on the trading floor. These independents are members of the Exchange who are not employed by any firm; their livelihood is gained by executing orders for firms or other brokers, receiving a negotiated commission for their service. The principal obligation of a floor broker is to get a "good fill": to execute an order at the best possible price. The main privilege of a floor broker is the opportunity to earn commissions for executing orders (or collect a salary if employed by a firm). A floor broker may not, however, trade securities for his/her own account.

Suppose the order received by a floor broker was "away from the market" (that is, the order specifies a price that is out of the range of current prices). The broker could turn the order over to the specialist in the security who would assume the obligation to execute the order if the market moved to the order's specified price. When the specialist received the order, he/she would enter the order into his/her "book"—a listing of unexecuted orders sequenced by price and time of entry. The specialist has the responsibility to execute any orders in the book when the market moves into their range. In this capacity, the specialist acts as a broker, executing orders for other brokers.

But the specialist operates in another capacity: a dealer permitted to buy and sell certain securities for his/her own account. As a dealer, the specialist is a market-maker. The specialist maintains a sizable inventory of the security (or securities) in which he/she specializes. The specialist is required to sell (buy) a security if a floor broker has an order to buy (sell) and the other "side" of the trade is not readily available. For example, a specialist would make a market if all orders in the book were away from the market. In such situations, the specialist acts as a monopolist: the specialist has considerable latitude in setting the bid-ask spread whenever making a market in a security. Some writers argue, however, that the specialist's latitude is circumscribed by competition from block positioners, regional exchanges, third-market dealers, as well as limit orders (Logue, 1975, p. 121).

The specialist enjoys a double privilege: generating commissions by acting as a broker and making profits through speculative trading by acting as a dealer. Correspondingly, the specialist has double obligations. First, the specialist must get a good fill for a customer's order; further, precedence must be given to a customer's order over the specialist's order. Second, the specialist is obligated to maintain "fair and orderly" markets. For example, the specialist must buy and sell from his/her own account—regardless of the impact on the specialist's profitability—to assure reasonable continuity in prices and to stabilize the market by buying if there are lots of sell orders and selling if there are lots of buy orders.

The specialist system has received mixed reviews in the financial and regulatory community. Proponents contend that the securities market would be much more volatile and erratic without the stabilizing influences of the specialists (e.g., Engel, 1977, pp. 96–98). Critics, however, claim that allowing specialists to act as brokers and dealers creates inevitable problems. For example, Neiderhoffer and Osborne (1966) discovered that the specialist can make superior profits from his/her knowledge of the book of unexecuted orders.

The market-maker system. The market-maker system is a relatively new and innovative way to organize trading, designed to obviate the problems associated with the specialist system. The market-maker system is used at the Chicago Board Options Exchange, the Midwest Stock Exchange, and the Pacific Stock Exchange. In this system, floor brokers operate in the same manner as they do in the specialist system, with the same obligations and privileges. The specialist's role, however, is divided into two roles: board broker and market-maker. The board broker assumes the brokering duties of the specialist; the board broker keeps the book of unexecuted orders. The board broker may be a member of the Exchange, earning brokerage commissions, or a paid employee of the Exchange. The board broker, however, is prohibited from acting as a dealer.

The market-maker assumes the ''market making'' duties of the specialist. Each market-maker is formally obligated to trade for his or her own account to maintain fair and orderly markets (known as ''affirmative obligations'') and avoid trading that would be inconsistent with this objective (Securities and Exchange Commission, 1978, p. 131). To fulfill these obligations, upon the demand of another actor in the marketplace, a market-maker must quote the prices at which he or she is willing to buy an option (''bid'') and sell an option (''ask''), and trade at least a certain minimum volume at a quoted price. A market-maker's main privilege is the opportunity to speculate in the market, trading for his/her own account. A market-maker may not, however, trade as a broker for others.

The market-maker system obviates several problems associated with the specialist system. Splitting up the specialist's role into formally separate broker and dealer roles avoids the inherent role conflict of the specialist. That is, a market-maker does not face the moral (or at least financial) dilemma of having to trade in the public interest when it conflicts with personal interest. The market-maker system also removes the monopolistic advantages of the specialist. While a single individual makes markets in a given security in the specialist system, multiple market-makers may trade the same security in the market-makers system, competing against one another as they establish their bid-ask spreads. Proponents of the market-maker system maintain that it results in a more efficient and competitive market. Critics argue that prices can become more volatile in the market-maker system because multiple traders rather than a unitary trader are making markets. Although no explicitly comparative evaluation has been made of the two human-mediated systems, it seems reasonable to assume that the market-maker system more closely approximates a perfectly competitive market than does the specialist system.

Electronic trading. For the past four years the Cincinnati Stock Exchange has been experimenting with electronic trading. The Securities and Exchange Commission recently granted permanent status to the Exchange's electronic system, and the Exchange has launched an ambitious expansion plan which includes increasing the number of listed stocks from 110 to 350 by the end of 1983 (''A Little Exchange,'' 1983, p. 100). In the futures industry, a new commodity futures Exchange—the International Futures Exchange in Bermuda—has implemented electronic trading in futures. But these cases of electronic trading are minor; the national markets in securities and futures are still dominated by Exchanges that utilize traditional methods of floor trading. Electronic trading on a grand scale is still only a possibility of the future.

Ubiquitous electronic trading would eliminate all need for human mediation in matching bids and asks. Orders to buy and sell would be submitted to a computer system in which all limit orders (the "book") would be displayed and an impersonal algorithm used to match bids and asks. Proponents contend that electronic trading would reduce transaction costs, improve information dissemination, and eliminate floor trading abuses (Burns, 1982; see also, Mendelson & Peake, 1979). In short, electronic trading would permit prices to be pure reflections of the supply and demand for securities. This market mechanism would embody the perfectly competitive market ideal.

The Formal Group Context of Trading

Several characteristics of a securities marketplace that utilizes floor trading create a *formal group* context of trading. First, the marketplace is spatially organized so that each security is traded at a unique physical location on the trading floor. Second, all floor brokers and traders who desire to trade a security must meet and stand at the location designated for trade in that security. Trading a security outside its designated locale is not permitted. Third, all participants must meet face-to-face and communicate their desires and intentions to trade securities by "open outcry"—publicly and orally announcing price quotes and filled trades. In other words, the securities marketplaces are "auction-type" markets. These three characteristics of trading combine to produce a formal group context of trading: the buyers and sellers who congregate at a location to trade securities form a group, an organized collection of participants who are quite similar in form to the hagglers in primitive marketplaces. These groups are labeled "crowds" in securities market parlance.

According to conventional wisdom, the fact that securities are traded in groups is inconsequential. Interactions among actors in a crowd are assumed to have no effect on the determination of prices; interactions are thought to produce only an objective matching of bids and asks—virtually the same as would be produced by an electronic market mechanism. This assumption was tested in the analysis presented in this chapter. The main focus of the analysis was "crowd dynamics": the patterns of interaction among actors in marketplace groups and their effects on price determination (Baker, 1982; 1984). The analysis demonstrates, as discussed below, that the formal mechanism of the market is enmeshed in "crowd dynamics" in ways that substantially influence the determination of prices.

CROWD DYNAMICS AND THEIR EFFECTS ON PRICES[1]

Rudiments of Trading Within Crowds

Orders drive the market; indeed, without a constant flow of orders, the market would cease to exist. But orders themselves have no standing in the trading arena, as Mendelson and Peake (1979) point out. In the trading arena, orders must be converted into *offers:* an offer to buy at a stated price (''bid'') or an offer to sell at a stated price (''ask''). Bids and asks, then, are the concrete elements brought together and intermeshed in the trading process.[2]

In the crowd, bids and asks are declared by ''open outcry''—loud shouts, often accompanied by hand signals and associated body language. The highest declared bid and the lowest declared ask constitute the market for a security at a given time; when these match, a transaction can take place (Mendelson & Peake, 1979, p. 33).

Brokers, who act as agents in the crowd for others, present bids or asks as directed in the orders they receive. Market-makers, in contrast, who trade for themselves, generate their own bids and asks in accordance with their profit-seeking strategies. In addition, since market-makers are formally obligated to do what their name implies—make markets—by always standing ready to buy or sell, they must establish and maintain their bid-ask spreads. Each market-maker, consequently, has an individual market: a price at which he or she is willing to buy, and a price at which he or she is willing to sell. The difference between these two prices represents potential profits to be made.

The trading process itself is a creation of dynamic tension. On the one hand, each market-maker attempts to establish wide markets, buying cheaply and selling dearly, in order to maximize profits. On the other hand, market-makers compete with one another in establishing their individual bid-ask spreads, resulting usually in a narrowing and convergence of spreads. An example will show how this dynamic process works. Suppose a broker enters a crowd comprised of two market-makers. The broker, let's assume, wants to sell the security, but this intention is not disclosed to the market-makers. The broker approaches a market-maker and asks ''What's your market?'' The market-maker replies, ''A quarter and a half,'' indicating a willingness to buy at ¼ and sell at ½. But the other market-maker may wish to make the trade and state a narrower market, saying ''⅜ and ½.'' Since the broker wants to sell high, he or she would accept the second market-maker's offer (''⅜''), and the first market-maker would lose the trade.

The dynamic trading process appears quite simple in the three-person case described above, but it becomes very complex when more actors are added: the interaction potential in a crowd increases multiplicatively as a crowd grows (Mayhew & Levinger, 1976). Consider, for instance, the enormous complexity of trading in some of the crowds that were observed to grow to 100 actors; in a crowd of 100 actors, there are 9,900 possible interactions. Such complexity, of course, is overwhelming, and actors in large crowds must develop ways to cope with it (see ''fragmented market'' below).

Four Types of Crowds

The various crowds and their markets may be classified into four main types: monopoly-monopsony, the negotiated market, the competitive market, and the fragmented market. Each type is represented by a characteristic pattern of roles and relationships with distinctive effects on price determination. Though all four types must be considered to appreciate the variety of crowds that occur on the floor, only two—the competitive market and the fragmented market—are enduring and regular patterns of relationships. The other two are transitory and fragile market patterns, emerging only on an occasional basis under specific and usually short-lived conditions. All four types are defined and described below; the two enduring types are then analyzed in detail in a subsequent section.

Monopoly-monopsony. Monopoly simply means "single seller" and occurs whenever a single individual, organization, or coordinated group enjoys exclusive ownership or control of the supply of a commodity. In this situation, the monopolist can dictate an artificially high price—i.e., a price higher than what should occur if there were many sellers in the market. Monopsony is the opposite of monopoly, occurring whenever a single actor is the sole buyer of a commodity. By virtue of his/her position, a monopsonist can dictate an artificially low price, a price lower than what should occur if many buyers were present and had to compete with one another.

On the floor of the Exchange, both monopoly and monopsony situations have been reported to occur on an occasional basis. In the simplest case, a monopoly can occur in a bull market where most actors want to buy but only one wants to sell. Similarly, a monopsony can occur in a bear market where most actors want to sell but only one wants to buy. These situations, however, are highly dependent on the direction of the market, and the temporary advantages enjoyed by the monopolist or monopsonist are lost as soon as new information arrives that indicates a change in the factors affecting prices—new orders, a news flash, corporate or government announcements, and so forth.

Monopolies can also take the form of market manipulations, such as a corner on the market where the monopolist owns or controls a substantial portion of a corporation's stock as well as a large number of options on the same stock. The monopolist can exercise the options, forcing the option writers (sellers) to sell stock to the monopolist. Assuming the option writers do not already own the stock, this means that they must purchase the stock in the marketplace. Of course, since the monopolist controls a large share of the underlying stock, he or she can force the option writers to acquire the stock at grossly inflated prices. This form of monopoly is less dependent on the direction of the market than the form discussed above, and it only rarely occurs (but see Commodity Futures Trading Commission [1983] for a successful similar manipulation perpetrated by floor brokers at a futures Exchange).

The more or less transitory nature of monopolies and monopsonies in the Exchange's marketplace points up an important difference between them and the more traditional forms of monopoly and monopsony. A traditional monopoly is based on an enduring and stable asymmetric relationship between the monopolist and the buyers. As the traditional monopolist is well entrenched in a position to exploit buyers, so the buyers are trapped in a position where they are forced to accept the terms dictated by the monopolist. This structural relationship is nearly impervious to alteration. In contrast, the monopolies that occur on the Exchange's trading floor are much more subject to changing external conditions, and are usually only fleeting affairs.

The negotiated market. The negotiated market is one in which actors in a crowd arrange trades or set prices by cooperative agreement rather than by open competition. Instead of competing with one another, actors have found it more profitable to work together to arrange how an order will be split up, or at what price trades will be made. For example, a market-maker described how a large order (say 20 options) might be divided among a number of market-makers:

> If it's not very active, we arrive at a negotiated arrangement. If there's three of us, market-makers that is, then each may be reluctant to buy the 20. And the floor broker comes in and says, ''Where can I sell X number of options?'' We talk among ourselves, and say: ''At such and such price, we'll buy so many . . .'' and so on. If no one has an ax to grind, if it's a neutral situation, then we'll buy them and split them up, even if everyone did not aggressively bid for them.

Thus, the market-makers cooperatively decide how transactions take place—who will buy, how much, and at what price.

Negotiating prices is more profitable for market-makers than is open competition. As noted in the section above on the rudiments of trading, the wider the bid-ask spread, the more profitable trading can be. In the negotiated market, actors can maintain a greater disparity between the bid and ask than they can in a competitive market. As one participant explained:

> You can make a wider market. For example, suppose you have a ''quarter market'' (say, bid at ¼ and ask at ½). An order comes in between (an offer to sell at ⅜). We wait, and the price goes down (to ¼), and everyone shares. In a large crowd, someone will pay up an eighth, and you lose out on the order.

To make this situation work, the actors must agree upon a specific bid-ask spread, and coordinate their trading so that they all wait until the floor broker drops his/her asking price.

Obviously, cooperation and coordination are necessary to create a negotiated market, and these can only occur in a small crowd. With a large number of actors it is not possible to achieve consensus on the terms of trade, nor is it possible to coordinate trading behaviors. Furthermore, actors must trust one another to abide by the informal agreements of a negotiated market (i.e., holding to the bid-ask spread and waiting for prices to drop); such trust only comes from a history of working together.

The competitive market. The empirical competitive market at the Exchange closely approximates the economists' theoretical model of the perfectly competitive market, one in which prices are determined primarily by the interaction of supply and demand forces (as represented by floor participants). Here one does not find monopolists (or monopsonists) artificially setting prices, nor does one find the terms of trade being negotiated. Rather, market actors compete with one another in forming their bid-ask spreads, and transactions only occur when the highest declared bid equals the lowest declared ask. As such, interactions within the crowd closely resemble the picture portrayed in the section above on the rudiments of trading.

Though the empirical competitive market approximates the ideal-type of market, it also deviates in some theoretically significant ways. For example, economists believe that competitive markets occur when there are large numbers of buyers and sellers, and that a market becomes more competitive as it grows (see Debreu & Scarf, 1963; Malinvaud, 1972). However, I found that a competitive market can only occur within a relatively narrow range of sizes. If a crowd is too small, a negotiated market will occur; if a crowd is too large, then communication among all actors breaks down, and it will fragment into subgroups (the "fragmented market" discussed below). Roughly, between 15 to 30 actors is the range within which competitive markets can form.

The effects of a competitive market on price determination, as elaborated in a later section, are quite beneficial. The competitive interactions of buyers and sellers tend to dampen the volatility of prices; that is, controlling for the volatility of underlying stock prices, the networks of trading tend to reduce the volatility of option prices. This dampening effect increases the orderliness of the market, which benefits investors and corporations alike (see Baker, 1984).

The fragmented market. A fragmented market occurs when a crowd is so large that actors are unable to communicate effectively and efficiently. In a large crowd, noise and the physical distance between potential trading partners prevent actors from hearing all the bids and asks announced in a crowd, and from transmitting their bids and asks to others. In addition, a large crowd means that an actor is faced with numerous potential trading partners. Though ideally an actor would survey all members of the crowd in search of the partner with the best price, in reality an actor cannot take the time to do so; instead, an actor must "satisfice" by taking the first good offer that appears.

To cope with noise, long distance between potential partners, and the complexity of dealing large numbers, actors must restrict their trading. One way participants restrict their trading is to trade with those in close proximity. As a veteran market-maker described:

> [What problems are there in trading in a large crowd?] Noise, static. The errors increase as an inverse square of the distance between brokers . . . You trade with people in close proximity

> to reduce the risk; there's money at risk. (For example) if a broker makes a certain percentage on a trade, and has an error, it might take 20 trades to make it up.

Trading with those in close proximity means that a large crowd will tend to break up into multiple subgroups (cliques); in short, it causes a large crowd to *fragment.*

Large size and fragmentation have a detrimental effect on the performance of the market. While the competitive market tends to dampen the volatility of prices, the large fragmented market has the opposite effect, causing the volatility of prices to increase dramatically. Trading in a large and fragmented crowd exacerbates the volatility of prices, reducing the orderliness of the market.

As the predominant types of crowds, the competitive and fragmented markets deserve closer examination. Let us now focus on the economic and social forces that create these market structures, presenting a view of the dynamics that underlie them.

The Dynamics of Crowd Size

The critical variable in the market is *size:* small crowds foster monopolies, monopsonies, or negotiated markets; medium crowds produce competitive market conditions; and large crowds produce fragmented market conditions (Baker, 1984). Size itself, however, is influenced by a number of factors. On the one hand, crowd size is largely determined by the profit-making opportunities perceived to exist in crowds; traders, who seek profits, will migrate to the crowds that contain the best chances of making money. On the other hand, groups of traders tend to "stake out" crowds as their own, and resist the efforts of other traders to enter them. While the migration of profit-seekers to crowds is the main determinant of size, the "territoriality" of crowd members—and the social control mechanisms they use—must also be considered.

Different economic indicators are used by traders to assess the profit-making potential of different marketplaces (crowds). For example, increased activity such as an increase in the volume of orders to the marketplace signals new opportunities to make money. Price volatility is also a major indicator of opportunities; generally, the more volatile prices are, the greater the profit-making opportunities that exist (Baker, 1984). Whatever indicators are used, traders will tend to migrate to the crowds where they perceive the best opportunities to be. As one floor broker observed:

> When it's inactive, there's a regular core of people there (in the crowd). When there's more action, more people come. You need lots more activity to get more floor brokers, and just a little more to get more market-makers. The market-makers are the first; the floor brokers won't show up until the firms don't have enough people to handle the orders.

As this floor broker noted, brokers too are involved in movements among crowds. The constant migrations of traders and brokers generate a vast ebb and flow of people on the floor; crowds expand or contract as the landscape of perceived opportunities changes.

The quantitative analysis (Baker, 1984), which focused on a small crowd and a large crowd, provided substantial evidence that differences in profit-making opportunities underlie differences in the size of crowds. Generally, underlying stock prices are much more volatile in large crowds than they are in small crowds. For example, stock prices were 3.5 times more volatile in the large crowd (in which an average of 71 actors traded in a two-hour period) than in the small crowd (in which an average of only 27 actors traded).[3] Furthermore, the large crowd grew as prices became more volatile, and shrank as prices became less volatile (though it always stayed big). The small crowd tended to remain stable. The large crowd created a fragmented market and the small crowd created a competitive market.

Immigrants are not always greeted with open arms. In fact, they are usually viewed as interlopers, a perception indicated by some of the terms regular crowd members use to describe the immigrants; as a broker pointed out:

> The swinging markets bring in newcomers. We have lots of names for them. We call them the carp, the boat people. The oldtimers have the rights, or so they feel, it's a kind of territoriality.

The oldtimers, who have a history of trading in a particular crowd, have staked out the crowd as their own. Most traders, even those with a chronic case of wanderlust, have a crowd of their own. As one veteran trader remarked: "Everyone has their stocks (crowd); we call it 'home'." And many traders will try to prevent newcomers from invading their "home."

Resisting the intrusion of newcomers requires the use of informal social controls; if they are successfully applied, the oldtimers can restrict the immigration of new traders and limit the size of their crowd. Several different examples of the social control of immigrations were reported in interviews. One widely-reported control mechanism involves the use of what may be called the "first" rule. The first person to orally respond to an offer is formally entitled to the entire volume offered (or any part thereof) at the offered price. Although others may desire to make the trade, they cannot preempt the person who responds first. The potential for social control is obvious. Even though a newcomer may be the first to respond to an offer, the offerer simply hears someone else as the "first." Thus, the "first" rule can be informally wielded to exclude anyone who tries to trade in the crowd.

The "first" rule is also used to increase the solidarity (and profitability) of the regular members of the crowd. As one trader said about the behavior of members of his crowd: "If one of us is really in trouble, then we hear him 'first' for whatever volume he wants." This rule may also be used to return favors. For example, some traders would absorb losses caused by errors made while trading. The beneficiaries of this largesse would return the favor by trading first with these traders. As one participant said:

> They would take the error (assume part of the loss) and when they wanted to trade, I would trade with them as long and as much as possible. If they took care of a mistake, I would hear them "first," no matter if they were first, or second, or last, or they didn't want to trade anything at all. I helped them out, regardless of who was first.

Thus, the "first" rule can be used as a way to benefit regular members of the crowd, as well as an exclusionary tactic.

Another control mechanism used by traders to exclude newcomers similarly utilizes a formal rule, this time the formal obligation of market-makers to make trades upon the demand of another member of the crowd (see above for a definition of a market-maker's "affirmative obligations"). One group of traders reported using the requirement of affirmative obligations to force a newcomer to trade repeatedly against his own position and thereby incur substantial losses. As one of the group recalled:

> We strained his (the newcomer's) capital. He has to make a market—what he's willing to buy at and sell for. So, we'd say 'What's your market?' And he'd say, '⅛ and ¼.' and I'd say, 'OK, *sold*. Now what's your market?' And he'd say, 'Well, uh, uh, . . .' and give us his market. Then we'd say, '*Sold*. Now what's your market?' And we'd drive him out; we strained his capital.

In the face of this onslaught, the newcomer had no choice but to leave the crowd and attempt to find a "home" elsewhere.

These social controls reportedly work well in restricting entry to the crowd.[4] When they are effective, they stabilize the size of the crowd, and place an upper limit on how large the crowd can grow. However, there are some limits on their effectiveness in controlling crowd size. It is reasonable to assume that they can prevent immigration if the number of immigrants is relatively small. But social control efforts would be overcome if many traders tried to enter a crowd at the same time. A substantial wave of immigration would occur if, for example, the volatility of stock prices suddenly shot up, and traders flocked to the crowd to take advantage of the new profit-making opportunities. In fact, many large crowds began economic life as small ones that grew as activity increased; and many small crowds were once large ones that shrank as activity dropped off.

To sum up, crowd size is determined by two factors: profit-making opportunities and social control efforts. Of these two, the former is the main determinant of crowd size; but, at least to some extent, crowd size is also influenced by the efforts of regular crowd members to exclude newcomers. A fragmented market occurs when stock prices are very volatile, and the crowd grows as a result. A competitive market occurs when stock prices are moderately volatile and therefore substantial immigration does not occur, and when entry is restricted by social control efforts.

The Structure of Competitive and Fragmented Markets

By structure I mean the recurrent patterns of interaction that characterize competitive and fragmented markets. Patterns of interaction are viewed on two levels: the *micro-level* which examines how buyer-seller dyads form in the market, and the *macro-level* which examines the overall patterns of interaction in the market.

At the micro-level, two characteristics need to be examined: the number of trading relationships each actor engages in (i.e., the circle of trading), and the strength of each relationship (i.e., the volume exchanged in each relationship). I found that actors in small and large crowds tend to trade quite similarly. On the average, each actor's circle of trading is almost the same in both large and small crowds (2.12 in the large crowd, 2.34 in the small crowd). Furthermore, the volume exchanged in each relationship is, on the average, virtually the same (about 5.8 option contracts per relationship).[5]

Holding constant both the average number of relationships per actor and the average volume per relationship, the potential for fragmentation increases as the size of the crowd increases. Therefore, I expected to find more fragmentation—multiple subgroup formation—in the large crowd than in the small crowd.[6] The macro-level structure of the large crowd is one of multiple subgroups trading within the overall crowd; the macro-level structure of the small crowd is one of a single group of participants. Figure 1 depicts these differences graphically.[7] During the period of trading represented by Figure 1, the large crowd (ABC) had split into two main cliques; though cross-subgroup trading did occur, the main feature is the division of a single crowd into two subgroups. The small crowd (XYZ) shown in Figure 1 was essentially a single group; this single group, as can be seen in Figure 1, was comprised of a core surrounded by a periphery of traders (a pattern which XYZ commonly exhibited).

There are, however, some differences in structure that occur throughout the typical day. Within the typical day of trading, there are patterned changes in market activity. Generally, the market is more active in the morning and afternoon than in the midday. In the small crowd, actor's trading circles enlarge to match diurnal changes in activity. Actors tend to engage in significantly more trading relationships in the morning and afternoon than in the midday; in other words, actors in the small crowd tend to intensify their trading with one another in the morning and afternoon. In contrast, actors in the large crowd hold their trading circles constant throughout the day. (In both crowds, though, actors do not vary the volume exchanged in a relationship.)[8]

The diurnal patterns of trading in the large and small crowd affect macro-level

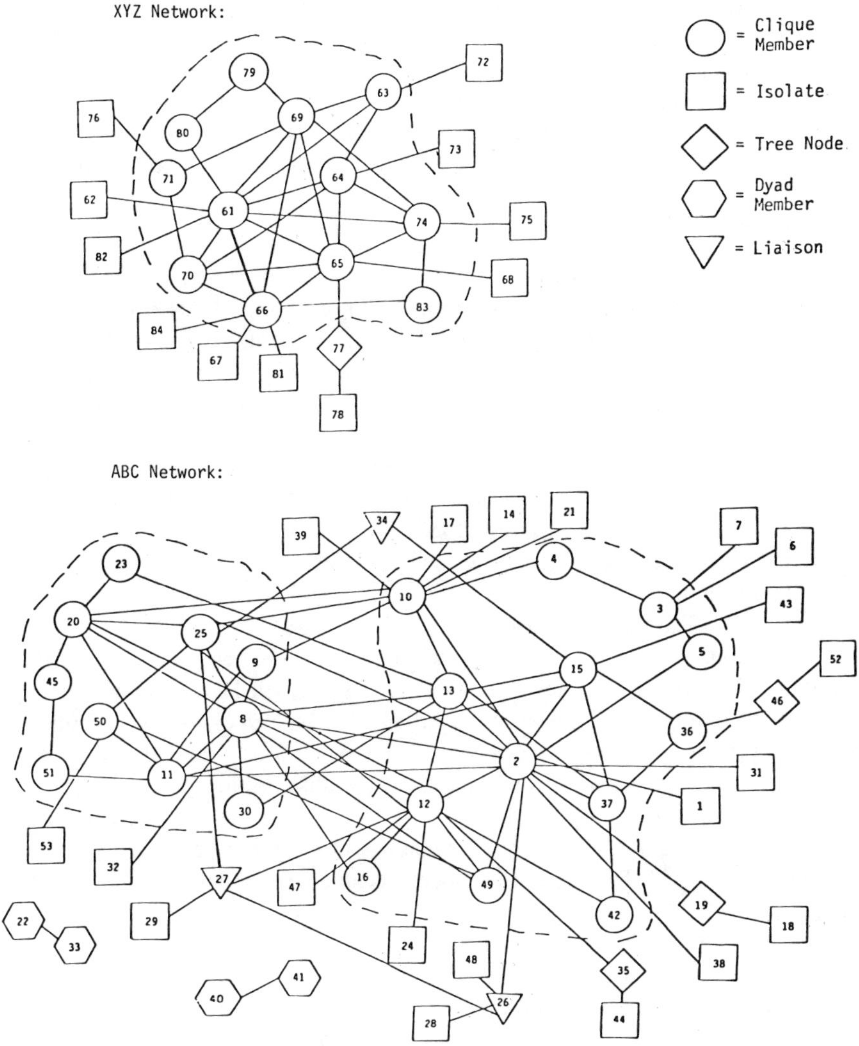

Figure 1. Empirical examples of XYZ and ABC market networks.*

*Graphic representations of actual networks of trading in XYZ and ABC marketplaces during the same afternoon period.

structure in different ways. In the large crowd, holding constant trading circles in periods of greater activity means that the large crowd is more likely to fragment in the morning and afternoon than in the midday. In fact, this is true. I found that a significantly larger number of cliques formed in the morning and afternoon periods than in the midday period. In the small crowd, however, there should be even less potential for fragmentation in the morning and afternoon because actors engage in more relationships during these periods. In fact, I found that the density of interaction within the core group increases significantly in the morning and afternoon compared with the midday. In sum, while the large crowd becomes more fragmented and decentralized in the morning and afternoon, the small crowd becomes denser and more centralized during the same periods.

Effects on Price Determination

Though the patterns of interaction within crowds are interesting in their own right, the typical investor is most concerned with one thing: the effects of these different patterns on price determination. Before considering the effects of social patterns on prices, however, one should pause to consider what conventional economics and finance have to say about what their effects should be. Essentially, conventional economics and finance have not focused on the effects of floor trading since it is typically assumed that floor trading is not a determinant of prices. Though a few economists have noted that human-mediated floor trading has inherent problems (e.g., Burns, 1982; Mendleson & Peake, 1979), floor trading has never been the subject of serious and systematic study. The neglect of floor trading should be kept in mind while reviewing the dramatic effects of the competitive and fragmented markets on prices.

Here I report the effects of market structure on one price characteristic: price volatility. While other variables were analyzed (Baker, 1981), price volatility is the main concern of sociologists (White, 1981).[9] In both markets, the volatility of option prices was partly determined by the volatility of underlying stock prices. That is, as stock prices became more volatile, option prices similarly became more volatile. But the volatility of stock prices is not the sole determinant of option price volatility. Crowd dynamics also affect price volatility.

In the large crowd, I found option prices became more volatile as the crowd grew in size.[10] Holding constant the volatility of stock prices, an increase in crowd size increased the volatility of option prices. Crowd size *exacerbated* the volatility of prices. In the small crowd, size did not affect option price volatility. But, as the density of the central clique increased, option prices became much less volatile. As trading intensified in the small crowd, the volatility of option prices dropped below that expected by the volatility of stock prices alone. Interaction density *dampened* the volatility of prices.

CONCLUSION

The analysis presented here has implications for three audiences: students of the market, investors, and policy makers. Students of the market should reevaluate the implicit assumptions of conventional economic and financial research in light of the findings presented here. While conventional research on the market implicitly assumes that floor trading has no affect on price determination, in fact crowd dynamics significantly influence how prices are made. In the negotiated market, for example, prices are determined by cooperative agreements rather than by open competition. Further, as demonstrated by the analysis of the fragmented and competitive markets, crowd dynamics can affect both the direction and magnitude of price volatility. A complete model of how the market operates, therefore, must include both social and economic variables.

Investors use price volatility as an important indicator of the risk of holding a security and of the intrinsic value of the assets represented by a security. Both exacerbated and dampened price volatilities present distorted information about the "true" volatility of prices—what volatility *should* be if crowd dynamics did not affect prices. Such distortions likely result in misallocations of funds among markets. Exacerbated price volatility makes a security appear to be much riskier than it should be; conversely, dampened price volatility makes a security appear to be less risky than it should be. Conservative investors, who are risk-averters, would tend to shun the first market and enter the second; speculators, who are risk assumers, would be attracted to the first market and tend to ignore the second. But since the decision of where to invest is based on distorted information about the true riskiness of a security, actors are placing their money in different markets than they would if crowd dynamics were not a factor in price determination (Baker, 1984).

Crowd dynamics also affect the corporations whose stocks are listed for options trading. One of the presumed merits of listing a corporation's stock for options trading is that an active options market reduces the corporation's cost of capital (Gastineau, 1979, pp. 192–193). This may happen if option prices are made less volatile by crowd dynamics. But exacerbated option price volatility may have a detrimental effect on underlying stock prices. If it did, the corporation's cost of capital would increase, and its ability to form new capital would be impaired (Baker, 1984).

Both the Exchanges themselves and their federal regulators base policy decisions on the presumption that securities (and futures) prices are not influenced by crowd dynamics. But as this analysis shows, crowd dynamics are an important factor in the market. Exacerbated price volatility, which indicates a decline in market orderliness, is inconsistent with the regulatory goal of "fair and orderly" markets. Thus, it is incumbent upon the Exchanges and their regulators to investigate crowd dynamics and attempt to ameliorate any detrimental effects. The effective regulation of securities markets must include some consideration of crowd dynamics and their effects.

ACKNOWLEDGMENT

I am grateful to many people whose suggestions and comments on the research underlying this chapter were extremely valuable. Among these, I would particularly like to acknowledge Albert Hunter, Allan Schnaiberg, Kent Smith, Harrison C. White and Christopher Winship. I would also like to acknowledge the editors whose comments on an earlier paper were very helpful for producing this chapter.

NOTES

1. The second section of this chapter is based primarily on research I conducted on a single market, the stock options market. Options are contingent claims to purchase stock ("call options") and to sell stock ("put options"). Only calls were traded in the marketplaces analyzed here. Since most Exchanges in the securities market utilize floor trading similar to that used at the Exchange I studied, the findings presented in the section on crowd dynamics can be generalized to most Exchanges.

2. There are many different varieties of orders. For example, as Mendelson and Peake (1979, p. 32) note: "Currently, the NYSE recognizes 21 kinds of orders divided into two types—"market" and "limit."

3. Ten days of trading in each crowd were analyzed. Each day of trading was divided into three two-hour intervals, resulting in thirty periods of trading for each crowd.

4. The effectiveness of social control efforts is difficult to observe directly or measure quantitatively. But the *existence* of social control in the market is not up for question if one can rely on the reports of the users and of the recipients of informal control. I located and interviewed traders on both sides of social control efforts, those who reported that they use the techniques I reported here to control immigration, and those who reported that they were cut out of trades and crowds by informal social controls.

5. The figures given for average number of relationships and average volume are means per period calculated over thirty periods of trading for each crowd.

6. Specifically, of the 30 periods of trading in the large crowd, multiple cliques formed in 36.7% of all periods, single cliques in 60.0% of all periods, and no cliques formed in 3.3% of all periods. Of the 30 periods of trading in the small crowd, multiple cliques formed in 16.7% of all periods, single cliques formed in 73.3% of all periods, and no cliques formed in 10.0% of all periods.

7. The analysis of macro-level structure was performed using a clique detection algorithm called NEGOPY (Richards & Rice, 1981). NEGOPY identifies four types of actors: isolates, who are connected only by a single link to another actor; dyad members, two actors connected only to each other; clique members, where a clique is a subset of at least three actors who trade more than 50% of their volume within the clique; and liasions, actors who fail to meet the 50% criterion for membership with any clique.

8. To evaluate daily patterns, each day of trading was divided into three two-hour periods: a morning period, a midday period, and an afternoon period. The means of selected variables were calculated for each period, and differences between periods were tested as differences between means using the t-test for paired samples.

9. For example, I also examined the effects of multiple subgroup formation on the "efficiency" of the market. I evaluated "efficiency" by focusing on periods of trading in which two or more cliques emerged. Since members of the cliques traded the same stock options, I was interested in determining whether the same option ever traded at one price in one clique but a different price in the other clique. I found that such disparities often occur. Potentially, it was possible to make profits by "arbitraging" between the two cliques, indicating a market "inefficiency" caused directly by the social structure of the crowd. However, due to irremedial problems of potential data nonsimultaneity, this finding is extremely tenuous; it only points to an avenue of future research. Note, however, that price disparities caused by multiple clique formation are reported by the participants themselves; as one observed:

In the really large crowds that are really active, it's possible to get trading in very different prices. (Why?) It's noisy; you can't hear. It happens when the stock is changing; some people trade, and they tell others, and then lots of people are coming over. There are some aberrations sometimes.

Another trader mentioned that it was possible to make "instant profit" by arbitraging between cliques, taking advantage of the price disparities that exist between the cliques.

10. Price volatility was calculated using Martin and Gray's (1971) measure of relative variability. Two price volatilities were calculated for each market: the price volatility of the option(s) traded in each crowd, and the price volatility of the stock(s) underlying the options. See Baker (1984) for details.

REFERENCES

Baker, W. E. *Markets as networks: A multimethod study of trading networks in a securities market.* Unpublished doctoral dissertation, Northwestern University, 1981.

Baker, W. E. *The effects of trading networks on the volatility of option prices.* Paper presented at the annual meeting of The American Sociological Society, San Francisco, September 1982.

Baker, W. E. *Intermarket structures: Modeling the interrelationships of markets and traders.* Paper presented at the annual meeting of The American Sociological Association, Detroit, September 1983.

Baker, W. E. The social structure of a national securities market. *American Journal of Sociology,* 1984, *89.*

Bohannon, P., & Dalton, G. (Eds.). *Markets in Africa.* Evanston: Northwestern University Press, 1962.

Burns, J. M. Electronic trading in futures market. *Financial Analysts Journal,* January/February 1982, pp. 33–41.

Commodities Futures Trading Commission. *News release.* New York: Author, January 12, 1983.

Debreu, G., & Scarf, H. Limit theorem on the core of an economy. *International Economic Review,* 1963, *4,* 235–246.

Engel, L. *How to buy stocks* (6th rev. ed.). New York: Bantam, 1977.

Gastineau, G. *The stock options manual* (2nd ed.). New York: McGraw-Hill, 1979.

A little exchange that's thinking big. *Business Week,* January 17, 1983, p. 100.

Logue, D. E. Market-making and the assessment of market efficiency. *Journal of Finance,* 1975, *1,* 115–123.

Malinvaud, E. *Lectures on microeconomic theory.* Amsterdam: North-Holland Publishing Company, 1972.

Martin, J. D., & Gray, L. N. Measurement of relative variation: Sociological examples. *American Sociological Review,* 1971, *36,* 496–502.

Mayhew, B. H., & Levinger, R. L. Size and the density of interaction in human aggregates. *American Journal of Sociology,* 1976, *82,* 86–110.

Mendelson, M., & Peake, J. W. The abc's of trading on a national market system. *Financial Analysts Journal,* September/October 1979, pp. 31–42.

Niederhoffer, V., & Osborne, M. F. M. Market-making and reversal on the stock exchange. *Journal of the American Statistical Association,* 1966, *61,* 897–916.

Polanyi, K., Arensberg, C. M., & Pearson, H. W. (Eds.). *Trade and market in the early empires.* Chicago: Henry Regnery Company, 1957.

Richards, W. D., & Rice, D. E. The NEGOPY network analysis program. *Social Networks,* 1981, *3,* 215–223.

Securities and Exchange Commission. *Report on the special study of the options markets to the securities and exchange commission.* Washington, D.C.: Committee Print, 96th Congress, 1978.

White, H. C. Where do markets come from? *American Journal of Sociology,* 1981, *87,* 517–547.

Williamson, O. E. The economics of organization: The transaction cost approach. *American Journal of Sociology,* 1981, *87,* 548–577.

STRUCTURED ANARCHY:
FORMAL ORGANIZATION IN THE COMMODITY FUTURES MARKETS

Mitchel Y. Abolafia

> No one has died on the trading floor since a heart attack killed a clerical worker in 1978, but the (paramedic) team regularly treats chest pains, stomach problems, anxiety attacks, and accidental stabbings—a consequence of traders in the crowded pits bumping into each other with sharp pencils.
>
> ("To Keep Future," 1982)

The history of financial markets is generally believed to exhibit a tendency toward increasing rationality and control. Even after more than a century of increasing rationalization following their establishment, the commodity futures markets still reflect their origins in mercantile capitalism. At the center of this industry (as described by Baker in chapter 6) are open auctions held in "pits," really three or four staired rings, where contracts for future delivery of such commodities as wheat, heating oil, gold, foreign currency, and U.S. treasury bills are traded. The image of these markets and the apparently anarchic behavior in them is dramatic. It was this drama which inspired novelist Frank Norris (1903, p. 98) to describe the scene at The Chicago Board of Trade just as the opening bell is rung.

> Instantly a tumult was unchained, arms were flung upward in strenuous gestures, and from above the crowding heads in the Wheat Pit a multitude of hands, eager, the fingers extended, leaped into the air. All articulate expression was lost in the single explosion of sound as the traders surged downward to the Centre of the Pit. . . .

While this description may seem overly dramatic, it differs only in style from the economist's image of the commodity futures market. To economists these gatherings of buyers and sellers are the representations of a perfectly competitive market. They are arenas where individual "articulate expression" is lost in the collective act of price determination. As such, futures markets are textbook examples for supply and demand. Note Samuelson (1964, p. 69) in this regard.

> Our curves of supply and demand strictly apply only to a *perfectly competitive* market where some kind of standardized commodity such as wheat is being auctioned by an organized exchange that registers transactions of numerous buyers and sellers. The Board of Trade in Chicago is one such example, . . . men from various brokerage houses are milling around on the trading floor while frantically giving hand and voice signals to the specialist who serves as auctioneer for each grain or company stock.

The action in the pits does indeed fit the economist's model of the competitive market. But the conceptual lens of the economist (and, by implication, the crowd psychologist) focuses on the near-anarchy in the pit without noticing the layers of organization, formal and informal, which surround and buffer this market. With a different set of conceptual lenses, those of sociology and of organization theory, the focus shifts to the context of all this dramatic action, a context which serves to structure and control the action.

The purpose of this chapter is to examine and analyze the organizational characteristics of the commodity futures industry. This will be accomplished through an ethnographic treatment of the complex social arrangements outside the pit which organize the competitive action. By looking at the larger system of organizational relations within which the market exists we will see how these markets, like all others, are part of an economic sector. Such sectors consist of horizontal and vertical relations between competitors, suppliers, consumers, public agencies, and other interested parties.[1] Following Scott and Meyer (1982, p. 11), the term "sector" is intended to refer to "a domain identified by similarity of service, product or function." Although sector is identified functionally, in a way equivalent to economists' definition of industry, the range of organizations in a sector goes beyond the list of competitors. It includes the regulators of the domain, e.g., the suppliers of input and distributors of output, as well as public agents of control. As such, a sector's components constitute a network of interorganizational relationships which constrains and facilitates the operation of the market.

In an earlier analysis (Abolafia, 1982) I examined competition and cooperation in the commodity futures industry. The present analysis will focus on the coordination and control aspects of this sector. We will look first at the formal structure and secondly at the processes of control in this sector. In the course of this analysis we will develop the unexpected finding that commodity exchanges exercise the monopoly power of cartels in the midst of this otherwise classically competitive industry.

STRUCTURED ANARCHY

In what sense can the commodity futures pits be characterized as anarchic? A visitor to the floor of any futures market would see a lot of physical chaos, as did Norris and Samuelson. But chaos can be misleading. We may attribute chaos to a group's behavior because we do not understand the situation as the actors themselves understand it. Traders' behavior is *not* unintentional or without direction. But few traders in the pit would deny that everyday life in the pits is anarchic and many admit that they wish to protect themselves against it. The anarchy is not only physical, it is cognitive.

The experience of anarchy in the pits is produced by conditions inherent in occupying the position of trader in a risky and active market. Transactions are stressful activities carried on by individuals in a crowd of other individuals. The nature of transactions is not collective, but rather highly individual. In the market, traders are confronted with a continuous conflict of interest with all other traders for acquisition of a scarce resource, i.e., transactions, at the most advantageous price. It is these multiple, simultaneous conflicts which account for the impression of an absence of order. The traders' individuality is only intensified by the crowd of surrounding rivals, thus giving the appearance of a lack of any sort of collective action.

In addition to the conflict of interest between traders, each individual trading for his or her own account carries the burdens of personal uncertainty, informational complexity, and limited rationality. The uncertainty exists on several levels. Most obviously, traders can never be fully certain of the direction that prices will take. Every trade therefore represents a financial risk. These risks are taken based on information. But the information itself constitutes an uncertainty. Is it complete? Is it correct? Has it changed? As Tarascio has noted in chapter 3, there is the problem of infinite regress: one cannot know everything. The uncertainty is compounded by complexity. There are a variety of types of market information and an ever-growing list of techniques for forecasting. Which form of analysis (e.g., fundamental, technical) should be chosen? Whose opinion about the future course of events is correct? The problem of complexity is exacerbated by the limited rationality of the trader. No individual can see all the market information, use all forms of analysis, hear all competing opinions and make perfect decisions, given the real limits on time, money, and cognitive ability.

At the same time that traders are overloaded and immersed in a continuous conflict with other traders, they are mutually dependent. They are dependent on their multiple exchange partners for completion of contract terms. They are mutually dependent to see that the market is maintained into the future so that each may continue to profit. And they are dependent on each other to see that the market is not monopolized, that it remains competitive so that all sellers may easily find buyers and all buyers may easily find sellers. This mutual dependence creates a paradox. Fiercely independent economic actors are, at the same time, reliant on one another.

This paradox is a central feature in the social organization of markets. Economic actors, whether they are commodity traders or firms, want a controlled and stable market while at the same time wishing to retain their autonomy and potential for profit. The result is the creation of social mechanisms which constrain and facilitate the operation of the market. These mechanisms include informal norms among traders, formal rules of trade, and organizational arrangements to coordinate collective action. In this chapter we will focus on the last of these, the organizational controls which members of the market use to structure their transactions into more certain and predictable relations.

The study of organizational controls in a market does not lend itself to conventional organizational analysis in terms of the familiar variables of bureaucratic structure. Rather, the technical language to be used here is derived from network analysis (Aldrich & Whetten, 1981; Benson, 1975; Evan, 1966; Scott & Meyer, 1982; Warren, 1967) and systems theory (Ashby, 1965; Buckley, 1967; Cadwaller, 1968; Parsons, 1978). The usefulness of this language lies in the preeminence of lateral flows between the formal structures of control found in an economic sector. Organizational control in the commodity futures industry consists of several levels. The first of these will be referred to as the coordinating system.

THE COORDINATING SYSTEM

This section will examine how the anarchy in the pit is structured into orderly business relations. This is not accomplished in the pit alone, but rather depends on the assistance of auxiliary organizations. The coordinating system consists of a core technology and the auxiliary organizational arrangements to move the product or service from input to output. The core technology in the commodity futures industry is the trading pit (see Figure 1). It is in the pit that the exchange of contracts, the financial service provided by the industry, actually occurs.

The technique used for the exchange of futures contracts is essentially identical from pit to pit across all eleven commodity exchanges in the United States. The technique basically involves an open auction where buyers and sellers stand facing each other in a multi-tiered ring. At the opening bell traders begin making offers to buy or sell. They use hand signals and strong voices to offer and accept

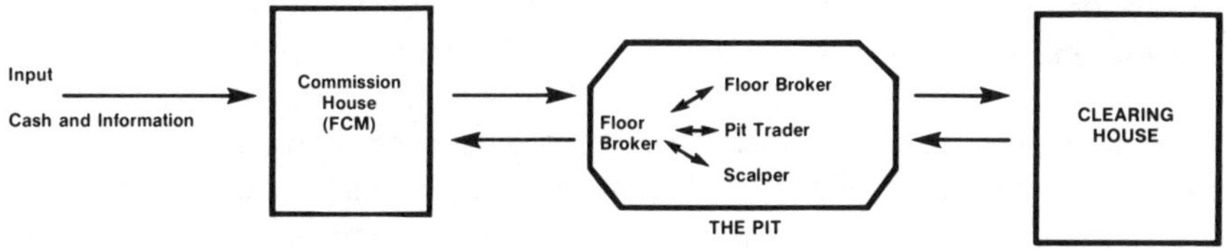

Figure 1. The coordinating system.

trades across the pit. These trades are recorded by each party to the trade. Trading does not stop after each transaction. It continues this way, more or less actively depending on the commodity, until the closing bell rings in the afternoon. The outlines of this process emerged at central markets for agricultural goods in pre-industrial Europe. These central markets were part of a mechanism which moved commodities from their producers to the ultimate consumers. The development of futures markets represents an elaboration of that marketing mechanism. The role of broker, for instance, developed as a middleman between producers and processors, one more part of a linear marketing channel.

The coordinating system in futures trading is a simple linear path. Cash, information, and later contracts, are passed along this path in a determined fashion. In the case of a trade initiated by a nonmember, such as one you or I might place, the input moves from our broker to a floor broker at the exchange. He or she buys or sells the contract(s). At the end of the day all trades are taken to the Clearing House where accounts are settled. Viewed in this manner, the futures market begins to look simple and its structural relations a bit overdetermined. By looking at each sub-unit in the coordinating system we may bring back some of the chaos and complexity generally associated with the market.

Commission House

When a customer, a potential trader, approaches the market, his or her first contact is with a commission house. The customer is not part of the system, but only a bearer of inputs whose cash and information are transformed into contracts, commissions and margin. The commission house acts as a gatekeeper who stands between the market and the resources flowing in. Commission houses that serve this function are members of one or more futures exchanges, and are officially referred to as Futures Commission Merchants (FCM). Customers usually refer to the person at the commission house whom they deal with as their broker or account executive. These are essentially salespeople for the FCM. The Chicago Board of Trade rules define an FCM as, "A member who makes a trade, either for another member or for a non-member, but who makes the trade in his own name and becomes liable as principal between himself and the other party to the trade" (Chicago Board of Trade, 1979, p. 403).

So the market is never directly linked to the thousands of non-member speculators and hedgers that use it. Rather, the FCM requires its customers to deposit a specific cash amount for each contract purchased or sold as a sign of good faith that all obligations will be met. The sum is usually ten to twenty percent of the value of the contract. This sum, the margin, must be maintained at some minimum level. If price fluctuation results in a loss the customer is required to deposit more funds with the FCM. In extreme circumstances the FCM may demand the additional deposit within as little as an hour. Commission houses usually try to keep the margin on account well above the minimum, but this varies.

In this way the FCM stands as a buffer between customers and the market. Customers have been effectively defined as outside the system. It becomes the obligation of the FCM to strain out the financially unstable and to secure access to the assets of those deemed reliable.[2] Such precautions are essential given that the FCM is legally liable for the contracts traded and thereby runs the risk of insolvency in the face of large losses. Thus, uncertainty is considerably reduced by knowing that all traders can be held responsible for their losses through the liability of the FCM.

In the Pit

Before there can be losses or profits the order must be placed. Once the customer has deposited a margin and agreed to be responsible for any losses, the account executive at the commission house will accept orders. These orders are phoned to the exchange where they are passed to a floor broker. The floor broker may represent the FCM exclusively or may freelance, trading for other members and for his or her own account. They are paid for each contract traded and therefore have an interest in cultivating business. They do this by developing a reputation for quick execution at the ordered price.

At this point in the coordinating system we have reached the pit, the technical core of futures trading. Here, in large open rings with descending steps, the chaotic outcry and gesturing of competing traders functions to determine the going price of a commodity. A hundred or more traders may gather around an active pit in soybeans, gold, foreign currency, or some other commodity, competing for their price.

The floor brokers are not the only participants in this scene, although their kind are usually the most numerous. Other members of the association, trading for their own accounts, add liquidity to the market. They often move in and out of the market, speculating on small price changes in the course of a few minutes, an hour, or a day. On the other hand, some floor traders, particularly those who are also involved with the cash commodity, may take large positions, occasionally influencing others to follow suit.

This then is the nearly perfect competitive market which economists study. Isolated from the buffers and strainers, it provides an arena for understanding price determination under competition. But the market does not and cannot work in isolation. The pit is but a component in an organizational system whose entire purpose is to maintain the integrity of the anarchy in the pit.

The Clearing House

Although the anarchy in the pit may be a natural coordinating mechanism for price, it does not necessarily coordinate human behavior. The result of the tumult in the pit is that contracts have been exchanged. These promises of future obligation must be sorted and settled. These tasks are accomplished by the clearing house, which Powers (1980, p. 253), with good reason, calls "the heart of any commodity futures exchange."

The clearing house may be a part of the exchange or a separate corporation, but whichever arrangement is chosen, it is directly linked to the pit. Membership in the clearing house consists of a subset of well capitalized members of the exchange. These members hold a stock in the clearing corporation and deposit a large sum in a guarantee fund. The clearing house is a not-for-profit corporation whose members oversee the financial integrity of the various contracts. The incentive for membership is that clearing members may profit from commissions paid them by floor brokers, although the clearing corporation itself does not profit.

The work of the clearing house begins at the end of each trading day when floor traders submit the list of all their trades to a clearing member. The trader typically has an ongoing relationship with some clearing member and has deposited clearing margin with that member. The clearing member hands cards representing each trade over to the clearing house staff where all trades are matched, recapitulating and verifying the buying and selling which occurred in the pit. At this point the clearing house becomes buyer to all sellers and seller to all buyers, thereby putting a buffer between the principals. Fulfilling of all contract obligations will, from this point until expiration of the contract, be guaranteed by the clearing house. No clearing house on an exchange in the United States has ever defaulted on this obligation. In most clearing houses one member's insolvency would cause an assessment on all other members until the obligation was met. This is informally referred to as the "good to the last drop" method of default recovery.

But the need for such measures rarely occurs. After the trades have been matched, the clearing house computes debit and credit amounts for all accounts. These are settled daily, just as in customer margin. If payment is due the clearing house it must arrive before the opening bell rings the next morning. The opening of trading may be delayed if all accounts are not settled. In this way the clearing house functions in the manner of a homeostatic mechanism (Ashby, 1965; Simon, 1981) or system regulator. Such a mechanism keeps the internal state of a system stable within fixed constraints. The constraints are the minimum margins which help guarantee the financial integrity of contracts against default. As Simon (1981, p. 12) states, ". . . the designer insulates the inner system from the environment, so that an invariant relation is maintained between inner system and goal, independent of variations over a wide range of parameters that characterize the outer environment."

In addition to sorting and matching the pit's output, the clearing house collects debts, dispenses credits and guarantees payment and delivery. Despite a continuous flow of inputs, the system remains stable within certain constraints. These are formal constraints which market members have chosen to structure their behavior and to provide rules within which the anarchy of competition may be played out. The straining and sorting components of the coordinating system insure that it is played out within fixed dimensions of time and space.

Of course, other possible sources of disturbance remain. Members may turn deviant, deciding that the incentive to violate the formal constraints excedes the incentive to conform. Disputes between members may demand arbitration. Most likely of all, environmental conditions affecting supply and demand may change so much that system constraints must be reset to guarantee the financial integrity of the market. While the coordinating system was adequate to regulate the *routine* flow of resources, for all these nonroutine disturbances there is a control system.

THE CONTROL SYSTEM

If the coordinating system, described above, was a closed machine through which energy flowed and was transformed, our analysis might stop with the linear chart in Figure 1. Once the system's parameters had been established by its designers, the system's major vulnerability would be entropy, a natural running down of the system due to lack of input. But the coordinating system is not a closed machine where the flow of energy can be wired and its course made invariant. First, it is an open system constantly receiving new input, i.e., customers' orders. Second, its constraints take the form of socially legitimized rules rather than calibrations. And third, its components consist of actors who make the rules and at the same time have an incentive to violate them. The constant flow of inputs keeps the system in negative entropy. As for the creation and maintenance of constraints, an elaboration is added to the open linear system: the exchange association. Looking at Figure 2, it is immediately obvious that the control system has added several new trajectories. These trajectories reflect the various proactive and reactive activities of the exchange association.

Both stock and commodity markets are organized by exchange associations. These exchanges are not-for-profit organizations owned and operated by the members. Members' shares in the association entitle them to act as floor traders, to pay reduced commissions, and to participate in governing the organization.

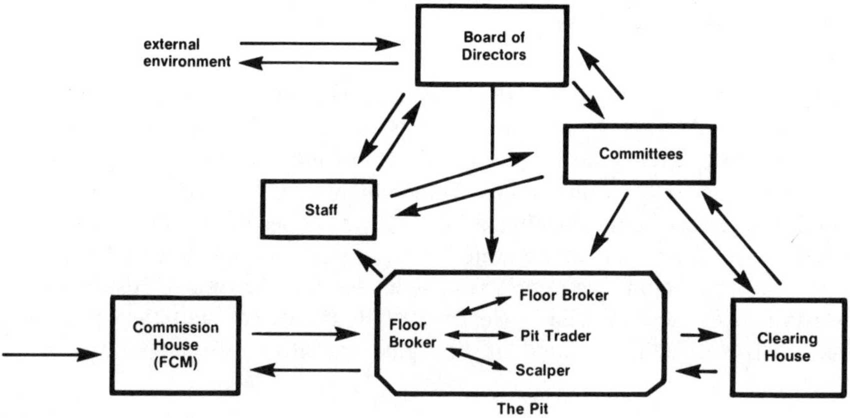

Figure 2. Formal structure of a futures exchange.

The function of the exchange is to establish and maintain competitive markets in financial instruments. The early history of these markets (Lurie, 1979; Taylor, 1917) indicates that increasingly rigorous constraints were found necessary to keep these markets from being cornered. The implication is that competitive markets do not emerge and maintain themselves "naturally." (If any tendency in markets exists, it is anticompetitive, as a result of the desire of successful competitors to reduce their uncertainty through monopoly.) Rather, it is *constraint* which is "natural" in the midst of competition. Commons (1959, p. 713) developed the notion rather elegantly.

> Competition is not Nature's 'struggle for existence' but is an artificial arrangement supported by the moral, economic, and physical sanctions of collective action. The theory of free competition developed by economists is not a natural tendency towards equilibrium of forces but is an ideal of public purpose adopted by the courts, to be attained by restraints upon the natural struggle for existence.

In this view the competitive market and its restraint are both equally artificial, i.e., social arrangements. Members, who draw their income from commissions, rely on the continuous operation of the market. They therefore have a vested interest in maintaining the market, which requires a limitation of the tendency toward monopoly. Of course, while the incentive of exclusive trading rights elicits conformity from the members, incentive systems are never perfect. As with any social system, someone is likely to test the system's limits. When the cost of such deviance is high, social systems resort to coercive control. The control system in commodity futures markets is highly formalized and hierarchical. This hierarchy will be examined in terms of its managerial and institutional functions.

Managerial Control

Managerial control in the commodity futures exchange consists of surveillance and corrective action. These functions are accomplished by committees made up of members of the exchange association. It is the responsibility of these committees to oversee activity in the pit and to control the operation in each pit by recording trades and posting prices. These committees are, for the most part, managers of information. Looking at Figure 2 we can see that information flows directly out of the pit and the clearing house, to staff and committees. The flow of both staff and committees represents a redundancy in the system. Historically, the committees were the chief managerial unit. It was not until 1948 that the Chicago Board of Trade hired its first paid executive officer (Hieronymus, 1971).

Surveillance. The surveillance function is common to all futures exchanges, although exchanges may differ on the names they use for committees. For the purpose of illustration we will look at the surveillance structure on the New York Mercantile Exchange.

Business Conduct Committee. This is perhaps the most controversial committee on a commodity exchange. It has general supervision over the business conduct of the members. In the course of supervision it may investigate ". . . the dealings, transactions, and financial conditions of members and member firms, may examine their books and records upon request, and shall prescribe such capital requirements as it deems appropriate" (New York Mercantile Exchange, 1979). Among the conduct forbidden in the by-laws is spreading of false rumor, noncompetitive trading, and fraudulent transactions with any member of the exchange.

Floor Committee. The Floor Committee is responsible for maintaining good order on the floor. This is mostly a matter of decorum and first violations are treated as a minor offense.

Membership Committee. This committee oversees all applications and transfers of membership. It conducts investigations into the qualifications and financial stability of the applicant.

At the largest exchanges the committees and staffs have, to some extent, a parallel structure. The Office of Investigations and Audits (staff) supplements and supports the work of the Business Conduct and Membership committees by gathering the investigative material needed for the committees' surveillance work. Guided by rules and by-laws, these and other committees assemble information on member's conduct, on the market positions they hold, and on the progress toward liquidation and delivery in various contracts. Once this information on members has been gathered, it is then redirected back at the board and its committees in their role as correction agents, so that deviation from the association goals may be punished by suspension, expulsion, or a fine.

Corrective action. The ability of exchanges to take corrective action is the key to managerial control. Many membership organizations have considerable surveillance capability but limited ability to take corrective action. Futures markets are remarkable for their flexibility in this area. The board and its committees have a range of actions at their disposal to adjust the system in the context of events.

In the short term the system reacts to rule violations and disputes between members. Rule violations are most often handled by the surveillance committees which are also part of the corrective feedback loop. In terms of internal disputes, the Pit Committee is the fire department of the exchange. It resolves any disputes arising from bids or offers in the pit. This is accomplished on the spot by the action of any two members of the committee. The Pit Committee may also levy fines up to $1000 for practices which are disruptive of orderly trading. The accused is entitled to a hearing, and appeal from the decision is to the board of directors. Larger disputes over a transaction involving either members or non-members may be brought before the Arbitration Committee, where an informal hearing is held. Such disputes are typically over the identity of trades, over prices, and over quantities. The committee hears both sides and assigns awards, where fitting, which are binding on the parties. In this way, conflicts arising are resolved internally so that trading may continue.

At another level, corrective action involves circumstances which threaten to interfere with the normal progress of a contract toward its final trading day. These circumstances include:

> (E)vents, conditions or positions which threaten a free, open and orderly market, the fair and orderly trading in any futures contracts, the orderly liquidation of or delivery pursuant to any futures contract, or a distortion of prices; a congestion, squeeze or corner or circumstances or positions which might result therein (New York Mercantile Exchange, 1979, pp. 2–20b).

Most exchanges have a Control Committee or its equivalent which assigns several members to monitor trading in each contract, assemble information regarding open positions and to ascertain from clearing members their customer's intentions as to liquidation or delivery of specific contracts. If investigation fails to eliminate the threat to orderly trading, the board may evoke its emergency powers.

Emergency powers are used to disrupt the flow of cash and information into the system. Action in the pit is constrained within specific limits until conditions in the market are deemed to have stabilized. Among the corrective actions available are, (a) limiting trading to liquidation only, (b) extending or shortening time for expiration of contracts, (c) ordering liquidation and fixing a settlement price, (d) ordering reduction of positions for any or all members, and (e) suspending trading. Such action is rarely necessary. Informal means of persuasion, directed by the committees at specific members, are often sufficient. When such extreme actions are taken, however, it is usually to avoid intervention from the regulatory environment (Abolafia, 1982). This brings us to the second function of the control system, institutional control.

Institutional Control

A control system, before anything else, is established to determine the operating policy in a market. This operating policy is the consensus by which the institution will be maintained. Since the founding of the Chicago Board of Trade in 1848, management of this consensus has been accomplished by the election of a Board of Directors, also known as the Board of Governors or Board of Managers on various other exchanges. These boards consist of between fifteen and twenty-five members and are elected from among the exchange membership. As part of setting policy, the board is responsible for making and changing exchange rules and for the management of all exchange property and finances. The board is also responsible for maintaining the legitimacy of exchange function and policy to the wider financial and regulatory environment.

Most of the work of the boards is done through committees which are made up of board members and other exchange members appointed by the board, usually for a one year tenure. Typically, the board meets once a month and an administrative committee exercises its authority to manage the exchange on a day to day basis. The board and its committees are assisted by a small hired staff.[3] The board itself may be called into special session when issues of management or rule interpretation are considered by the Chair to warrant such action.

Such extraordinary circumstances are the exception. Most policy action involves incremental changes in contract terms, margin, and permitted daily price fluctuations. These things are likely to be handled at the committee level. Constituting the greatest part of the policy making process, incremental changes are really a result of feedback from the technical core (see Figure 2). The policy making process is represented by a loop running from the board through the committees to the coordinating system and back again. The committees' centrality lies in their ability to receive information needed for policy making and to transmit the board's will.

The board itself is most likely to respond to outside pressure from its political or economic environment. Under government pressure it may be required to amend a contract or change a procedure which the government feels is anticompetitive. On the other hand, the board is increasingly concerned with turning the tables on the regulatory environment. It is actively involved in commenting on new federal regulations, testifying before Congressional committees, and lobbying the regulatory commission for approval of new contracts. As for rival exchanges, the board must assess competition from its rivals in various contracts and make the decision to develop new contracts. As competition and the regulatory environment have become more turbulent, these issues have become the predominant focus of board policy making. Thus, the board is becoming more of a buffer between the exchange and its environment, leaving internal control to the committees.

Whereas managerial control was concerned with the maintenance or restoration of market efficiency, institutional control is basically oriented to the long term survival of the market. In the short term, market order is maintained by the managerial functions of surveillance and conflict resolution. Institutional control, however, is dedicated to managing symbols more than people. Under the auspices of the board, (1) by-laws are written and amended; and (2) policies are defended in public appearances and through the dissemination of documents. These activities are more concerned with survival than efficiency. Markets, like other forms of social organization, do not continue to exist without reaffirmation of their goals and their legitimacy. It is the incremental but continuous adjustment of policy and the promotion of that policy in public forums that insures survival. In the next section we will examine the process by which futures markets act as institutions, attempting to control both internal and external affairs.

THE PROCESS OF CONTROL

To this point we have seen that a rather well articulated structure exists for coordinating and controlling the anarchy of futures trading. The competitive markets in the pit are only one component in the futures system. The pits are surrounded by buffers and sorters, surveillance agents and enforcers. The combined structures of the coordinating system and the control system constitute a *market control system.* A market control system comprises the rules of conduct and formal structures established by market members to reduce the level of uncertainty in their markets. As such, market control systems are tools of collective action established for the benefit and protection of the membership. Having studied the *structure* of market control, we are now ready to examine the actual process of market control.

It is appropriate to begin by turning to the oldest and largest of the eleven commodity futures exchanges in the United States, the Chicago Board of Trade. The CBT accounts for approximately 50% of all futures trading in the United States. In specific contracts, such as soybeans and corn, it holds as much as 87% and 91% of the market, respectively (Chicago Board of Trade, 1977). In fact, until recently there had been very little competition between exchanges over contracts in specific commodities.[4] Exchanges tend to specialize by commodity so that each has a dominant position in some group of commodities. The next largest exchange, the Chicago Mercantile, accounts for about 25% of trading futures, so that together the CBT and CME handled 75% of all trades in 1980 (Futures Industry, 1981).

Indicators of the powers of exchanges are not limited to market share. Each exchange is the only means of access to trading in its particular commodities (futures contracts). They allow no trading outside the exchange floor or after the hours specified by the exchange. The members own the exchange. They are able to limit membership, establish rules, and change them at will.[5] Going further, the most powerful elite insiders of the exchange are able to exact, within limits, supercompetitive profits (Abolafia, 1982; Noll, 1982). Exchanges are, as such, legal monopolies which have retained their dominance not only through existing economies of scale but through active maintenance of the market to assure the survival of the institution for the long term.

Of course, the cartel-like behavior of commodity exchanges has not gone undetected. In a 1905 decision, the U.S. Supreme Court recognized that the CBT was restraining dissemination of its price quotes but found that the exchange had a right to retain price quotes as its private property, even though this would eliminate competition from the prevalent off-exchange "bucket shops." In 1918 the court affirmed the right of the CBT to establish its own rules of trade, even when they restrained behavior in the market. In this classic decision Justice Brandeis found that in some cases market control is a *reasonable restraint of trade* in that its intention is the maintenance of market conditions (Abolafia, 1981). The important precedent here is that firms may cooperate on a variety of rules of trade, as long as they continue to compete over price. More recently, the efforts have been made to narrow the range of cooperation permissible. In 1972 the Department of Justice brought suit against the CBT under antitrust law for price-fixing by setting minimum commission rates. These minimum rates inhibited competition between brokers, and, claimed the suit, kept commissions artificially high. By mutual agreement the exchanges have slowly phased out minimum commission rates. The effect has been an increase in competition and the appearance of "discount rates" from new as well as older brokerage houses. Since 1975, a new federal regulatory agency, the Commodity Futures Trading Commission, has been responsible for discovering the anticompetitive behavior of exchanges (Johnson, 1977).[6]

Thus, there is a long history attached to exchanges' active control of market conditions, and the objections to this system have existed almost as long (Cowing, 1965; Lurie, 1979). But the survival and success of such a system can not be taken for granted. Underlying any market control system are active efforts to define its boundaries and, at times, to defend them. An essential part of the process of control in a market system, especially one as formalized as a commodities exchange, is boundary maintenance.

Boundary Maintenance

The boundaries in a market are defined by custom, precedent, rules and assumptions. They form the outline of what is deemed appropriate in the product and in the way it is exchanged. Participants recognize each other by these shared product and transactional definitions. Boundary maintenance refers to the process by which these "working rules" are tested and redefined. In the first futures market, at the Chicago Board of Trade, these rules were derived from mercantile custom. These customs established the norms of market control and reciprocity which were institutionalized by the exchange association.

How are such boundaries maintained? New actors come and old actors leave. Products, in this case the futures contracts, develop, improve and decline. Definitions of what is appropriate change. This market metabolism would lead to an expectation of continuous change. Yet, the market, as a social entity, retains a limited range of behaviors which do not fluctuate very widely. This stability is the result of three control processes: socialization, routine investigation, and boundary crises.

The limits of what one can "get away with" are constantly being tested in a competitive market. For this reason committees and staff are constantly monitoring behavior in the pits. In most cases minor infractions are punished very lightly; often with a reprimand. Such infractions include under-margined accounts or a commission house (FCM) falling below the capital requirements. More serious violations require stronger action. In February 1979 the Chicago Board of Trade fined a member firm, Clayton Brokerage, $30,000.

> At a meeting yesterday, the exchange's directors found Clayton engaged in 'reckless and unbusiness-like dealings' and 'acts detrimental to the interests and welfare of the association.' Specifically, the directors held that Clayton 'traded systematically against the orders and positions of its customers;' executed orders without obtaining margin, or security deposit, from its customers; didn't adequately monitor an account to assure that trades were suited to the account's financial resources, and made misstatements upon material points to the Business Conduct Committee of the exchange ("Board of Trade Fines Clayton Brokerage," 1979)

Such incidents are infrequent, this one being the only highly publicized one to occur during a three-year period of research. A principle actor in the above affair was later expelled from the Chicago Board of Trade and it was noted that it was the first expulsion in six years. But the effects of such incidents are not lost on members. They are a topic for discussion throughout the industry. Members are made aware of the efficacy of the self-regulatory machinery and the boundaries of acceptable behavior are reaffirmed.

On occasion these boundaries are sufficiently threatened to invoke a *boundary crisis*. Powerful actors inside or outside the market may call into question the "working rules" of the market. Such action elicits a collective response by members of the market who feel threatened. These crises appear as conflicts between the accused deviants and the defenders of the status quo. In futures markets these sides are often represented by venturesome speculators on one side and those who stand to lose on the other. It is in such crises that market members negotiate the acceptance or prohibition of products and behaviors. Two examples of boundary crises will be used to show how the market members maintain their most favorable positions. Our first example will examine the details behind the 1905 Supreme Court case already mentioned. The second example examines a recent case of boundary maintenance in the 1980s.

Bucket shops. Bucket shops first made their appearance around 1879, by which time futures trading was already thriving in Chicago.[7] They were an attempt to profit from commodity speculation without playing by the working rules of the exchange. In the practice of bucketing one takes the opposite side of a customer's order without ever executing it on an exchange. Bucket shops were storefronts where people gathered to speculate by making bets on the direction a commodity's price might take on the exchange. Unlike exchange trading, one could bet any amount of money, had no worry about delivery, and needed no broker. For a commission the proprietor of the shop took the other side of all trades.

At first the Chicago Board of Trade paid little attention. The fact was that it was not uncommon for members of the CBT to bucket orders themselves. But as the shops grew and attracted more customers it became clear that they were objectionable on at least three bases:

1. they provided competition for exchange members who made their living from the commissions paid by customers;
2. they reduced liquidity in the pit and thereby affected market efficiency; and
3. they threatened the legitimacy of exchange trading by equating commodity speculation with gambling in the minds of the public and its officials.

This last was potentially most threatening because it questioned the ability of the exchange to regulate the market and gave ammunition to reform groups, mostly farmers, calling for the abolition of futures trading.

The boundary crisis was of a dual nature. The CBT had first to decide on the practice of bucketing within the exchange and then to face the challenge from the political environment. By 1882 the directors had noted the "demoralizing" effect of the shops and "their injurious effect on the business" (Lurie, 1979, p. 80). In 1883 the CBT finally approved a rule against those members who bucketed by the close vote of 281 to 251. Although this rule proved difficult to enforce, this construction of new boundaries to member's behavior set the stage for a protracted struggle to eliminate the external threat.

Efforts to control information through denial of telegraphic price quotes outside the exchange proved worthless. Bucket shops contrived ways to get the quotes, even using wire taps. Telegraph quotes were soon resumed. In 1894 the Directors finally decided to put an end to bucketing within the exchange by suspending and expelling bucketers. After this the CBT was able to fight the bucket shops in court, raising their illegality according to Illinois law as an issue. This legal struggle culminated in a 1905 Supreme Court decision in the case of Chicago Board of Trade vs. Christie Grain and Stock Company (a bucket shop). Oliver Wendell Holmes, Jr. writing for the majority, found that quotations are the property of the exchange and that the exchange's activities were clothed with a legitimate public purpose.

This decision ended this boundary crisis. It signalled the end of the bucket shops and thus the elimination of serious external competition. More importantly, it established the legitimacy of the exchange as a self-regulating body with a public function. As the next example shows, legitimacy is an increasingly critical part of a market's boundary maintenance.

Margins. Perhaps the single most important tool that exchanges have for maintaining the financial integrity of the market is their ability to set and change the margins paid by brokers and customers. They are the cornerstone of self-regulation. A challenge to the appropriateness of exchange-based margins might be felt as a challenge to the competence of the market control system in general.

Just such a challenge occurred in Spring, 1980. As in the example of the bucket shops, the threat was external, but this time it was from the federal government. In the interim between these two crises the boundaries of the market changed little, except perhaps in that custom and precedent made them more solid. But starting in the 1920s these boundaries were codified in federal law, so that their violation might be made a public matter. By 1975 the codification had been strengthened to include an independent federal regulatory agency, the Commodity Futures Trading Commission (CFTC). At this point the conditions for a new boundary crisis between the exchange and the government were set.

The precipitent to the boundary crisis was a threat to the integrity of the silver market. A monumental struggle between buyers and sellers of silver was being played out. This threat not only questioned the self-regulatory ability of an exchange, but played havoc with a commodity of great importance to the U.S. Treasury and Federal Reserve Board. As such, both Congress and the CFTC began to raise questions about appropriate self-regulatory behavior on the New York Commodities Exchange (Comex). The Board of Governors of the Exchange had raised margins, set limits on speculative positions and finally ordered trading for liquidation only.

The issue was whether Comex had acted with sufficient alacrity. It was claimed that while Comex members were making money on the high volume trading, the Board was reluctant to take action to cool off the market. Rumors began to circulate in the industry that the power to set margins might be transferred to the Federal Reserve Board, where margin setting for the securities industry is determined. During a Senate hearing on the adequacy of regulatory action during the "silver situation" Comex representatives took great care to forcefully defend their competence and thereby their boundaries.

> In reviewing the history of the Federal Reserve Board in establishing securities margins it is interesting to note that there has not been any change in the 50% stock margin requirement for over five years. During the seven months in question, Comex changed original margin requirements regularly to keep pace with a dramatically moving and volatile silver market. To establish futures margins, regular review of futures market and a constant awareness of economic factors within the markets is essential. No entity is more appropriate to discharge that responsibility than futures exchanges. As evidence of the effectiveness of futures exchanges in establishing margins, it should be noted that there has never been an incident of brokerage firm failure resulting from commodity defaults (Commodities Exchange, 1980).

Comex was not going to depend on the success of this presentation to defend its boundaries. One month later it was reported that "the CBT, CME, and Comex have joined forces to retain a high-powered Washington lobbying firm, Charles Walker Associates, in an effort to head off Senator William Proxmire's efforts through S.2704 to shift margin setting authority to the Federal Reserve Board" (Futures Industry, 1980). When the dust finally settled and the silver market had recovered, the exchanges had lost none of their self-regulatory powers.

The two cases discussed above indicate several notable aspects of boundary maintenance. Both were set off by activity which was part of the industry's operation. Both were the product of deep conflicts between traditional actors in the industry. What separated this activity from all others was that it threatened the continued autonomy and legitimacy of the market control system. In both cases the exchanges rallied their resources and fought to defend their boundaries.

Both the bucket shops and the collapse of the silver market were in themselves damaging to the exchanges. Both caused a reduction in customers, the key resource input of the market. The exchanges took action to eliminate the problem but found opposition from outside public or private agents. When this opposition threatened the legitimacy of industry custom and behavior, a boundary crisis could be said to exist. At this point the exchanges responded by quickly resolving their own affairs, i.e., the conflicts, and defending the issue of their actions in a public forum. In maintaining their boundaries the futures markets have aggressively sought and acquired legitimation. As the public interest in particular markets increases, the process of boundary maintenance may be forced into public arenas more frequently.

Finally, it is important to note that both of these efforts restored competition to the market. Futures exchanges can never afford to stray too far from conditions of free and open markets. By eliminating the practices which were most costly to market members they sustained competitive conditions. That those practices eliminated were also those which society found least legitimate has helped these institutions of market control to survive despite opposition from Populism, Progressivism, and more recent reform movements.

CONCLUSIONS

In this chapter we have used the perspective of organization theory to study formal structure in the commodity futures industry. The organizational ethnography presented here has shown that behavior in this industry is, in fact, highly structured. Futures trading is a competition carried on within strict rules. These rules are created and enforced within a well-articulated set of organizational arrangements. Players are sorted, surveilled, and even punished on occasion. By stepping back from the pit, one begins to see the construction of the competitive arena and the institutional arrangements for insuring the reproduction of that competition.

It can also be concluded that the shape these arrangements take is not arbitrary. Organizational arrangements are isomorphic with the market structure. Futures markets are organized as exchange associations. In these associations, control is formally democratic, access is formally open, and members share equally in the decision making. This, of course, mirrors the perfectly competitive market where all are equal and all have equal access to the process of price determination. But in the context of organizational arrangements, the free market ideals of unfettered trade are selectively displaced by considerations of maintaining the market and protecting the personal advantages of membership. The maintenance of competitive conditions, from which traders earn their living, requires the ability to control that competition, to routinize it, and to exclude those forms of behavior which threaten it.

Another conclusion is that these organizational arrangements may be conceived of as a market control system. As Figure 2 indicates, the various parts of the coordinating and control systems are linked by flows and feedbacks of cash and information. It is the system as a whole that maintains the market mechanism. Judging from the survival of markets like those at the Chicago Board of Trade, the system is highly effective.

The market control system really has three interrelated tasks. In the pit, where financial contracts are exchanged, efficiency is the central task. In fact, futures markets are most familiar to economists as exemplars of efficient transaction. In the coordinating system and managerial control committees the task is discovering problems in the pit (e.g., under-capitalized traders or market concentration) and taking whatever corrective action is necessary to *protect* market efficiency. The task of the Board of Directors is the management of the material and symbolic assets of the system as a whole. This includes the management of exchange property, the production of new and innovative contracts to keep the exchange attractive to customers, and the maintenance of organizational autonomy in the face of potential government regulation. Each of these tasks contributes to the overall effectiveness of the market control system.

Finally, it is important to ask whether the kind of structuring of uncertainty found in the commodity futures markets can be generalized to other markets, and if they too exhibit some form of market control system. Data on the anarchic conditions on the floors of stock and options markets (see Baker, chapter 6) would certainly lead us to expect similar control structures.[8] From a sociological perspective, economic actors, whether they are traders of financial instruments or large industrial firms, are unlikely to tolerate the uncertainty of the market without resorting to some form of collective organization. It is for this reason that markets, and volatile financial markets in particular, cannot be fully understood without attention to the layers of social organization, formal and informal, which surround and buffer them.

NOTES

1. The concept of an economic sector carries with it many of the same problems that the concept of an industry has (Scott & Meyer, 1982). The analyst must decide what products are to be included in the category, i.e., which products are in some sense substitutable. He or she must also choose a level of specificity, e.g., the educational sector or the graduate education sector. In our case, we are concerned with the financial sector in terms of the dollar value of transactions in all financial instruments (Smith, 1971). Although stock and futures do not have a substitutable product, they may logically be compared because of their similar cast of participants and formal structures. Both are organized as membership associations linked to the brokerage industry and backed by a clearing house.

2. Merrill Lynch suggests to prospective futures clients that they have at least $50,000 in speculative capital before they begin. It is not unusual for commission houses to keep treasury bills and other easily liquifiable assets on deposit as part of the margin account. Smaller houses may ask for only the minimum required by the exchange.

3. On the four largest exchanges, which account for more than 90 percent of trading, the staff was between 13% and 18% of the size of the total membership in 1980. The largest of the four had 254 staff people, the smallest had 50.

4. Competition began to heat up in the mid 1970s over the development of future contracts in financial instruments, such as treasury bills and bonds, Government National Mortgage Association Certificates, and most recently, stock indexes. It appears that existing economies of the scale at the CBT and Chicago Mercantile Exchange will eventually allow each to overcome competition from the New York exchanges and to dominate in particular commodities.

5. The establishment of the federal Commodity Futures Trading Commission in 1975 has inhibited their freedom in rule changing to a degree, in that the exchanges must now submit all rule changes for approval.

6. Elsewhere (Abolafia, 1981), I have discussed the agency's reluctance to intervene in the exchange's market control system. Recently, the agency has been forced by events covered in the press to attend to the conflicts of interest which may occur when members of the board of directors use their rule-changing power to affect trading in a contract in which they hold positions.

7. This account of the bucket shops is based on the historical account by Lurie (1979).

8. At a further remove, it would appear that the trade associations, professional associations and cartels are also types of market control systems. More research is needed to develop a broader understanding of the structuring of the anarchy in financial and other markets.

REFERENCES

Abolafia, M. Y. *Taming the market: Self-regulation in the commodity futures industry.* Unpublished doctoral dissertation, State University of New York at Stony Brook, 1981.

Abolafia, M. Y. *Self-regulation as market maintenance.* (Working paper 82-2.) Davis: Graduate School of Administration, University of California, 1982.

Aldrich, H., & Whetten, D. Organization-sets, action-sets, and networks: Making the most of simplicity. In P. Nystrom & W. Starback (Eds.), *Handbook of organization design.* Oxford: Oxford University Press, 1981.

Ashby, W. R. *An introduction to cybernetics.* New York: Harper & Row, 1965.

Benson, J. K. The interrorganizational network as a political economy. *Administrative Science Quarterly,* 1975, *20,* 229–249.

Board of trade fines Clayton brokerage. *The Wall Street Journal,* February 21, 1979.

Buckley, W. *Sociology and modern systems theory.* Englewood Cliffs, N.J.: Prentice-Hall, 1967.

Cadwaller, M. The cybernetic analysis of change in complex social systems. In W. Buckley (Ed.), *Modern system research for the behavioral scientist.* Chicago: Aldine, 1968.

Chicago Board of Trade. *Commodity trading manual.* Chicago: Author, 1977.

Chicago Board of Trade. *Rules and regulations.*Chicago: Author, 1979.

Commodities Exchange. *Chronology of activities relating to the silver market from September 1979 through March 1980.* New York: Author, 1980.

Commons, J. R. *Institutional economics.* Madison: University of Wisconsin Press, 1959.

Cowing, C. B. *Populist, plungers, and progressives.* Princeton, N.J.: Princeton University Press, 1965.

Evan, W. M. The organization-set: Toward a theory of interorganizational relations. In J. D. Thompson (Ed.), *Approaches to organization design.* Pittsburgh: University of Pittsburg Press, 1966.

Futures Industry. *III* (1, June 2, p. 4). Chicago: Author, 1980.

Futures Industry. To nobody's surprise, 1980 was another record volume year. *IV* (2, January 19). Chicago: Author, 1981.

Hieronymus, T. A. *Economics of future trading.* New York: Commodity Research Bureau, 1971.

Johnson, P. F. Antitrust in the commodities field: After Gordon. *Hofstra Law Review,* 1977, *6,* 115–128.

Lurie, J. *The Chicago board of trade, 1859–1905.* Urbana: University of Illinois Press, 1979.

New York Mercantile Exchange. *By-laws and rules.* New York: Author, 1979.

Noll, R. Comments on self-regulation as market maintenance. In R. Noll (Ed.), *Regulatory policy and the social sciences.* Unpublished proceedings of the NSF Conference on Regulatory Policy and the Social Sciences, Washington, D.C., 1982.

Norris, F. *The pit: A story of Chicago.* New York: Doubleday, Page & Co., 1903.

Parsons, T. Three levels in the hierarchical structure of organization. In W. Evan (Ed.), *Interorganizational relations.* Philadelphia: University of Pennsylvania Press, 1978.

Powers, M. *Getting started in commodity futures trading.* Waterloo, Iowa: Investors Publication Inc., 1980.

Samuelson, P. A. *Economics: An introductory analysis* (6th ed.). New York: McGraw-Hill, 1964.

Scott, W. R., & Meyer, J. *The organization of institutional sectors* (Stanford University Report No. 82-A16). Stanford, Cal.: Institute for Research on Educational Finance and Governance, 1982.

Simon, H. *The sciences of the artificial.* Cambridge: MIT Press, 1981.

Smith, P. F. *Economics of financial institutions and markets.* Homewood, Ill.: Dorsey, 1971.

Taylor, C. *History of the board of trade of the city of Chicago.* Chicago: R. O. Law, 1917.

To keep future healthy, exchanges have medics on hand. *The Wall Street Journal,* October 28, 1982, p. 33.

Warren, R. The interorganizational field as a focus for investigation. *Administrative Science Quarterly,* 1967, *12,* 369–419.

PART IV

INSTITUTIONAL DIMENSIONS OF THE MARKET

THE MEDIA AND THE MARKET

David A. Snow and Robert Parker

The purpose of this chapter is to explore the relationship between the mass media and the stock market by examining the impact of two kinds of news pertinent to the stock market.[1] The first type refers to media-disseminated news about events and happenings in the world. This "general news" is typically featured on radio and television newscasts and on the front page of the major dailies throughout the country, including the *Wall Street Journal*. The second type of news refers to "news about the market," such as is found on PBS's Wall Street Week and in the newsletters of investment advisors. Our concern is not with the media's construction and dissemination of these two types of news,[2] but with the presumed linkage between the general news and the market and the manner in which the market is portrayed by the media.

Underlying these concerns are two interrelated observations. The first has to do with the commonsense belief that the market is directly affected by news about other events and activities. The second pertains to the media's widespread and continuous coverage of the market. With the exception of the weather and sports, few if any other domains of activity receive such extensive media coverage. Whether driving to or from work, one is likely to learn via the radio where the Dow Jones Industrials closed or opened in comparison to yesterday and whether the average price per share was up or down on the New York and American Exchanges. The latest information about the market is also summarized routinely on the morning and evening network news programs. For those who desire to follow the market more closely, PBS boasts *Wall Street Week, The MacNeil-Lehrer Report* and its *Nightly Business Report,* while Cable TV offers Financial News Network, Ted Turner's Cable News Network with its three business shows—*Moneyline, Moneyweek,* and *Inside Business,* and Satellite News Channel with its report on business twice each hour. Should individual investors or money watchers miss one of these programs or wish to scrutinize the ebb and flow of their pet securities, they can always turn to the print media and its various and sundry offerings. In addition to the hundreds of daily newspapers with their various market reports, there are a number of business and financial newspapers such as Dow Jones and Company's *Wall Street Journal* and *Barron's National Business and Financial Weekly.* As if these radio, television, and newspaper offerings were not enough, there are weekly discussions of the market and related business news in the general interest magazines like *Time, Newsweek,* and *U.S. News and World Report,* not to mention the specialized business and financial magazines such as *Business Week, Forbes, Fortune,* and *Dun's Review.* Finally, at the end of this media smorgasbord of information on the market, there are numerous newsletters put out by various financial houses and by an array of market gurus, such as Granville, Kaufman, and Zweig.

When this extensive media coverage of the market is considered in conjunction with the phenomenal amount of research on the individual and societal effects of the mass media,[3] it seems reasonable to expect that the relationship between the media and the market would be well understood. That is not the case, however. For whatever reasons, social scientists have devoted scant attention to the linkage between the media and the market. As a consequence, it is difficult to give straightforward answers to questions concerning the impact of the general news on the market, the media's depiction of the market, the accuracy of that imagery, and the like. The aim of this chapter, then, is to examine systematically such questions so as to further our understanding of the linkages between the media and the market. We begin by considering whether the market reacts to the "general news" and, if so, how and why, and then turn to a critical examination of the "news about the market."

THE GENERAL NEWS AND THE MARKET: A LINEAR RELATIONSHIP?

To what extent does the general news influence the market? Are turns in the market precipitated by changes in this kind of news? And if so, is it the news in general or a particular news item that affects the market?

At first glance such questions seem pointless. At least that is the commonsense position. This position was clearly reflected in casual conversations with a small nonrandom sample of seventeen lay investors. As one informant put it:

> The news and the market dance together. Occasionally they get out of step. But most of the time important news items influence the market.

That these lay investors, and presumably others as well, would subscribe to the notion that the market reacts to the general news is not surprising given the media's constant linkage of the two. Though news reports on market activity do not always address the question of underlying precipitants, when such factors are mentioned, as when there is a significant increase or decline in trading, newscasters typically preface their comments with the phrase of "news that" or "news of." In other words, the tendency is to attribute market turns to "news of" or "about" some coterminous event or happening. Consider, for example, the following statements excerpted from radio newscasts:

> The market rallied today on news of a decline in the prime interest rate.
>
> News that the gross national product fell 2.5% in December drove the Dow Jones Industrial Average down 11.59 points today.

The linkage of market rallies and declines to particular items of news is also commonplace in newspapers, as is clearly reflected in the following headlines appearing atop the *Wall Street Journal's* "Abreast of the Market" column:

> Industrials Add 12.24 in Late Rally, Spurred by Oil, U.S. Budget News
>
> Early surge is Dampened by News of Israeli Attack
>
> Stock Slips as Early Rally Founders On News Of Firm's Chapter 11 Filing

The question of concern is whether such attributions are correct. Does news of various sorts really cause the market to rally or decline? Is this commonsense belief that is routinely promulgated by the media empirically on target?

RESEARCH FINDINGS

The first and most systematic examination of this issue was conducted by Klein and Prestbo (1974). This study consisted primarily of a comparison of market trends with the general news over the six year period 1966 through 1972. As their barometer of market activity, Klein and Prestbo used the Dow Jones Industrial Average.[4] As a measure of the news, they developed a news index based on systematic weighting of both the placement and content of the material appearing in the "What's News" section (which includes a column on "World-Wide" nonbusiness developments and a column on "Business and Finance") and in the three feature stories carried on the front page of the *Wall Street Journal*.[5] The placement of the material was weighted by giving "a score of three (3) to the lead, or top, story in both "What's News" columns, a score of two (2) to stories that appear above the fold that divides the paper in half horizontally, and a score of one (1) to stories below the fold" (Klein & Prestbo, 1974, p. 54). The content of the material evaluated was scored according to whether it seemed good or bullish for the market (+), negative or bearish (−), or neutral or indifferent (0). To illustrate, a "What's News" lead item that was "deemed favorable for stocks received a plus three, a negative lead item a minus three, and so on down" (Klein & Prestbo, 1974, p. 55).

The study's major findings are summarized in Table 1, which shows the degree of correspondence between the flow of the general news and the eight major market turns that occurred between the beginning of 1966 and the end of 1971. Considering first the relationship between the news flow and the major upturns of this period, we see that in the 24 weeks preceding these upturns the news was decidedly negative (62% of the days and 75% of the weeks), whereas in the 25 weeks following the upturns the news was decidedly positive (63% of the days and 80% of the weeks). This rather dramatic shift in the tenor of the news after the four upturns prompted Klein and Prestbo (1974, p. 68) to suggest that "when the flow of the news abruptly reverses itself, from very negative to very positive, the market is bound to stop falling and start rising." If so, then the obverse pattern ought to hold for downturns. That is, a dramatic increase in negative or bearish news ought to be associated with a major decline in the market. When we examine the downturn columns that is, in fact, what we find. Although the news was skewed slightly but not significantly in the postive direction in the weeks before the downturns of the 1965–71 period, it was overwhelmingly negative in the 24 weeks (73% of the days and 96% of the weeks) after the market had reached its peak and had begun to plummet downwards.

Table 1
News Flow Before and After Major Upturns and Downturns January 1966 to January 1972*

	Market Turns			
	Upturns		*Downturns*	
News Flow	*Before*	*After*	*Before*	*After*
Number of Days	117	123	119	117
Positive (+)	29%	63%	46%	20%
Negative (−)	62%	29%	45%	73%
Neutral (0)	9%	8%	9%	7%
Number of Weeks	24	25	24	24
Positive (+)	25%	80%	42%	4%
Negative (−)	75%	20%	50%	96%
Neutral (0)	0%	0%	8%	0%

*This table is based on figures derived by Klein and Prestbo (1974) and presented in Tables 5-A (p. 67) and 6-A (p. 82).

Klein and Prestbo also found that this pattern of directional correspondence, whether upwards or downwards, between the flow of the news and stock price movements manifested itself 80% of the time throughout 1972. Taken together, these findings strongly suggest that the news and the market tend to move together and, as a consequence, "that stocks can't continue to fall in the face of a sustained dose of good news, nor continue to rise when the news is decisively bad" (Klein & Prestbo, 1974, p. 108).

Since these observations pertain to the relationship between the market and the news in general, one might reasonably wonder about the effects of particular items or kinds of news, such as news of a Presidential election outcome, of military buildup in a foreign country, or of corporate fraud, bankruptcy or mergers. Klein and Prestbo also considered this issue by examining the impact on the market of news regarding the Vietnam War, four presidential elections, and three corporations. Here it was found that while news concerning single issues may affect the stocks or industries involved, if any, such particularized news tends not to affect the market as a whole.

Klein and Prestbo's central finding, then, was that major turns in the market are associated not so much with news of particular events or happenings, but with pronounced changes in the general flow of the news. As they concluded:

> Sudden, momentous events hardly ever trigger major turns in the market. President Kennedy's assassination in 1963, for instance, caused just a momentary lapse in the bull market of 1962–66, and the impact of the Arab-Israeli Six-Day War, in June 1967, was equally transitory, in the short run. Sometimes big news gets credit for precipitating a basic shift in market direction because the news and the shift occur at the same time, but a closer look usually reveals that a change in the *flow* of the news is responsible. (Klein & Prestbo, 1974, p. 71)

Since the state of the economy during the early 1980s differed rather remarkably from the comparatively upbeat economic climate of the 1966–72 period, we thought it would be useful to see whether the aforementioned findings and observations obtain today. We thus examined the correspondence between the market and the general news for a five month period beginning July 1, 1982, seven weeks before the historic August upturn, and extending through November 1982. We employed essentially the same measures and weighting procedures used by Klein and Prestbo as described earlier. The only major difference was that the news index we developed was based on an analysis of the placement and content of only the two "What's News" columns on the front page of the *Wall Street Journal*.[6]

Our findings, which are summarized in Table 2, provide only minimal corroboration of Klein and Prestbo's observations. Inspection of Table 2 reveals that prior to the August upturn the news was decidedly negative, whereas in the weeks following the upturn there was an increase in the volume of positive or bullish news, from 13 to 23 percent of the days and from 0 to 25 percent of the

Table 2
News Flow Before and After Upturn Beginning
August 17, 1982

News Flow	*Before Upturns*	*After Upturns*
Number of Days	31	74
Positive (+)	13%	23%
Negative (−)	84%	68%
Neutral (0)	3%	9%
Number of Weeks	7	16
Positive (+)	0%	25%
Negative (−)	100%	75%
Neutral (0)	0%	0%

weeks. This shift is in a direction consistent with Klein and Prestbo's findings, but it does not constitute a highly significant shift in the flow of the news, much less an "abrupt reversal" of the kind they found. To the contrary, the news remained predominantly negative (68% of the days and 75% of the weeks) following the upturn. Thus, rather than finding directional correspondence between the news and the market, our research revealed a news flow mired in a bog of negativity during a period in which the market was spiralling upwards to record heights. Simply put, we found the simultaneous existence of a sustained dose of negative news and a bullish market.

Since these findings are inconsistent with both the commonsense position and Klein and Prestbo's findings, we think several revised, albeit tentative, conclusions are in order: First, though the general news and the market may move together, as Klein and Prestbo demonstrated, such directional correspondence is neither automatic nor fully predictable. Second, though market trends generally may be more responsive to the flow of the news than to particular items of news, this is not always the case, as is clearly illustrated by the meanderings of the market after the upsurge of the summer of 1982. And third, during some periods the direction of the flow of the news and market activity may be divergent rather than correspondent.

Conceptual and Theoretical Observations

The foregoing findings and conclusions, however tentative, give rise to a number of questions that require clarification if we are to better understand these findings in particular and the relationship between the media and the market in general. One such question has to do with the factors that account for temporal and directional variation in the relationship between the general news and the market. If that connection is neither linear nor fully predictable, then are we to assume that it is random, or that it is mediated instead by various intervening factors? And if the relationship between the general news and market is mediated, then what are the intervening factors at work?

In considering these questions, it is important to be precise about what it is that requires explanation. Thus far we have referred to such phenomena as the market, market trends, and upturns and downturns rather loosely and broadly, treating them as if they were independent and autonomous things rather than products of the decisions and actions of an aggregation of individual and institutional investors. To continue to proceed in such a manner is to reify market trends and to thereby gloss over the factors that influence their relationship to the news. Accordingly, what requires examination is not the relationship between the general news and the market *per se,* but the relationship between that news and individual and institutional investors.

In addressing the above questions, our intent is not to detail the full range of plausible explanations accounting for the connection between general news and the market. Rather, it is to present what we consider to be several of the more important factors that modify the impact of the general news on investment behavior and thereby affect market trends.

Expectations, Market Theories, and Self-Fulfilling Prophecies

A core assumption of the symbolic interactionist perspective in sociology is that human beings seldom respond directly to the things or stimuli they encounter but respond, instead, primarily on the basis of the *meaning* those things or stimuli have for them (Blumer, 1969; Meltzer, Petras, & Reynolds, 1975; Stone & Farberman, 1981). Human behavior is thus seen as resting in part on an interpretive process involving the assignment of meaning to the objects encountered. Rather than responding automatically, immediately and absolutely, we take note of what is perceived, define it in terms of some interpretive scheme and the constraints of the situation, and then act or respond accordingly.

The implications of this premise for understanding the relationship between general news and investment behavior is that it suggests that how investors, whether individual or institutional, respond to the news, if at all, is partly contingent on the meaning the news has for them. Since the meaning of any particular object is not intrinsic to it, but is conferred upon it according to some perspective, it follows that how the market reacts to the news is partly dependent on investors' ideas about how the market works in general and their views about the relationship between the news and the market in particular. As has been noted in previous chapters, there is relatively little consensus about how the market works. The problem is not a lack of market theories or interpretive schemes, but rather an overabundance of such schemes (Smith, 1981).

Just as these theories differ in terms of their general ideas about what moves the market, so too they differ in terms of the significance attached to the news.

The fundamentalists, who believe that market activity reflects developments in the real world, pay rather close attention to the news so as to keep abreast of the developments that presumably affect the market. At the other extreme are the technicians or chartists who attach relatively little significance to the news. Because they believe that the market has a life of its own, the key to defining its movement is thought to reside in the analyses of their elaborate charts, graphs and formulas, not in news about love and hate, war and peace, and boom or bust. In between these two schemes are the contrarians and the random walkers. Contrarians, who operate on the principle of going against the grain, attend to the news not because they think there is some invariant connection between it and stock prices, but because they need to see what others are up to in order to plot their divergent course. Random walkers, on the other hand, pay scant attention to the news, but not for the same reason it is disregarded by technicians. The random walkers concede that the market reacts to the news, but argue that it makes little sense to attend to it because its effects are so sudden that by the time most investors decide to act on it, it has already been factored into the prices.

The existence of these contrasting perspectives suggests that not only may the significance attached to the news vary considerably, but that the same news or "facts" about the world in general or the market in particular may have completely different meanings. At the level of the single investor, this means that the impact of the news on investment decisions is likely to be filtered through some favored perspective. At the aggregate level, this means that the relation between the news and market trends may vary considerably depending on the popularity of one perspective vis-a-vis the others. If one perspective is currently in vogue,[7] then it is likely that the market will conform to its expectations. If either numerous individual investors or a handful of institutional investors believe, for example, that an increase in the Consumer Price Index is bearish news, then the market is likely to respond in a bearish manner. If, on the other hand, contrarian views hold sway, then such bearish news may precipitate an upturn. In either case the result is a self-fulfilling prophecy; for what moved the market was not news *per se,* but the meanings attached to the news.

The point, then, is that at the individual level the relationship between general news and investment decisions is mediated by one's expectations regarding the impact of the news on the market, whereas at the aggregate level the relationship between the general news and market movements is mediated by the confluence of shared definitions and expectations among numerous investors or a few investors with large holdings.

Ambiguity, Market Gurus, and the Two-Step Flow of Communication

In emphasizing the interpretive function of various market theories, we do not mean to suggest that most lay investors actually approach the market with a working understanding of one or more of these theories. Indeed, there is good reason to assume the contrary. The exceedingly volatile nature of the market, the array of conflicting theories about it, and the great volume of information on it give rise to a domain of activity that is characterized, at least on the surface, by considerable ambiguity and disorder. Such a situation seems more conducive to confusion and uncertainty, especially to outsiders, than to understanding and certainty. As a consequence, it seems reasonable to assume that most lay investors find themselves, much like participants in many collective behavior situations (e.g., riots, panic and crazes), looking for guidance as to what to do. Perhaps this, among other things, is why many of the market professionals interviewed by Smith (1981), in his intensive examination of their philosophies, practices and views, held their clients in relatively low esteem insofar as their understanding of the market was concerned. As Smith (1981, p. 63) noted in discussing an informant's attitude towards his customers:

> Some of his customers, he feels, have no understanding of the market whatsoever. Others have a degree of sophistication, most of which they have gained from him. Few, if any of them, he feels could survive on their own. When one of his customers begins to "second guess" him he likes to let them go on their own for a while just to teach them a lesson. Usually they fall into line fairly quickly.

These observations are particularly revealing because they direct attention to the role of market experts as both interpreters and purveyors of news about the market. That various market professionals would function in this manner is not particularly surprising given the organization of market activity, with the intermediary function of brokers, and the ambiguity that pervades the market. It is also quite consistent with what is referred to in mass communications research as the "two-step flow of communication," a process involving the flow of communication from the media to various "influentials" or "opinion leaders" who in turn digest and interpret this information and then relay it on to those individuals who presumably respect their specialized competencies and judgments. This process was discovered quite by accident during the course of Lazarsfeld, Berelson and Gaudet's (1948) now classic study of the role of the mass media in affecting voting decisions in the 1940 presidential election. In a reexamination of the study some twenty years later, Lazarsfeld and Menzel (1963, p. 96) summarized its major aim, expectation, and finding thusly:

> This study went to great lengths to determine how the mass media brought about such changes. To our surprise, we found the effect to be rather small. . . . People appeared to be much more influenced by face-to-face contact with people . . . than by the mass media directly.

Although subsequent investigations of the two-step model in a variety of communication situations have suggested a number of limitations and modifications,[8] we think the general idea of a two-stepped or multistaged communication process is particularly applicable to the relationship between news about the world in general and investment behavior. This is because the intense desire of investors to know what is going on, coupled with the previously mentioned ambiguity that shrouds the market, gives rise to an almost frenetic search for inside or specialized knowledge about what to do.

While this clamoring for news about the market has probably always been a salient characteristic of investor behavior, we suspect that it is even more pronounced today because the recent increase in the volume of televised information on the market (Canape, 1982) has, in all likelihood, accentuated rather than diminished the ambiguity. As has long been noted by students of collective behavior, and particularly the rumor process (Rose, 1951; Rosnow & Fine, 1976; Shibutani, 1966; Turner & Killian, 1972), too much news, like too little news, can create considerable confusion about what to believe and what to do. The result is that today, probably more than ever before, the market situation has something of the character of many collective behavior situations wherein there is a tendency to look for and "play follow the leader since no one knows what is going on but believes that others do" (Smith, 1981, p. 142). That this is indeed the case is illustrated by the number of market experts who have assumed a guru-like status. Recent events indicate that some of these gurus even have the power to drive the market up or down by directing their devotees to buy or sell.

The archetypical case of such a market guru is Joe Granville. Granville, author of the Granville Market Letter, reached a pinnacle of notoriety on a January evening in 1981 when he issued a "Sell Everything" signal to more than 30,000 clients of his early-warning market advice service. The next morning brought with it an extensive small-investor sale of securities. On a day when market volume set a record, many stocks, such as GM, AT&T, and IBM, were delayed in opening as brokers and specialists were swamped with sell orders. At the end of trading, the Dow was down by 23.80 points, reflecting a paper loss of $40 billion. Granville, in making a sharp reversal in his advice to sell, irritated many of his 15,000 regular subscribers (who were paying $250 yearly for his wisdom) who were still following his advice of January 3, which was to "do some aggressive new buying." Nevertheless, he defended his position and stated that, "with me or without me, the market would have gone down Wednesday, maybe not 23 points, but at least 8 to 10" ("SEC Finds Granville's," 1981, p. 2).

For the time being, Granville, once reknown for his vaudevillian stage performances, doesn't need to worry about being humble or downplaying his incisiveness. He's largely discredited now, gone the way of others like him, to a place where initiates and reporters stop seeking him out. This guru's downfall came in the Autumn of 1982 when he insisted on identifying the market surge as a "bubble," and thus remaining essentially bearish. In August, after the rally was under way, he told ABC's Ted Koppell that "the probability is you'll see between 550 to 650 on the Dow index sometime between September 1982 and

January 1983.'' Given the market's actual performance, even disciples had to acknowledge that ''Joe really missed it this time'' (Putka, 1982, p. 21).

But while Granville's star was fading, another guru's was shining brightly. The Autumn upsurge marked the national emergence of Henry Kaufman, chief economist and head of research at Salomon Brothers (Wall Street's largest financial partnership). Kaufman has, by most accounts, been the most important credit market forecaster since the 1973–75 recession. It was during this time that he attracted considerable attention by frequently and correctly predicting higher interest rates. His assertion in October 1974 that rates had peaked was accurate to within two weeks. Later, on four separate occasions in late 1980 and early 1981, Kaufman was credited with precipitating declines in the stock market after uttering bearish sentiments (Ross, 1981, pp. 92–93). But his most spectacular achievement to date occurred on August 17, 1982, when he finally changed his long-term prognostication for high and rising interest rates (Kaufman had been predicting rising interest rates, with short-term exceptions since 1977). Kaufman's move, it is important to recognize, grew from a fundamental pessimism about the overall state of the economy. His essential argument was that an economic recovery was ''not likely to materialize'' and that corporate borrowing would therefore remain depressed, keeping upward pressure off interest rates. The aura that surrounds the actions of a guru of Kaufman's stature is captured in this depiction of that August day:

> On Tuesday morning, rumors whirled through Wall Street that Henry Kaufman had . . . changed his mind on interest rates. . . . Salomon Bros. officials, who had been besieged by telephone calls all morning confirmed at 10:41 that Kaufman was releasing a new forecast that predicted further declines in interest rates. By 11:10, the Dow was up almost 9 points, and the rush to buy was on. (''Oh, What a Beautiful Rally,'' 1982, p. 19)

The Granville and Kaufman episodes indicate that perhaps the famous advertising slogan, ''When E. F. Hutton talks, people listen,'' is correct, but with one qualification: it applies more accurately and dramatically to various market experts or gurus who clearly function as important determinants of the news that comes to investors' attention, of the meanings and credibilities attached to that news, and of the action that should be taken in light of it.

These observations suggest several qualifications of the two-step thesis with respect to the relationship between the news and the market. First, the two-step process does not hold for all news, but applies primarily to the general news. And second, a major, and perhaps the most important, factor mediating the connection between the ''general news'' and market trends is ''news about the market,'' including that which is generated and disseminated by market experts such as those discussed above. If indeed the impact of the general news on the market is mediated by news about the market, then we must look more closely at that news and how it portrays the market.

MEDIA PORTRAYAL OF THE MARKET

In examining news about the market as a mediating influence, we are interested in whether the images projected by that news are historically and empirically sound. From closely inspecting news about the market over a six month period, we have identified several misleading or distorting tendencies that we think characterize the media's portrayal of the market. In addition, we have identified several functions of this portrayal which are critical to the market's operation and viability.

MEDIA DISTORTIONS

Exaggerating the Market's Relevance

At the outset of this chapter it was noted that the media's coverage of the market is more extensive than for nearly any other domain of social life. Just the radio and television news programs alone constantly remind us, with their continuous summary reports, that there is a stream of activity called the stock market and that its course, however tranquil or turbulent, predictable or unpredictable, is an important phenomenon and is therefore something we should monitor. We think that this implication that the market is of considerable importance to the average news consumer is highly questionable. Several empirical indicators suggest this contention. First, only about 30 million Americans are shareholders, compared with, for example, the more than 100 million people who count themselves as workers. On the Big Board, 30% of the stock is held by large corporations whose own stocks are listed there, and another 50 percent is controlled by institutional investors.

Given this shareholding distribution, it is clear that as chapter 2 shows, individual investors now play a comparatively small role in securities trading. At the turn of this century, however, it was a very different situation. At that time, almost all the equity capital in America was in the hands of individuals. But in the 1950s institutions began to turn to the market for investments. By 1963, approximately one-fifth of all equity capital was either owned or managed by an institution. In 1965, there was an average of just nine block trades executed daily.[9] By 1969, the figure was up to 61 blocks daily, or about 20% of total volume. Ten years later 27% of transactions on the New York Stock Exchange were block trades ("Stock Exchange Composite," 1981, p. 11 and "Stocks' Record-Breaking," 1983, p. 7). But these numbers are dwarfed by recent transactions made by institutional investors. Consider, for example, that on October 7, 1982, when 147 million shares traded hands on the New York Stock Exchange, 287 block orders were placed before the first hour of trading had begun. Before the day was over 2,413 block transactions had been executed.

This trend, as clearly indicated in chapter 2, is expected to continue throughout the next decade. In fact, the current chairman of the SEC has confidently predicted that before too long block trades will comprise roughly 60% of market activity—a figure that dramatically highlights the growing distance between market activity and the average news consumer.

This increasing distance is reflected also in the changing financial assets of households. Commerce Department data demonstrate that stocks as a form of financial holding is diminishing for most households. In 1961, for example, stocks accounted for 45% of household financial assets, followed by deposit accounts, which made up 23% of the total. But by 1981, these two categories were reversed, with deposit accounts comprising 39% of all household financial assets and corporate stock accounting for 23% of the total.

As a consequence of these trends, stock trading has become even more of an elite activity. It is important to emphasize, however, that the whole notion of a stock exchange has long aroused feelings of suspicion and even hostility among many American citizens. A New York Stock Exchange-commissioned Roper poll released in the late 1940s showed that most Americans did not trust Wall Street. According to Sobel (1977, p. 104), "fixed upon the public mind" was "the image of the stock broker as a polished crook, and the New York Stock Exchange as a nest of thieves."

An early advocate of cleaning up Wall Street's image was Charles Merrill, founder of the brokerage house Merrill Lynch Pierce, Fenner, and Smith. During the 1940s and 1950s, Merrill became the first of many brokers to launch a large-scale advertising campaign designed to "educate" the public about the New York Stock Exchange's operation. Merrill also took measures to ensure that his brokerage offices were attractive and comfortable. All of these tactics had the same objective—to transform the image of the brokerage business from catering to gamblers and the wealthy into serving a prudent middle-class social group.

In keeping with this effort to legitimate the market in the eyes of working and middle class America, New York Stock Exchange President Keith Funston championed "People's Capitalism" in the 1950s and 1960s. Under his leadership, the Exchange urged small investors to put money in the market as a way of building a strong economy and helping in the struggle against the Soviets. As NYSE Vice-President Frank Coyle put it: "A regular dividend check is the best answer to Communism" (Sobel, 1977, p. 107). In the fast growth economy of the 1960s, a strategy of encouraging small investors to buy stocks did produce gains for many. But coinciding with a sputtering economy in 1970, the market dropped some 300 points as the decade unfolded. Seven years later the Exchange had three million fewer small retail investors. Relatedly, the number of registered representatives employed by NYSE commission houses fell by about 20% during the same time.

Throughout this period the media generally accepted uncritically the propaganda disseminated by Funston, Coyle, Merrill and others. But while the media have provided close attention and publicity for the market, many small stockholders, not to mention the majority of nonstockholders, do not see the market in such a patriotic and positive fashion. As Sobel (1977) summarizes the situation:

> Two decades ago Wall Street urged the nation to own shares of American business, as though this would be a way to participate in its benefits and fight Communism. . . . Some investors—usually newcomers—actually believe this, but most arrive at a different view of affairs shortly after coming to the Street. The owner of 100 out of the more than 600 million shares of American Telephone and Telegraph would be foolish if he thought he was patronizing his own establishment when he made a dime call. (pp. 158–159)

Ahistorical Orientation

As the news media reports each day's market activity, it often performs a disservice by failing to place market movements into an intelligible context. An historical perspective is essential in allowing news consumers to make reasonable judgments about the quality of the stock market and its gyrations. But the media, especially the broadcast media, do not provide this kind of viewpoint. Instead, they engage in fetishistic exercises that dramatize the market's functions. Because of this daily preoccupation, any long view of where the market has been and what it means today has long been obscured.

The lack of an historical perspective manifests itself in the media in a variety of ways. For example, in the late summer and fall of 1982, much was made about the 250–300 point ascendency of the Dow Jones Industrial Average. After that, the media gushed with enthusiasm when the Dow passed the 1100 mark for the first time. But this emphasis on the Dow's historic high distorts the real value of the market average. In real terms, the Dow would have to exceed 3000 to set a new all-time high. It makes as much sense to talk about record highs on the Dow as it does to talk about workers' wages being at record levels. Neither are very meaningful without some insight into inflation's impact. As the *New York Times* noted in the midst of the Autumn 1982 advance:

> When the Dow average achieved its previous record in 1973, the 'constant dollar' Dow (January 1913 as the base) was 242.10. But in September 1982, when the monthly range based on closing prices was 934.79, the Dow on a constant-dollar basis was only 93.70. (Sloane, 1982, p. 31)

Thus, in real terms, the Dow, despite the considerable advance, was only at about its 1950 level. Yet, that message is often concealed by the media's fixation on the market's activity in the early 1980s. As a result of this narrow focus, the media's coverage of stock activity tends to exaggerate the significance of both price advances and declines over the short term. An illustrative case is the media's coverage of stock trading conducted on October 25, 1982. On that day, the Dow Jones Industrial Average slid 36.33 points, a fall exceeded only by (by two points) the record plunge set on October 28, 1929. Most of the media had a field day with the story, waxing emotional and making comparisons with that fateful day back in 1929. As one local paper's headline read: ''Worst day since '29 hits stocks'' (''Worst Day Since '29 Hits Stocks,'' 1982, p. 1). In reality, however, there was little basis for such a comparison. On that day in 1929, the market fell some 13% compared to only 3.5% in 1982. For the October 1982 decline to be truly comparable with the collapse in 1929, the market would have had to have slid almost another 100 points. Similarly, the media was exuberant a week later when the market rose a record 43.41 points. But again, this increase of four percent, although uncommon, was also not a record climb for one day.

A final oversight illustrating the media's ahistorical orientation is its neglect of other, more fundamental, long-range trends. For one, as has already been noted, the shift from individual to institutional investment has had a profound impact on the market. It has, by all accounts, greatly increased the volatility of the market.[10] Swings of 15–20 points are no longer unusual for an hour of trading, and of course even wider swings have occurred recently over a full day's worth of transactions. Coinciding with the market's growing volatility has been a sharp increase in market volume. Record volume days in 1981 are only moderate ones in 1982. In 1981, there were 11.85 billion shares traded on the New York Stock Exchange, whereas in 1982, the number was up to 16.46 billion, a 39% increase (''Stocks' Record-Breaking,'' 1983, p. 7). But the media rarely report either historical variation in trading volume or the factors associated with it.

Overgeneralizing the Market's Benefits

The view that the stock market is a reliable guide to economic vitality and a general indicator of national well-being is deeply entrenched in the media. However, the upturn of the summer of 1982 vividly demonstrates that market advances are not always the result of optimistic anticipation about the economy. As noted by Bleakely (1982, p. 31),

> To most Americans, the stock market's rally in late summer and early fall in the face of dour economic news stretched the bounds of reason, seeming like a chapter out of 'Extraordinary Popular Delusions and the Madness of Crowds,' a book published in 1841 that chronicled such investment frenzies as the South Sea Bubble and Tulipmania.

As we noted earlier, Kaufman's prediction of declining interest rates, which functioned in part to trigger the market advance, was founded on the belief that economic activity was so weak that demand for capital would remain depressed indefinitely. And indeed, the 1982 fourth quarter (October–December) was the weakest of the early 1980s recession.

That the market advanced so strongly amid such widespread economic weakness did not go unnoticed by the media, yet the tendency was to treat stock market activity as if it were directly and profoundly related to economic recovery. Typical headlines during the period read ''Market Surge Cited as Boom to Households'' (1982, p. C10) and ''Stock Boom Favorable Sign'' (1982, p.

D32). But what the articles fail to ask is ''Which households?'' and ''Favorable sign for whom''? Indeed, the stories behind the headlines suggest that the strong market meant an imminent economic recovery. With greater temerity, they often imply that the market upsurge added something like $400 to $600 ''to the wealth of every American household.'' Surely this came as great relief to the less fortunate and growing numbers of workers who found themselves without jobs during this very time.

There is, of course, some element of truth in the proposition that the stock market serves as a leading indicator of the economy. In fact, the Commerce Department uses the more widely-based Standard and Poor's 500 stock index as one component in its index of leading economic indicators. Further, as measured by the S&P 500 stock index, an economic recovery has followed the bottom of a market cycle within five months or less in five of the seven recessions since World War Two.

The more important point, however, is that the connection between the market and one's welfare is true primarily for those who are in a position to exploit the market. Consequently, ''news about the market'' has become increasingly pertinent only to an elite audience—wealthy individuals and large institutions.

Functions of the "News About the Market"

Earlier we suggested that the news about the market functioned importantly to mediate the relationship between the general news and the market. We would now argue, in light of the distorting tendencies identified above, that the news about the market also serves a number of additional functions that are critical to the market's operation and viability.

First, and perhaps most obvious, the media's coverage and portrayal of the market functions to stimulate investment confidence and activity by emphasizing that stocks are generally a lucrative investment for the citizenry at large, by suggesting that the market is a major source of investment capital, and by suggesting that the market can be beaten if one is familiar with the correct theory or has the right information. Each of these beliefs or contentions is highly questionable, however. The notion that stocks are generally a lucrative investment is only a partial truth at best. Over the past decade an investor would have done better in terms of annual rate of return by investing in anything from U.S. coins and stamps to gold, silver, or farmland. Between 1972 and 1982, when consumer prices rose 9% annually, stocks were moving upward at an annual rate of just 4%. Moreover, the Dow Jones Industrial Average's current value, as noted earlier, is only roughly comparable to its 1950 value. But the media seldom apprise us of such useful facts because of its preoccupation with the moment.

The notion that the market is a major source of investment capital (what economists have referred to as ''optimal allocator'') and therefore provides the basis for "regenerating the nation's industrial base" ("Collectibles vs. Other Investments," 1982, p. 11) is equally questionable. Though it is true that rising stock prices may ease a firm's acquisition of investment funds, there is no direct relation between market activity and the creation of investment capital. Between 1975 and 1979, for example, only 7% of the money corporations raised from outside their own operations came from selling stock. Most of the funds came from long and short term debt. Further, the issuance of new stock comprises only a small percentage of total stock sales. In 1980, for instance, sales of all new issues of corporate stock were worth about $23 billion, a considerable figure to be sure, but one that is overwhelmed by the 522 billion dollars of stock transactions involving sales between different investors ("Bullish On America," 1982, pp. 3–5). It thus follows that the belief perpetuated by the media and some economists that buying stock represents an investment in American industry is only nominally true.

The notion that the market is something other than a crap shoot, that it can be beaten with the right theory or if one has the right information is also questionable. Nonetheless, the perpetuation of such a belief is vital to the market's image and the confidence of both the lay and professional investor.

As a consequence of these beliefs, particularly the latter one, along with the widespread coverage of the market, the media function to help produce and sustain the very ambiguity that accounts in part for the market's volatility and that is conducive to the operation and influence of market experts and gurus such as Granville, Kaufman, and Zweig among others. In performing the above functions, the media are also playing an important role in legitimizing and sustaining the network of financial houses, security analysts, and brokers that thrive on the current structure and functioning of the market.

Finally, and more generally, by overstating and overgeneralizing the effects of market upturns, the media perpetuate the correspondent beliefs that a strong market and a strong economy go hand in hand and that a rising market translates into general economic well-being for most Americans. On the surface it would certainly appear that a rising market could not imply anything other than enhanced investor confidence. Yet, as we have already noted, a rising market alone does not mean economic recovery, an end to or decline in unemployment, or an advance in the standard of living for all or even the majority of Americans. The Fall rally of 1982 makes patently clear that a strong market alone does not necessarily translate into a strong economy.

To suggest, as we have, that the media's portrayal of the market is both distorted and critical to the market's functioning is neither particularly surprising nor radical. To the contrary, both observations are quite consistent with the longstanding sociological theorem that major domains of social activity are functionally interdependent. They are also quite consistent with previous research on newsmaking, especially the finding that what is disseminated as "news" is typically an assembled and constructed reality, and the finding that news is generally an ally of the legitimate and more powerful institutions, such as large corporations and governments (Altheide, 1974; Fishman, 1980; Gans, 1979; Tuchman, 1978). Accordingly, it seems reasonable to conclude that, not only are the market and the news about it inextricably interconnected, but that the market's viability is partly contingent on the way it is portrayed by the media.

CONCLUSIONS

Throughout this chapter we have attempted to further understanding of the connection between the media and the market by examining, first, the assumption that the market reacts to the general news and, second, the manner in which the market is portrayed by the news about it. Drawing on prior research and on both secondary and primary data derived from systematic analyses of various media sources, we have arrived at three general conclusions. First, though the market and the flow of the general news frequently move together, such directional correspondence is neither automatic nor always predictable. Second, the relationship between the market and the general news can be best conceptualized as a two-step or multistaged process that is mediated in part by market theories, especially those in fashion at a particular point in time, and in part by various market experts or gurus who function simultaneously as interpreters of the general news and as purveyors of news about the market. And last, we have argued that by exaggerating the relevance of the market to the average American, by overgeneralizing its effects, and by focusing primarily on daily market activity to the exclusion of historical considerations, the media present a distorted picture of the market that functions to perpetuate and sustain certain beliefs and practices that are critical to the market's functioning.

NOTES

1. By the market we refer primarily to the New York Stock Exchange and, to a lesser degree, the American Stock Exchange.
2. For detailed analysis of the processes by which "news" is located, gathered, packaged, and disseminated, see Altheide (1974), Fishman (1980), Gans (1979), and Tuchman (1978). These works indicate, among other things, that the "news" is a socially constructed or manufactured reality, not merely a portrayal of reality or depiction of selected "facts" about the world.
3. For a review of this voluminous research and some of the issues involved, see Comstock et al. (1978), Davis and Baran (1981), DeFleur and Dennis (1981, pp. 273–385), and Liebert, Sprankin, and Davidson (1982).
4. Though the Dow Jones Industrial Average is composed of only 30 bluechip stocks listed on the New York Stock Exchange, Klein and Prestbo selected it over other possible indexes because it has not been proven to seriously distort market trends and because it is clearly the most popular measurement of market activity, as evidenced by news analysts' frequent reference to it.
5. The *Journal* was selected over other possible news sources because it is published every day the market is open, it covers business in more detail than any other daily, and because it is a national newspaper that is available to security analysts and investors throughout the world.

6. We excluded from our analysis the three feature stories on the Journal's front page because Klein and Prestbo did not describe fully their coding procedures for these columns.

7. What theory is in vogue hinges heavily on the state of the business cycle and the stock market itself. During rapid rises in market prices, for instance, fundamentalists begin to seem ''old-fashioned'' and fall out of favor, often to be replaced by technicians. Technicians can largely ignore fundamental points, and are thus more popular when, as in 1982, the market seems to move beyond what anyone would expect given the general news.

8. For discussion of the research on the two-step model, the model's shortcomings, and suggested modifications, see DeFleur and Dennis (1981, pp. 294–298), Rogers (1979), Robinson (1976), and Weiman (1982).

9. Block trades, which are the key barometer of institutional activity, refer to sales of 10,000 shares or more.

10. See, for example, Carrington and Hertzberg (1982, p. 1) and Lowry (chapter 2).

REFERENCES

Altheide, D. L. *Creating reality: How TV news distorts events.* Beverly Hills: Sage, 1974.

Bleakely, F. R. There's room for more zoom in stocks. *The New York Times,* December 12, 1982.

Blumer, H. *Symbolic interactionism: Perspective and method.* Englewood Cliffs, N.J.: Prentice-Hall, 1969.

Bullish on America? Making sense of the stock market. *Dollars and Sense,* November 1982, pp. 3–5.

Canape, C. Putting stock in TV business news. *Washington Journalism Review,* November 1982, pp. 38–42.

Carrington, T., & Hertzberg, D. Stock prices become more volatile as role of institutions grows. *The Wall Street Journal,* November 30, 1982, p. 1.

Collectibles vs. other investments. *The New York Times,* December 12, 1982.

Comstock, G., Chaffee, S., Katzman, N., McCombs, M., & Roberts, D. *Television and human behavior.* New York: Columbia University Press, 1978.

Davis, D. K., & Baran, S. J. *Mass communication and everyday life: A perspective on theory and effects.* Belmont, Cal.: Wadsworth, 1981.

DeFleur, M. L., & Dennis, E. E. *Understanding mass communication.* Boston: Houghton Mifflin, 1981.

Fishman, M. *Manufacturing the news.* Austin: The University of Texas Press, 1980.

Gans, H. J. *Deciding what's news.* New York: Pantheon Books, 1979.

Klein, F., & Prestbo, J. A. *News and the market.* Chicago: Henry Regnery, 1974.

Lazarsfeld, P., Berelson, B., & Gaudet, H. *The people's choice.* New York: Columbia University Press, 1948.

Lazarsfeld, P., & Menzel, H. Mass media and personal influence. In W. Schramm (Ed.), *The science of human communication.* New York: Basic Books, 1963.

Liebert, R. M., Sprankin, J. N., & Davidson, E. S. *The early window: Effects of television on children and youth.* New York: Pergamon Press, 1982.

Market surge cited as boon to households. *Austin American Statesmen,* November 6, 1982, p. C10.

Meltzer, B. N., Petras, J. W., & Reynolds, L. T. *Symbolic Interactionism.* London: Routledge & Kegan Paul, 1975.

Oh, what a beautiful rally! *Time,* August 30, 1982, pp. 19–20.

Putka, G. Joe Granville's followers defecting as he sticks with bearish outlook. *The Wall Street Journal,* November 12, 1982, p. 21.

Robinson, J. Interpersonal influence in election campaigns: Two-step flow hypothesis. *Public Opinion Quarterly,* 1976, *40,* 304–319.

Rogers, E. M. Mass media and interpersonal communication. In G. Gumpert & R. Cathcare (Eds.), *Inter/Media.* New York: Oxford University Press, 1979.

Rose, A. M. Rumor in the stock market. *Public Opinion Quarterly,* 1951, *15,* 461–486.

Rosnow, R., & Fine, G. A. *Rumors and gossip.* New York: Elsevier, 1976.

Ross, I. How Henry Kaufman gets it right. *Fortune,* May 18, 1981, pp. 92–98.

SEC finds Granville's market role troubling but doesn't see violations. *The Wall Street Journal,* January 9, 1981, p. 2.

Shibutani, T. *Improvised news: A sociological study of rumor.* New York: Bobbs–Merrill, 1966.

Sloane, L. Friends and foes of the Dow. *The New York Times,* November 4, 1982, p. 31.

Smith, C. W. *The mind of the market.* Totowa, N.J.: Rowman & Littlefield, 1981.

Sobel, R. *Inside Wall Street.* New York: W. W. Norton, 1977.

Stock boom favorable sign, analyst say. *Austin American Statesman,* October 8, 1982, p. D32.

Stock exchange composite: Trading summary for 1980. *The Wall Street Journal,* January 2, 1981, p. 11.

Stocks' record-breaking '82 rally hid a multitude of market flaws. *The Wall Street Journal,* January 3, 1983, p. 7.

Stone, G. P., & Farberman, H. A. *Social psychology through symbolic interaction* (2nd ed.). New York: Wiley, 1981.

Tuchman, G. *Making news: A study in the construction of social reality.* New York: Free Press, 1978.

Turner, R. H., & Killian, L. *Collective behavior* (2nd ed.). Englewood Cliffs, N.J.: Prentice-Hall, 1972.

Weimann, G. The two-step flow of communication. *American Sociological Review,* 1982, *47,* 764–773.

Worst day since '29 hits stocks. *Austin American Statesman,* October 26, 1982, p. D32.

FALSE SECURITY:
DEVIANCE AND THE STOCK MARKET

Robert Lejeune

The basic premise of this chapter is the sociological observation that every system of human action generates patterns of deviance which reflect its particular institutional arrangements. This occurs in at least three ways. First, any community, by setting up a system of rules for its members, also defines any behavior as deviant which breaches these rules. By creating an entity called "property" society must of necessity create an entity called "property crime." Indeed, as Durkheim eloquently argued, if society is to maintain a moral order and the sentiments which preserve it, it must accept some deviance from this moral order as an essential and normal outcome (Durkheim, 1964, pp. 47–75; see also Erikson, 1966). Property could not exist without property crime any more than health could exist without illness.

A second sense in which the patterns of deviance of a group depends on its institutional arrangements relates to the values that support these arrangements. If we understand by "values" those central and shared sentiments of a community which define what are desirable and undesirable goals to pursue, then clearly both conforming and deviant behavior will be influenced by these values. If a community values wealth it will organize itself around the attainment of wealth, and greed will be a powerful motivator for its members. A strong single-minded emphasis on a valued goal is often associated with lesser concern with the legitimate means for its attainment (Merton, 1957, pp. 131–160). More specifically, Bonger, a criminologist, hypothesized that "commerce" as a form of exchange breeds an "egoism" that manifests itself in lying, fraud, and lack of compassion for others (Bonger, 1969, pp. 37–38).

Thirdly, the social arrangements of a group are realized through its social structure, the system of statuses and roles which organizes the activities and relationships of group members. In any social group the ways in which deviance is expressed will depend greatly on the opportunities for illegitimate activities that are built into the social structure, as well as the characteristics of the social control mechanisms intended to curb these activities. Such factors as the visibility of role performance, the size and effectiveness of the rule-enforcement apparatus, and the extent of built-in conflict of interest situations, will affect what types and amounts of deviance are to be found in a given social system.

In order, therefore, to examine the nature, extent, and likely causes of deviance related to the exchange of securities it is necessary to grasp how the institutional arrangements of the stock market operate. A brief and necessarily schematic overview of the principal rules of the game will set the stage for a more detailed analysis of some of the concrete patterns of cheating.

THE STOCK MARKET AS A GAME

In its barest outline the modern securities market can be viewed as a game organized around the exchange of two basic currencies, money and shares of stock, neither of which has any intrinsic value. On the one hand, the value of money rests on shared expectations, continually tested in the marketplace of commodities and services, concerning the amount and quality of a vast array of desired goods and services that can be exchanged for its fixed units. The value of stocks, on the other hand, is only remotely linked to actual commodities that can be consumed or used. The price of a share of stocks is determined by the collective assessment of current "players" concerning what other "players" will be willing to pay for it in the near or distant future. This, in turn, depends largely on the *beliefs* of the buyers and sellers concerning present and, more importantly, future fortunes or profits of the corporations which issued the stock. Those players who consider only short-term value are called traders. Those who take a longer view are called investors. Both types, viewed as the extremes on a continuum, from day traders to conservative investors who purchase stocks for a lifetime (and beyond), buy or sell stocks on the basis of expectations, or beliefs about future events. It is the conscious intent of all players, irrespective of their time frame, to utilize their presumed ability to predict future events as a resource for increasing their personal wealth or the wealth of those for whom they act as agents (as in the case of institutional investors).

Securities are created and enter the market initially as offerings issued by corporations in order to help raise capital for their operations. However, most of the volume of daily transaction involves the trading of existing securities, on the various stock exchanges, in what is known as the secondary market. The rapid matching of buyers and sellers in this market is made possible by a special category of players, the broker-dealers (brokerage houses). As the name indicates, the individuals who hold this position, and the firms which they represent, are involved in the stock market game in two principal capacities. First, in their role as brokers they, in return for commission, buy and sell shares of stocks for all other players, acting essentially as a clearing house. Their fortunes as brokers depend largely on the volume of play, irrespective of whether or not the play results in a win or loss for their "clients." Secondly, in their role as dealers, they may buy and sell securities for their own accounts, with the added advantage that as members of the exchange in which they trade they do not have to pay commission.

As can readily be seen from this simplified account of what is in fact a very complicated game, one way to be successful as a player is to use current information to predict both future events and the likely effects of these events on the buying and selling decisions of other players. By extension, any one who has access to information that enables him or her to forecast relevant events more accurately than others has a distinct advantage over other market players. Such an "insider," if free to use such information, can obtain great financial gains, with little or no risk of loss.

An Attitude of Deception

If access to and control of information is a key to wealth in the stock market it should not be a surprise, given the way the game is structured—the value of stocks depending so much on players' perceptions and beliefs—that anyone who is in a position to withhold accurate information or to disseminate false or misleading information is also in a position to obtain great advantage over the other players. This road to riches is one which historically has been well traveled. Dreman relates one such "exciting coup" which stands for innumerable other, though less dramatic, instances of the use of deception in stock market play:

> Sometimes making money has appeared simple. On June 19, 1815, for example, the Rothschilds learned via carrier pigeons that the French had been crushed the previous evening at Waterloo many hours before the news reached London by more customary means. When the market opened that morning, Rothschild agents buzzed the news of a major British defeat, and Nathan Rothschild himself began to sell, which triggered a large break. Near the low point, other inconnu family agents began to buy heavily, not long before the expected arrival of more conventional couriers. The market that day closed considerably higher than it opened, further adding to the family coffers. (Dreman, 1979, p. 3)

Clearly then, deception can play an important part in the stock market game. But whether or not deception *per se,* in its many forms, is to be considered deviant or criminal depends on the particular rules of the game. In games such as poker—indeed in most games—it is not only permissible to deceive the other players, but it is rather an integral and prescribed part of successful play (Hayano, 1982). Similarly, in a very real sense, stock market transactions, if the players are playing to win, tend to require an attitude of deception on the part of both buyers and sellers (Leff, 1976, pp. 13–15; Slater, 1980, pp. 19–20). The seller sells on the belief that in the exchange of his stock for money he has bested an anonymous buyer, whereas the buyer believes the opposite. What may or may not be acceptable within the rules of the game is the active misrepresentation of facts, such as in the above Rothschild coup.

TOWARD A TYPOLOGY OF STOCK MARKET FRAUD

What I have been leading up to and now wish to make explicit is that the vast majority of deviant practices related to the stock market—and particularly those most interesting sociologically—involve the manipulation of information for illicit gains. The institutionalized spirit of greed, which is the lynchpin of a capitalistic economy, combines with the attitude of deception in the stock market to create a fertile ground for deviance. The types of criminal activities to be discussed here represent variations of fraud, to be contrasted to crimes involving force. They involve in all instances, as white-collar crimes generally do, the violation of trust; in the very special sense that one of the parties to a transaction knowingly intends to withhold or manipulate information so as to deceive the other party in a way that has been deemed illegal by the relevant regulatory agencies.

In addition to a climate of greed and deception, the likelihood of deviance is further enhanced by structured inequalities that are built into the stock market game. While all players, from the smallest to the largest, may in various ways engage in fraudulent practices, the positioning of the players, both with respect to financial resources and their assigned roles in the game, creates differential opportunities for deception and deviance. Concretely, as will be examined below, two broad overlapping categories of players, the broker-dealers and the managers and directors of corporations that issue stock, share a distinct advantage in the perpetration of fraud.

Broker-Dealer Fraud

For broker-dealers the stock market is not just a game, it is big business. As of January 1, 1981 the market value of all stocks traded in the United States, on the listed exchanges and over the counter, was $1.4 trillion (*Wall Street Journal,* January 2, 1981, p. 20). During 1979 the volume of shares traded on the U.S. exchanges was nearly eleven billion, and worth more than $300 billion. To handle this large volume of business the brokerage industry employed nearly

68,000 registered representatives, affiliated with 4,697 broker-dealers and 6,519 branch offices (Securities and Exchange Commission, 1981).

For the individual who is financially able and wishes to play the stock market, the way of entry into their game is usually through his/her stockbroker. The latter, once referred to as the "customer's man," has in recent years been rechristened with the more professional-sounding title of "registered representative." This individual, usually male, is first and foremost a salesman (Smith, 1981). He spends much of his time on the telephone soliciting business from clients and placing their orders to buy or sell stocks with specialized brokers located on the various exchanges, "the specialists" in the particular stocks. While there is obviously a great deal of variation in the behavior and the ethical standards among persons who practice this trade, the public image of brokers lies somewhwere between that of confidence men and used car salesmen. Published accounts of their activities, some written by would-be advisors to investors, including stockbrokers themselves, are nearly unanimous in cautioning the greatest of care in the selection of a stockbroker, and continued caution throughout the duration of one's relationship with him. *Caveat emptor,* rather than trust in his professional advice and judgment, is the rule (cf. Baruch, 1971; Brutus, 1971; Dreman, 1979; Goldberg, 1978; Hagin & Mader, 1973; Harper, 1926; Kelly, 1930; Mayer, 1980; Schwed, 1940; Tucille, 1980).

As early as 1880, a stockbroker, writing an anonymous exposé of Wall Street, warned would-be investors of the unscrupulous nature of many of his fellow practitioners preying on the gullibility and the greed of the public:

> Acting . . . for the benefit of all who were interested in stocks, or who intended to be so, we necessarily watched closely any publication claiming to be of [reputable] character, and yet bearing evidence of some tricks and false representation which have done so much during the last dozen years, to discredit an honest profession, and reduce it, in many minds, to the level of the very lowest gambling. It was entirely in such interest that we proposed a deal, with ungloved hands, with those who gave evidence of prostituting the business of stock dealing to something very like the "confidence" of police courts . . . (*Fraud and Fair Dealing,* 1880, p. 1)

The above was of course written before the crash of 1929, which led to the formation of the Securities and Exchanges Commission and the enactment of the Securities Act of 1933, the Securities Exchange Act of 1934, and various other legislations since. Nonetheless, and with good reasons, the image of an industry shot through with unethical and illegal practices has persisted. Baruch, in his 1971 study of the ten largest and most prestigious brokerage firms, found a pattern of accepted business practices unlike that of any other regulated industry. Large sums of money, left by customers to make future stock purchases, or as proceeds from sales of stocks, as well as stocks held for "safekeeping," were routinely used by brokerage firms to finance their day-to-day operations, to purchase securities for their own accounts, or as collateral to secure bank loans. Baruch, who at the time of his research was a Special Counsel for the Securities and Exchange Commission, summarized his own views on the stock market game, and the role of the broker-dealers, in a way that was even less flattering than that of our anonymous broker in 1880—before regulations:

> In any well organized game for high stakes there will usually be two classes of players who bear symbiotic relationship to each other. The professionals control those aspects of the game which are not left to chance, and they keep it going by maintaining the illusion that the amateurs have a reasonable chance of winning. In return for this illusion and the excitement of the game, the amateurs are expected to furnish a living for the professionals. What is quite unique about the stock market is that the amateur players in the market stake the professionals with the cash and securities they need for playing the game! (Baruch, 1971, p. 118)

As many observers of the stock market suggest it is useful to an understanding of the types of deviance that occur in this arena of the transaction to recognize the similarities between the stock market, gambling, and the confidence game (see especially, Leff, 1976, pp. 64–76). Throughout the vast literature which is addressed to those who would become rich, or at least not become poor, through this medium of exchange, are repeated warnings to control the passions—greed and fear—which, combined with gullibility, are likely to transform the "investor" into a gambler or "mark."

In gambling there appears to be two primary motives on the part of players: greed and the desire for excitement. In the confidence game the mark is suckered out of his money by greed, pure and simple. In the stock market the purchases of "hot issues" or more speculative instruments, usually with the added incentive of leverage, such as options or commodities contracts, attract the players interested in quick profits and excitement. Their psychological involvement in the market is very similar to that of the gambler or mark. The alternation between the lure of quick profit and the fear of financial loss, which the vicissitudes of the stock market engenders, makes such players particularly vulnerable to both the legitimate and illegitimate ploys of "insiders" who have greater access to and control over the information likely to affect the future prices of stock. But even the conservative investors are certainly not immune to the deceptions of more "sophisticated" players, nor to the effects of greed and fear. More importantly, they too play in a game which the boundaries between legitimate and fraudulent deception are frequently crossed, or never clearly defined.

In most gambling operations all players lose to the house in the long run, and most players lose in the short run. Similarly, in the confidence game the mark is strung along until he or she loses all to the con man (Nash, 1976). In the stock market these analogies are only partial in that some players, in addition to the house, can and do win, both in the short and long run. But, whether the players win or lose, the house always wins as long as the players continue to buy and sell. The greater the volume of the play, the greater the profit for the house, since, with each transaction, the house takes a percentage in the form of commission.

In addition the house can increase its profits by adding elements of the confidence game. Certain gambits are built into the stock market game which places the house and its representatives, the brokers, in the position to manipulate information in such a way as to (1) increase the volume of play to its advantage and to the detriment of some of the other players and (2) to pit some of the players against the house in such a way that the players will generally lose and the house will always win.

The first rule of selling is to generate volume (see, for example, Smith, 1981, p. 71). Without it neither the brokerage house, nor its registered representatives, can survive. Given the intangible nature of the product being sold, an expectation of future gain more than a present reality, the greed which such a product evokes in the would-be buyer, and the desire on the part of the salesman to generate high volume business, the pressure to misrepresent is overwhelming. It is therefore not surprising to find that Wall Street has had a long history of boiler room or bucket shop operations which, through deception and high-pressure tactics, have sold over the years billions of dollars of worthless or near worthless securities to the public.

Before the invention of the telephone, the swindlers used the mail to recruit the gullible nouveau riche and the not so rich in the countryside. In the booming America of the late 19th century there appears to have been an endless line of suckers waiting to be taken. In the words of one stockbroker living at the time:

> The quickness with which the money has been made and lost in Wall Street offered as exceptional field for the sharpers, through various modes of stock operations, and the glittering comparisons of what might have been done, when placed in skillfully-worded circulars. Books and papers made easy prey of country dealers; while the results of the swindle has been passed by, by the majority, in their desire to cover from their friends and employers the fact that they were "gambling in stocks." Thus the swindles continue, with "fresh fish" indefinitely, the very opportunities for being warned thus going out of the chances. (*Fraud and Fair Dealing*, 1880, pp. 14–15)

A century later the securities industry attempts to present itself, through its public relations and advertising, as reputable and low-pressured. It relegates bucket shop tactics to the past or to fly-by-night operators on the fringe of the industry. The reality is quite different. High volume has always been, and remains, the principal means to high profits for most brokerage firms. It leads, as a minimum offense, to the pervasiveness of high-pressure selling by brokers. A 1981 *Forbes* article details, for instance, how a growing number of the more prestigious brokerage firms rely on squadrons of salesmen, including unemployed actors, reading from "scripts" to sell stocks by telephone to well-to-do individuals (Stern, 1981, pp. 167–171). Such a practice is not illegal, but reading excerpts from the "script" used by such firms as Lehman Brothers, which has developed this form of selling to a fine art, one cannot help but note a sophisticated attempt to play on greed and gullibility of the prospects. The attitude of deception hangs over the whole operation, as the following brief excerpt from the Lehman Brother's script illustrates:

> Says the customer: 'Send me information or a report.' Replies the salesman: 'Mr. ____________, I am sure you know that when a company such as ours publishes a report on ____________ it may have a beneficial effect on the price of the stock. We prefer to accumulate quietly.' Flash two or three highlights of the stock recommendation and say 'Wouldn't it be nice for once in your life to get there ahead of major institutions?' (Stern, 1981, p. 171)

It is a short step from the pressure for high volume and the attitude of deception which permeates the Wall Street community to practices which are illegal as well as unethical. Clearly, as a very large number of observers and regulators of the industry have noted for more than half a century, there is a built-in conflict between the self-interest of the broker-dealer and that of the client. The issue is well summarized by a former Enforcement Attorney for the SEC:

> In a very real sense, a brokerage firm when dealing with a commission transaction, is like a poker casino or a pari-mutual horse track—the owners take their cut and just can't lose. What they have in common is that the more action, the higher the total amount of the cut and the greater the ultimate profit. However what these three financial institutions are definitely *not* supposed to have in common is the same attitude toward the customer—poker player, horse bettor and securities investor. In the last instance of a security investor, the broker-dealer is deemed a fiduciary who is charged with the duty of loyalty to its customers. (Goldberg, 1978, pp. 1–2)

The concept of the fiduciary lies at the heart of all occupations that claim the prestige and the other privileges of "professional" status. Such professions are granted autonomy, specifically, to greater or lesser extent, the right to regulate the activities of their own members, in return for the obligation of placing the well-being of their clients above their own economic self-interest (Parsons, 1939, pp. 457–67). Such a claim has been made by and largely granted to the securities industry (as shown in chapter 2), and the fiduciary relationship between broker and customer is an explicit premise of the laws and regulations enacted since the Securities Act of 1933:

> The relationship between broker and customer is fiduciary in nature . . . In the performance of his duties, the broker is held to the same high standards of conduct as the law imposes upon attorneys, administrators, executors, guardians, bankers, public officials, and other persons vested with fiduciary power. (Securities and Exchange Commission, 1936, p. xiv)

This ethical assumption which is part of the legal bedrock of all stock market regulations introduces a problematical element in the stock market game. As I have noted earlier, pure market exchanges are grounded in an attitude of deception on the part of the players. By contrast, a fiduciary relationship requires trust and trustworthiness as the governing elements in the relationship. Consequently, as students of the securities industry have observed over the years, the structuring of the roles of broker-dealer in the stock market makes the implementing of a fiduciary relationship virtually impossible (Elias, 1971; Evan & Levin, 1966; Mayer, 1980; Securities and Exchange Commission, 1936).

Foremost, and probably most frequent, among the types of illegal violations of the fiduciary relationship is "churning," i.e., "a fraudulent practice which occurs when a broker-dealer uses its influence over one of its customers to induce excessive trading for the purpose of generating high commissions" (Goldberg, 1978, pp. 1–2).

What makes this practice particularly pernicious, compared to some other forms of stock market deviance we will examine, is that the victims are usually the naive small investors, such as the retired, who have entrusted their life savings to a broker. The fate of such investors is usually sealed when their trust in the industry's claim of a fiduciary relationship leads them to make their accounts "discretionary," i.e., to give their broker the legal right to make all buy and sell decisions.

As in the case of most types of stock market deviance it is difficult to know precisely the point at which legal behavior ends and criminality begins. The definition of churning, which on the first examination seems simple, hinges on a series of factors which are difficult to define precisely, and even more difficult to measure. For instance, two central elements in the definition of churning are that the trading be "excessive" and that the investor be "unsophisticated." In addition to these, Goldberg lists seven additional criteria, all equally subjective and imprecise, as elements to be weighted in any legal decision (Goldberg, 1978, pp. 1–3). A jury or judge must, for instance, in deciding that churning has occurred weigh the trust and confidence that the investor had placed in the broker-dealer. Consequently, while there are many documented cases of blatant churning in the files of the SEC, the full extent of this practice is unknown, and possibly unknowable, since the definition of the crime rests largely on subjective assessments of situations. All that can be said with certainty is that the temptation on the part of the stockbrokers to churn their accounts is great, discovery is unlikely, and the penalties are minimal.

One form of stockbroker fraud must be discussed here since it bears directly on the structural causes of deviance that are built into the dual role of broker and dealer. Because brokerage houses and individual brokers are themselves "players" in the market, and can derive a significant part of their profits from their own portfolio transactions, they are in the position to benefit not only from the volume of stocks bought and sold but also from the upward movement of stocks that they have accumulated (or from the downward movement of stocks they have sold short). In such a situation the potential for stock manipulation is ever present. With the added likelihood that some brokers have access to "inside" information prior to their customers, the combination can be lethal for the naive investor who accepts the broker's recommendation as if it were truly to the "client's" interest. One such case, as described by Elias, is instructive. It illustrates both the conflict that is built into the role of broker-dealer and the remarkable laxity with which this type of fraud is treated by the regulatory agencies:

> Kleiner, Bell had recommended to investors that they buy the stock of a conglomerate, Commonwealth United Corporation, while all the while the firm was selling the stock on the basis of inside information. During 1968 and part of 1969, Commonwealth United stock had risen sharply, but unknown to investors the company was expected to lose $61 million in 1969 alone. . . . The SEC [also] charged that in 1968 Kleiner, Bell manipulated the price of Omega Equities stock by bidding for it and then purchasing it at increasingly higher prices. All the time Kleiner, Bell was making its sham transactions it was recommending to its customers that they buy Omega shares. (Elias, 1971, pp. 205–206)

For these and other offenses, including improper disclosure, trading on inside information, and the illegal use of customer securities as collateral, no one was ever tried. The firm's registration as a broker-dealer was suspended, but it was permitted to continue in its investment banking capacity. None of the investors who had purchased shares of Commonwealth United Corporation and Omega Equities were ever compensated (Elias, 1971, p. 206).

Fraud by Corporate Management

Just as stockbrokers are in the position to defraud other "players" by virtue of the special advantages that are built into their role, so too are corporate officers, members of boards of directors and, in general, the upper level managers of corporations in positions that provide the opportunities to obtain information (or to disseminate false information) in such ways as to fraudulently profit on the stock market. The two major types of criminal activities engaged in by corporate management therefore involve either the use of insider information—i.e., the use of information about the corporation before it is made public to the other players or the giving out of false information to the public.

As I have emphasized above, the value of stocks rests on beliefs. These perceptions are largely shaped by the information that corporations disseminate about themselves. A fair market is one in which all the players have an equal access to true, accurate, and complete information about the corporations whose stocks they intend to buy or sell. Consequently, corporations that issue stock to the public are legally bound to present, in their annual and quarterly reports and through other public announcements, information concerning the risks, liabilities, assets, profits, and other data likely to influence the price of their stock. Through such disclosures, it is claimed, all prudent investors who avail themselves of public information approach the stock market game on an equal footing; their gains and losses result either from their judgment or luck in picking stocks.

Even a casual reading of financial publications suggests that this has never been and is never likely to be; that public information is seldom as useful as private information; that by the time information is fully disseminated throughout the system its value is nil (Manne, 1966). As the term "insider" connotes, some are in the know more than others. And none are more in the know than the managers of corporations. Information concerning sales volume, anticipated mergers, major discoveries of natural resources, and many other events and situations likely to affect stock movement generally come to the attention of management prior to public disclosure. Consequently, corporate officers are frequently in the position to enrich themselves in the stock market in ways not available to most other investors.

In an attempt to make the stock market game as fair as possible the SEC has interpreted and the courts have supported the antifraud provision of the Securities and Exchange Act of 1934 (Rule 10b–5) as making unlawful the practice of buying and selling stocks (or leveraged instruments, such as options) on the basis of information known to corporate officers and other insiders, but not yet made public (Ratner, 1978, pp. 120–134).

Nonetheless insider trading is probably the most prevalent form of stock market deviance. It is also the one instance of stock market fraud which, in certain situations, can be detected in the aggregate, although, ironically, individual acts are difficult to apprehend. The best evidence for this type of fraud is found in the case of merger situations. It is generally the rule that the stock of one company being taken over by another will appreciate, often dramatically, upon public announcement of the takeover bid. Such situations, while they represent only a small fraction of cases where inside information can be used for illegal gains, provide us with objective data concerning insider trading and a method for extrapolating the extent of fraud in corporate America. Two recent and independent studies published in *Fortune* (Louis, 1981, pp. 72–82) and *Barron's* (Merjos, 1981, p. 11) show unequivocally that insider trading occurs more often than not in takeover or merger situations. Louis summarizes the method and essential findings from the *Fortune* study:

> We took a retrospective look at the trading patterns of target companies in 20 recent tender offers and acquisitions, selected at random. In almost every case the formal announcement of a proposed takeover was *preceded* by large gains in the stock price—implying that someone knew what was going to happen and acted on that information. . . . Only in one case out of 20 was there no eye-catching movement in the target company's stock price. (Louis, 1981, p. 72)

These two systematic studies, as well as innumerable news items which have appeared in recent years (Quinn, 1983), indicate that insider trading is the rule rather than the exception. Moreover these studies capture only the tip of the iceberg, for the overwhelming portion of insider trading cannot be detected in the aggregate, and is even more difficult to pinpoint in individual cases. The extent

of undercounting of this type of stock market crime very likely dwarfs the "dark figure of crime" which criminologists have indicated for decades results in massive undercounting of criminal acts in official statistics (cf. Pearce, 1976, pp. 77–105). Such a large amount of undetected, and even larger amount of unapprehended, criminal behavior by corporate officers and other insiders does square, however, with our growing knowledge of the extent of crime committed by management in their own interest and in the interest of the corporations they manage. For instance, Clinard and his associates, in one of the more recent and thorough studies of illegal corporate behavior in America, details and documents a widespread pattern of criminal behavior among corporations, both large and small. Using only data on corporate crimes *which became known to enforcement agencies* (and which therefore grossly underestimates the actual amount of corporate crime), sixty percent of a sample of 1059 corporations, including 477 from the *Fortune* 500, were charged with at least one federal violation in a 2-year period. Of those corporations with at least one criminal violation the mean number of violations was 4.4 during the 2-year period 1975–76 (Clinard, 1979, p. 82).

Trading on the basis of inside information violates the principle of public disclosure, intended to give all market participants equal access to relevant corporate information. It represents the passive manipulation of information for the private gain of insiders. The other side of corporate fraud, often more dramatic, involves the active manipulation of information about the corporation so as to benefit corporate officers; the dissemination of fictitious data concerning actual and anticipated profits so as to convey the false appearance of corporate growth. Such deception, if successful, can enrich managers who own large blocks of their own company's stocks, to the ultimate financial detriment of outside investors. These types of manipulations may also cover up the outright embezzlement of funds by corporate officers.

Two of the most notorious schemes of recent years, the Home-Stake Oil fraud and the Equity Funding swindle, will be reviewed here to illustrate this type of stock market manipulation. Both involved complex and blatant manipulation of information over many years, resulting in millions of dollars of loss to investors. The complexity and scope of these operations can only be suggested in this account, but both reveal structural flaws in the system which purports to regulate financial dealings.

The Home-Stake Oil swindle, masterminded by Robert Trippet, the company's president, with the assistance and complicity of dozens of associates, deceived hundreds of mostly wealthy and sophisticated investors from April 1955 to January 1974. The scheme lured high tax bracket individuals to participate in tax-sheltered programs based on oil drilling ventures, with the prospect of immediate tax reduction on current investments and the promise of large dividends from future oil finds (Ehrbar & Schiff, 1974; Galbraith, 1977; McClintic, 1976, 1977).

In reality, only a small fraction of the money collected from program partici-

pants and from common stockholders was ever expended for drilling operations. From four to six million dollars—the exact amount is still unknown to this day—was embezzled by Robert Trippet through a complex scheme of dummy corporations, established solely to syphon money out of Home-Stake. Over $100 million was used to maintain the appearance of a legitimate venture, the money from later investors being used to pay "dividends" to earlier investors, as if the corporation was actually profit-making. The swindle literally required thousands of acts of deception, including fake oil pipes, the falsification of annual reports to investors, and the complicity and/or bribery of outside accountants, engineers, lawyers, bankers, and salesmen over an eighteen year period. During that time many of the earlier investors became suspicious when their dividends failed to match the promises that had been made in person or in the sales literature. Some were either bought out (and bought off) or settled out of court. Others were induced to donate their near-worthless shares to unsuspecting charities for further tax deductions, at inflated prices concocted by Home-Stake and its bribed outside "engineering consultants." Although some of the investors were heavy losers, the government—i.e., the taxpayers—lost more heavily. When finally, in 1974, faced with overwhelming evidence of fraud and precipitated to action by an expose in the *Wall Street Journal,* the SEC brought criminal charges against Trippet and seven other corporate officers and outside accomplices, the Home-Stake swindle came to an end.

The outcome of all criminal trials completed in 1977, showed once again, a few years after the Watergate conspiracy, the great profit and low risks of white-collar crime in high places. As a result of a combination of factors—legal maneuvering by the defendants, judicial bias in favor of white-collar criminals, and SEC ineptitude—no meaningful criminal penalties were ever imposed on the swindlers. Trippet and two of his associates spent one night in jail before sentencing. They were then put on probation, ranging from one to three years. In addition, Trippet, who had embezzled millions and masterminded one of the two most brazen known swindles of recent years—the other to be discussed shortly—was fined $19,000 and required to pay $100,000 into a fund for civil claims by investors.

The Home-Stake case represents one of the dramatic swindles of recent time, maintained for some eighteen years, which deceived hundreds of "sophisticated investors," holding high-ranking positions in America's largest banks and corporations, as well as an equally large number of naive investors from the entertainment world. Although Home-Stake had its common stock listed on the American Stock Exchange, the major part of the swindle resulted from its oil drilling programs sold as tax shelters, outside of the normal Wall Street brokerage house channels. It therefore leaves unanswered whether or not such a massive and long-term fraud can be perpetrated by the allegedly more closely watched and regulated corporations whose stocks are traded on the New York Stock Exchange. The answer is evident in the Equity Fund swindle.

Equity Funding was one of the most widely praised NYSE listed corporations in the late sixties and early seventies and its stock was among the most highly recommended by Wall Street analysts at that time. Acclaimed as a ''new concept'' corporation, Equity Funding was in the seemingly conservative business of selling life insurance and shares of mutual fund. As part of the ''equity concept'' individuals who purchased mutual fund shares were also persuaded to use these shares as collateral for loans with which they purchased life insurance from Equity Funding. This enabled the purchasers to build equity, through the mutual fund, and to obtain life insurance, without any additional cash outlay—a legitimate, if not particularly astute, investment. The fraud, however, was perpetrated not on the customers, but on the stockholders who presumed that they would be the beneficiary of the company's apparent success. Financial analysts viewed the linkage of life insurance to mutual fund equity as a major reason for the (apparent) dramatic growth of yearly earnings of Equity Funding from March 1965, when the company was founded, to March 1973, when trading in the stock was halted by the SEC (Blundell, 1976; Dirk & Gross, 1974; Seidler, Andrews, & Epstein, 1977).

As most newspaper readers of that era know, Equity Funding was in fact losing money all along, beneath the appearance of huge profits and growing assets. For the eight year period that the corporation functioned, company president Stanley Goldblum, with the assistance of several dozen employees and corporate officers who had varying knowledge of the fraud, perpetrated a massive deception on the investing public, on stockholders, on Wall Street analysts and, of course, on the SEC regulators. The corporation reported nonexistent assets ($120 million by 1973) and ever-growing fictitious profits. As in the Home-Stake swindle, investors were paid their dividends from their own equity rather than from profits. Throughout, the fraud was abetted by a series of outside accounting firms who certified financial statements they knew to be fraudulent and who failed to report financial irregularities to the SEC.

To perpetuate the fraud Goldblum and other corporate officers engaged in a complex scheme of forgeries and lies. In addition to false financial statements reported to investors and to the SEC, fake life insurance policies were created and then resold to other insurance companies as a way of raising cash. Subsequently a portion of these phantom policy holders were ''killed off'' so that Equity Funding could collect. The effect of these and other manipulations was to drive up the price of Equity Funding stock and thereby enrich Goldblum and other company officers, who then sold some of their large holding at inflated prices. (Goldblum alone realized a profit of $4.7 millions from his sales.) When the fraud was finally uncovered, thousands of investors, large and small, lost millions of dollars, recovering on the average only one-fifth of their original investments.

Unlike the Home-Stake swindlers some of the perpetrators of this fraud did receive stiffer than average penalties—compared to the light, or more usually nonexistent, prison sentences meted out to those apprehended for stock manipulation. Goldblum was sentenced to eight years in federal prison and fined $20,000. Five other defendants who had been his accomplices in managing Equity Funding and its frauds were sentenced to as many as five years. In addition three outside auditors, without whom the fraud could not have been perpetuated, also went to jail. Their firms were assessed in excess of $40 million dollars in civil suits.

THE SOCIO-CULTURAL CONTEXT OF STOCK MARKET FRAUDS

I have chosen to focus on the Home-Stake Oil and the Equity Funding swindles since the scope and publicity of these two frauds have resulted in ample documentation and since the essential factors which permit such large swindles to be perpetrated can also be found in the smaller but more numerous stock market swindles reported periodically in the pages of such publications as *The Wall Street Journal* and *Forbes*. Frauds implemented by corporate management, whether large and "ingenious" or small and prosaic, but involving the theft of millions of dollars, have at least three underlying factors in common:

1. the relative ease with which it is possible to deceive investors by falsifying public information;
2. the low risk to the perpetrators; and
3. the large profits which can be obtained by illegal means.

These underlying elements of all stock market frauds are in turn embedded in a larger socio-cultural matrix which supports, indeed encourages, swindling. It is to the more general framing of the problem that we now turn.

The Spirit of Greed

If operators and insiders prey on the gullibility, fear, need for excitement and, particularly, the greed of their victims, they do so in a social context that fosters and facilitates their operations. Sustained by the values of a capitalistic society, the participants in any of the various financial markets, whether bonds, stocks, commodities, or options, can feel—indeed are encouraged to feel—that they are taking part in an activity essential to the well being of the society. Capitalism has institutionalized greed. A private vice is transformed into a public virtue, as Adam Smith concluded. In the value system of Wall Street, it is only excessive greed which is condemned and excessive greed is indicated primarily, and conveniently, as the mark of the loser. The familiar Wall Street adage sums up the philosophy: "A bull can make money. A bear can make money. But a hog never can."

Social Darwinism—survival of the fittest—remains entrenched on Wall Street. A market is impersonal; it is the financial outcome, the bottom line, that counts. Such a perspective, which so highly values economic success, also tends to encourage looking the other way when it comes to an examination of the morality and legality of the means for its attainment. Success rather than morality is the prime value, or, perhaps more accurately, success *is* morality. The loser indicates his own moral failing by the very act of losing; his individual greed, gullibility, or fear indicate the fatal flaw of the loser. In this ideology of the stock market the "odd lotter" (i.e., small investor) is nearly always assumed to be wrong and his market behavior is closely watched as a contrarian indicator. When the odd lotters are selling, it is time to buy, and vice versa. Likewise one should watch the "specialists" when they are buying or selling, for invariably they are the elite, guided by knowledge and rationality to buy and sell against the crowd, free of the sins of gullibility and greed. The dictum that "a hog never wins" is easily transformed into "all losers are hogs." Winners, by contrast, exemplify The Protestant Ethic, and the virtues presumed to be essential to success in the marketplace: caution, rationality, and the ability to defer gratification.

Such a value system glosses over the facts that most participants in the market are driven by greed and that success depends greatly on positional advantage, if not outright fraud. In terms of the perspective on deviance and its control this ideology has further consequences. It leads to limited compassion for the victims of fraud, a cavalier attitude toward offenders and, consequently, only perfunctory attempts at the apprehension and punishment of rule breakers.

Regulations are either grudgingly accepted or held in great contempt by Wall Street professionals and business in general. Because the industry accepts the economic model of the competitive market as best guided by the "invisible hand," members regard outside regulation as the main enemy of the bottom line, of freedom and the American way. The pages of *The Wall Street Journal, Forbes, Barron's,* and other financial publications read by the business and investing elite, repeatedly hammer out the theme of the evils of government regulation of business. *Barron's,* probably the most influential publication addressed to investors and Wall Street professionals, is particularly strident in its editorial attacks on all forms of government regulations. For instance, soon after the inauguration of Ronald Reagan as President, *Barron's* ran a full page editorial entitled "In Praise of Sweatshops: Everyone Should Have the Right to Work" (Grant, 1981, p. 7). A few months later it turned its big gun, in-house reactionary, Robert M. Bleiberg, against the "ecological nuts" and government regulators. The result was another one page editorial: "Bring Back DDT and Wipe Out a Decade of Regulatory Excess" (Bleiberg, 1981, p. 7).

Such an ideology is all too often, in a moderated version, part of the mental set of the regulators themselves. Largely drawn from corporate management, or from elite law firms with close ties to American corporations, the commissioners who formulate policy for such regulatory agencies as the Securities and Exchange Commission (SEC) and the Commodities Future Trading Commission (CFTC) are often at best ambivalent toward systematic and strict enforcement of the law. This was most recently and dramatically illustrated by the paralysis experienced by the CFTC in the months preceding the near-crash of the stock market on March 27, 1980—"Silver Thursday."

As has been discussed in previous chapters, throughout the late seventies Bunker Hunt and other members of the Hunt family, in league with oil-rich Arabs, manipulated the silver market with the intent of cornering it (Fay, 1982). By September 1979 the CFTC was aware that the Hunts were using secret accounts, in clear violation of the law, and were making unusually large purchases of silver contracts, with the obvious purpose of inflating the price. Yet the commission did nothing for four months while it watched the price of silver rise from $13 to $50 an ounce. It was unwilling to place position limits on traders, much less close the market, although the manipulation of the Hunts was explicitly outlawed by the Sherman Antitrust Act and the Commodity Exchange Act of 1936 (Fay, 1982, pp. 111–117). In January 1980, when the situation became so critical that it threatened the financial markets, the CFTC passed the buck to the Comex (the commodities market where most silver contracts are traded), which was forced to impose position limits in order to avoid a crisis.

The paralysis of the regulators stemmed largely from the ideological orientation of two of the four CFTC commissioners. One of the two, David Gartner, made the following observation to journalist Stephen Fay, subsequent to the events:

> If Joe Schmoe is going to corner the market in widgets, and he happens to have five billion dollars, is there a law to stop him? If the Hunts have some paranoia about the dollar and want to leave some money to their children, what do you do about that? (Fay, 1982, p. 117).

Without impugning the integrity of many diligent and ethical staff members of the regulatory agencies, it is clear that commissioners of the SEC and CFTC have not always represented the most judicious presidential appointments. The first chairman of the SEC was Joseph Kennedy, notorious for his stock market manipulations. More recently William Casey, later appointed director of the CIA, had been linked to alleged market manipulations prior to his appointment as SEC chairman by Richard Nixon. Another Nixon appointee to the SEC, G. Bradford Cook, was forced to resign as chairman when it was discovered he had been instrumental in suppressing information concerning swindler Robert Vesco's contribution to the Nixon Campaign (Dirk and Gross, 1974, p. 277). Even when the regulators are willing to act and enforce the laws, they are often plagued by a sense of powerlessness in view of the magnitude of the task and the limited resources at their command. Since the penalties for illegal activities related to the stock market are generally minor—or at least existing enforcement practices result in only minimal sanctions—both the enforcers and the potential violators of securities laws perceive such deviance as relatively risk-free. This perception is well summarized by John Fedder, the director of the SEC's enforcement division as he analyzes the risks of trading on the basis of inside information from the point of the perpetrator:

> What are the risks? If the SEC sues me, what can they do? They might disgorge my profits, but they don't bring any criminal proceedings. The only thing I'm really jeopardizing is my reputation. (Green, 1982, p. 46)

The Role of "Regulations" in Perpetuating a Climate of Deviance

The general pessimism about the effectiveness of enforcement, as well as the laxity of actual enforcement, raises the issue of the latent function of regulations and the regulatory agencies *as presently constituted.* When so many crimes are committed, so few criminals are apprehended—and those that are seldom prosecuted—one must raise some questions about the primary function of the regulatory system. In fact one must doubt that its main function is the vigorous enforcement of the law. Clearly, governmental regulation of business, and of the securities industry in particular, is seen as the last resort to curb fraud by those who are charged to administer the law. Their preference is for "self-regulation." Such a philosophy is freely acknowledged, for instance, in a recent SEC Chairman's report to Congress:

> Thanks to the unique disclosure and self-regulatory framework established by Federal securities law, *the Commissions relationship with the private sector has traditionally been more one of oversight than prescription—more cooperative than adversarial.* . . . The ultimate purpose of Federal securities law is, after all, to ensure the confident, efficient, and fair securities markets that foster the capital formation process which underpins our prosperity and our democracy. (Securities and Exchange Commission, 1981, pp. ii–iii, emphasis added)

Thus, it seems that the financial community and its regulators share a set of public values and beliefs which have as a latent function the sustaining of a high incidence of fraud in the securities market. These values and belief are in effect subcultural fictions which facilitate fraud, under the cover of largely ineffective regulations.

One such fiction is the publicly expressed belief that insider trading can be regulated under the existing system. This belief has been translated into law, SEC rule 10b–5, which prohibits purchases or sales of securities by persons who have access to information not publicly available (Ratner, 1978, pp. 120–135). In reality, most Wall Street professionals, as well as SEC officials, view the efforts of the SEC to deter as well as to punish this very lucrative activity as largely ineffective. As one SEC official readily admits, off the record: "These are tough cases to prove. We have to be able to determine that the insider acted on the basis of that information rather than a dozen possible alternative explanations'' (Miller, 1980, p. D1). A partner in one of the largest Wall Street firms which deals with corporate mergers is even more candid in describing the difficulties in enforcing rules concerning insider trading:

> If a person has inside information and tells a friend about it, and that friend tells another friend about it, and transactions are done through nominee accounts [in which the actual owners of the stock are not identified], detection becomes very hard, if not impossible. (Noble, 1981, p. D1)

This kind of cynicism about regulations concerning insider trading clearly reflects the reality. Although, as was documented above, the practice of trading on inside information is rampant, the actual number of apprehensions is small and the number of prosecutions is even smaller. From August 1978 to March 1980 the SEC initiated only seventeen court actions and two administrative proceedings against persons accused of inside trading (Miller, 1980, p. D3).

Another public fiction relates to the role of the broker-dealer. As we have seen above, the broker-dealer is in a position to sell stocks from his own inventory, or to even to ''unload'' stocks which he knows, on the basis of inside information, are about to drop in market value (Elias, 1971, pp. 205–206; Ratner, 1978, pp. 149–151). This situation is clearly not in the best interest of customers. The institutionalization of such conflicts of interest is particularly evident with respect to the role of the specialists—those individuals and their firms who are floor brokers, charged with maintaining an orderly market in the stock in which they specialize. The fiction is that their behavior is in the interest of the trading public. Yet it is a Wall Street truism that knowing which stocks specialists are buying and selling for their own accounts is an accurate predictor of the future movement of these stocks. The reason for this is clear. The structuring of the role of specialist provides the incumbent with an information advantage which permits him to have advance knowledge of market trends for the particular stock in which he specializes. In his ''book'' the specialist keeps a record of all standing orders to buy and sell stocks at specified prices. Consequently (as noted in chapter 6), he knows before all other market participants the extent of the supply and demand in his particular stocks, and is in a position to profit thereby (Hagin & Mader, 1973, pp. 167–175).

These permissive structural arrangements are supported by, and probably could not exist without, the prevailing belief that the market is regulated and therefore ''fair.'' Put another way, it appears that the regulatory apparatus, whether it be the SEC or the internal regulatory bodies of the various markets, functions to deter not deviance but a close scrutiny of the structural factors contributing to deviance in the securities industry. Indeed, from this perspective, the existence of regulatory agencies staffed with honest and dedicated personnel has the ironic effect of increasing the extent of stock market deviance, for they lull the investing public into a false sense of security.

As I have noted above, the stock market has elements of both gambling and the confidence game, in addition to the more easily recognized purpose of providing capital for the development of industry. For any "con" to work, the "mark," invariably driven by greed, must believe in the high likelihood of profit. Similarly the gambler must believe that he has a good chance of winning. Any sense that the "game" is heavily stacked in favor of the house would reduce the inclination of the public to participate, and therefore reduce the number of potential "marks." It is a matter of simple public relations to maintain the illusion that the game is a fair one and that all market participants share equally in the risks as well as the profits. Whenever the public strongly doubts that the market is fair it tends to withdraw its participation. This reduced participation is obviously not to the interest of insiders. The brokers need high volume in order to make commissions. The insider depends on the outsider to bid up the price of the stock once private information is made public. The specialist cannot sell short on low volume.

Consequently the regulators are an intrinsic aspect of the public relations game which maintains the view that despite sporadic abuses the market is essentially honest and fair, following the laws of supply and demand, rather than the laws of fraud and manipulation. Regulators, as they presently operate, serve less to control or prevent abuses than to maintain investor confidence. As Edward Herlihy, one regulator in charge of the SEC division charged with controlling insider trading notes, failure to regulate is detrimental to the securities industry:

> Insider trading is like going to the track and knowing which horse will win the race before placing the bet. It's precisely the kind of overreaching that jeopardizes investor confidence in the integrity and fairness in the market. (Miller, 1980, p. D6)

CONCLUSIONS

In this chapter the focus has been on fraud, deviance and criminality. The stock market is much more than that. It is excitement, panic, drama and boredom. It evokes a selected segment of human emotions—fear and greed—and reflects some of the major economic, political, and social forces in the society. Most of all it is a necessary institution for the maintenance of liquidity in corporate investments; neither institutions nor individuals would invest in stocks without the knowledge that their investment can at any time be reconverted to cash. The stock market is a necessary underpinning of capitalism. It therefore evokes many of the same vices as the system it supports, often magnified by the peaks of emotionality it engenders.

While the market, as capitalism in general, cannot thrive without unleashing greed and deception neither can it operate without the appearance of fairness and rationality. In an uncertain world humans search for certainty. And since the future price of any investment is always uncertain to some degree, the market elicits the gullibility of even the most sophisticated, as their desire for profits lures them into schemes which promise riches but often deliver grief.

Greed, fear and gullibility are only the starting point in an understanding of stock market fraud. These human traits express themselves more in some social contexts than in others. Securities transactions are imbedded in a socio-cultural matrix which encourages deviance. The greed which motivates legitimate risk taking essential to the functioning of capitalism—and legitimate only within the contexts of the values and norms of that system—is also a motivating force in the type of deviance discussed above. Similarly the deception, which is an essential part of the stock market game, spills over the boundaries of what is defined as fair play by the rules of the system and becomes, of course, an essential and integral part of stock market fraud. The drift from legitimate to illegitimate activities is easily negotiated when the attitudes required for one are the same as for the other. This is all the more so when the boundaries between conforming and deviant behavior are so ill-defined. When does high-pressure selling leave off and churning begin? At what point does "creative accounting" become outright fraud? The rules are complex and subject to human interpretation.

Finally, as I have indicated above, the mental and emotional orientation, the subculture of Wall Street (and of commerce in general), which is so favorable to deviance, is only one of the two main classes of factors which encourage stock market fraud. The other is the structure of opportunity, including the costs and benefits to be derived from illegitimate activities. Stock market crime is rational crime. The ease with which information can be manipulated for profit, given the built-in structural advantages of the roles of broker-dealers and corporate managers, is half of it. The other half is the limited risks which such manipulations engender. Discovery of stock market fraud is minimal compared to its prevalence. Penalties, when crime is uncovered, are not severe enough to have a meaningful deterrent effect. In short, the amount and types of crimes related to the stock market reflects the mentality and social organization of its participants.

REFERENCES

Baruch, H. *Wall Street: Security risk.* Washington, D.C.: Acropolis, 1971.

Bleiberg, R. M. Bring back DDT and wipe out a decade of regulatory excess. *Barron's,* June 29, 1981, p. 7.

Blundell, W. E. Equity funding: I did it for the jollies. In D. Moffits (Ed.), *Swindled! Classic business frauds of the seventies.* Princeton, N.J.: Dow Jones, 1976.

Bonger, W. *Criminality and economic conditions.* Bloomington: Indiana University Press, 1969.

Brutus. *Confessions of a stockbroker.* Boston: Little, Brown, 1971.

Clinard, M. B. *Illegal corporate behavior.* Washington, D.C.: Government Printing Office, 1979.

Dirk, R. L., & Gross, L. *The great Wall Street scandal.* New York: McGraw-Hill, 1974.

Dreman, D. *Contrarian investment strategy.* New York: Random House, 1979.

Durkheim, E. *The rules of sociological method.* New York: The Free Press, 1964.

Ehrbar, A. F., & Schiff, L. The Home-Stakes case: Where was the SEC? *Fortune,* September 1974, pp. 95; 98; 100.

Elias, C. *Fleecing the lambs*. Chicago: Henry Regnery, 1971.

Erikson, K. T. *Wayward puritans*. New York: Wiley, 1966.

Evan, W. M., & Levin, G. Status set and role set conflict of a stock broker: A problem in the sociology of law. *Social Forces*, 1966, *45*, 73–83.

Fay, S. *Beyond greed*. New York: Viking Press, 1982.

Fraud and fair dealing in stocks. New York: John Thompson, Jr., 1880.

Galbraith, J. K. Crime and no punishment. *Esquire*, December 1977, p. 88.

Goldberg, S. C. *Fraudulent broker-dealer practices*. New York: American Institute for Securities Regulations, 1978.

Grant, J. In praise of sweatshops: Everyone should have the right to work. *Barron's*, March 16, 1981, p. 7.

Green, R. Selling in the rain. *Forbes*, April 26, 1982, pp. 45–46.

Hagin, R., & Mader, C. *The new science of investing*. Homewood, Ill.: Dow Jones-Irwin, 1973.

Harper, H. H. *The psychology of speculation*. Burlington, Vt.: Fraser, 1926.

Hayano, D. *Poker faces*. Berkeley: University of California Press, 1982.

Kelly, F. C. *Why you win or lose*. Burlington, Vt.: Fraser, 1930.

Leff, A. A. *Swindling and selling*. New York: Free Press, 1976.

Louis, A. M. The unwinnable war on insider trading. *Fortune*, July 1981, pp. 72–82.

Manne, H. G. *Insider trading and the stock market*. New York: Free Press, 1966.

Mayer, M. Broker dealer firms. In Twentieth Century Fund (Ed.), *Abuses on Wall Street: Conflict of interest in the securities market*. Westport, Conn.: Quorum Books, 1980.

McClintic, D. The biggest ponzi scheme: A reporter's journal. In D. Moffits (Ed.), *Swindled! Classic business frauds of the seventies*. Princeton, N.J.: Dow Jones, 1976.

McClintic, D. *Stealing from the rich: The Home-Stake oil swindle*. New York: M. Evans, 1977.

Merjos, A. Clear crystal ball? Many stocks show handsome gains in advance of takeovers. *Barron's*, January 2, 1981, pp. 11; 23–24; 105.

Merton, R. K. *Social theory and social structure*. Glencoe, Ill.: Free Press, 1957.

Miller, J. S.E.C. cracking down on trading by insiders. *The New York Times*, March 7, 1980, pp. D1; D6.

Nash, J. R. *Hustlers and con men*. New York: Grossman, 1976.

Noble, K. B. Stalking stock-trading abuses. *The New York Times*, March 6, 1981, pp. D1; D3.

Parsons, T. The professions and social structure. *Social Forces*, 1939, *17*, 457–467.

Pearce, F. *Crimes of the powerful*. London: Pluto Press, 1976.

Quinn, J. B. The inside story. *Newsweek*, February 7, 1983, pp. 11E–11G.

Ratner, D. L. *Securities regulation in a nutshell*. St. Paul, Minn.: West Publishing, 1978.

Schwed, F., Jr. *Where are the customer's yachts?* New York: Simon & Schuster, 1940.

Securities and Exchange Commission. *Report on the feasibility and advisability of the complete segregation of the functions of dealer and broker*. Washington, D.C.: Author, 1936.

Securities and Exchange Commission. *Annual Report 1980*. Washington, D.C.: U.S. Government Printing Office, 1981.

Seidler, L. J., Andrews, F., & Epstein, M. J. *The equity funding papers*. New York: Wiley, 1977.

Slater, P. *Wealth addiction*. New York: E. P. Dutton, 1980.

Smith, C. W. *The mind of the market*. Totowa, N.J.: Rowman & Littlefield, 1981.

Stern, R. L. Wall Street has your number. *Forbes*, October 26, 1981, pp. 167–171.

Tucile, J. *Mind over money*. New York: William Morrow, 1980.

TOWARD A SOCIOLOGY OF FINANCIAL MARKETS

Patricia A. Adler and Peter Adler

Earlier we argued that a void exists in the social science literature pertaining to the sociology of financial markets. Our purpose in this book has been to offer a sociological perspective of this economic arena which is diverse in its approach while comprehensive in its coverage. Moreover, we have tried to show how sociological analyses of financial markets offer different conceptualizations from models previously advanced by rationalist economists and crowd psychologists. Sociology facilitates this by offering us insights into the concrete dynamics of human individual, group and organizational behavior. With this goal in mind, let us now summarize some of the major themes which have been emphasized throughout the preceding chapters, clarifying and extrapolating on the direct and indirect implications they have offered.

THE SOCIAL DYNAMICS OF FINANCIAL MARKETS

Symbolic Behavior

Abstract constructs, such as political or business events and levels of price fluctuation, do not interact with each other on a direct basis. It must be understood, when any causal correlation is attempted, that the interaction between these social facts is necessarily mediated by the concrete actions of people. Humans, as Snow and Parker (chapter 8) have noted, react to the plethora of events and information which surround the market in a highly subjective manner. People's varying perceptions of these events lead them to form socially-derived interpretations which give these events meaning, thus enabling them to make decisions on how to act. Throughout financial market dealings however, the process of selecting a course of action is further complicated by the variety of speculative choices and abundance of competing belief systems available (fundamental, technical, contrarian and random walk analyses), all of which offer conflicting strategies of interpreting and reacting to news and events. The point here is clear: it is through people's divergent reactions to the everyday world that market liquidity is maintained, by ensuring that there will always be someone believing that they should sell when there is someone wanting to buy. Thus, the relationship between outside events and market movements is neither direct, linear nor predictable, because the process of individual decision making is influenced by the *subjective* process of symbolic behavior. This challenges the economists' Efficient Market Hypothesis, which is based on the belief (in all three forms) that the market *objectively* reacts efficiently and perfectly to the release of new information.

Collective Dynamics

The problems of uncertainty and ambiguity have been repeatedly cited as pervasive to financial markets (chapters 5, 8; cf. also Glick, 1957; Smith, 1981). This structural characteristic causes market participants to exhibit certain forms of collective behavior. As Klausner notes (chapter 4), when faced with the cognitive dissonance of having their belief systems challenged by the unpredictable vagaries of the market, individuals often react by engaging in social comparison. Spurred by fears and doubts, and surrounded by others in a similar state, people become highly susceptible to suggestibility and social contagion. Almost by instinct these individuals herd together, conforming to the group by fitting their lines of action together. Through this process market groups come to follow two types of leaders: individuals like themselves who either act assertively or who are perceived as successful, or people who are thought to have superior knowledge and power, such as market gurus (chapter 8) or a group of mysteriously defined insiders known as "They" (chapter 5). This "sheep mentality" becomes strengthened by people's fear of making a wrong decision and either taking a loss or missing a profit, coupled with the emotional comfort they feel of "going with the group." Thus emotions and emotional reactions often come to dominate when rationality is not clearly emergent, causing such collectively induced phenomena as: random shocks; overreactions; lagged adjustments; fad and fashion; pendulum swings, and momentum, in the fluctuation of prices. The fact that people tend to herd together and sometimes irrationally imitate each others' behavior is a well known fact among market participants. Maxims such as "you can't fight the market" illustrate how the collective dynamics of people's financial behavior can serve as a self-fulfilling prophesy: if people believe that a collective reaction is going to push prices in one direction (despite objective indicators to the contrary), they will adjust their holdings to support the trend, thereby reifying the initial belief.

These kinds of group dynamics and their effects contradict the economic view of markets as perfect adjustors. Rather than routinely moving to the level rationally calculable as "true" value, *the market is influenced by the collective features of human behavior to display imperfect price levels.* These aberrations are alluded to in what Tarascio (chapter 3) has described as the EMH's semi-strong form, but can go beyond the mere "lagged adjustments" referred to therein. The behavior patterns underlying these group dynamics also go contrary to the presupposition that "economic man" is motivated solely by short-term financial gain. A range of other motivations such as *excitement, greed,*[1] *comfort, admiration* and *doubt* thus motivate market participants to behave in this seemingly nonrational manner.

The Informal Social Structure

In several dimensions, levels, areas and ways it has been noted here that *the formal market structure is supplemented and occasionally subverted by an informal social structure or network of roles, relationships and social organization.* Baker (chapter 6) shows this in his discussions of group loyalty, territoriality, and the way floor traders act to maintain the most desired crowd size. When he describes how traders drive away unwanted market-makers or violate the "first" rule to aid colleagues, he points out that financial markets are necessarily social arenas, populated by individuals who must interact with each other on a daily basis. The relationships which form out of this regular interaction and the feelings traders develop about each other as people combine to generate a social cohesion which affects the way members perceive, interpret and organize their actions.

This informal social organization of floor trading stands in contrast to the view commonly held by laymen, rationalist economists and crowd psychologists, that behavior in the pits is anarchistic. According to the latter's image, trading may begin rationally, but it quickly degenerates into unreasoning, mass chaos. And curiously, while economists have a highly structured and formalized image of the market's macro organization, they too consider the actual face-to-face exchange of commodities and securities to be without patterned order. It has been one of the tasks here, then, to look beyond the formal depictions of how markets are *intended* to function, to recognize the informal system of operation which provides meaning for the actions of everyday participants.

Another dimension of financial markets' informal social structure can be found in the communication networks which govern the diffusion of information between groups of market participants (chapter 5). Facts that pertain to the market can spread unevenly according to the status hierarchy of the group involved, insiders having higher prestige and greater access to information than outsiders. Thus what becomes known to members of one group may not be discovered by a second group for several days and never be realized by a third. This status hierarchy of information diffusion challenges the EMH's view of the market as an efficient information processor. While economists assume that all market participants have instantaneous access to pertinent information so that they may act on it to discount price levels, we see that informal networks of information dispersal prevent this from being the case.

Social Supports to Market Functioning: The Visible Hand

Although the market has been ideally described by economists as a perfectly competitive arena, we find that this is not intrinsic to its functioning. *Throughout the history of financial markets, conscious human intervention has been required to artificially maintain the competitive nature of this arena.* On the micro level, Baker (chapter 6) describes how markets naturally drift away from the conditions of pure competition, aided and abetted by the subtle actions of floor traders. For traders, the greater control they can exert over the trading situation, the greater their profit making opportunities will be, even if the degree is only slight. They therefore prefer the ''monopolistic-monopsonistic'' and ''negotiated'' market conditions, where they have a better chance to corner and squeeze a market or to conspiratorially hold fast to an extended price spread. Trying to effect a negotiated market situation, they employ informal social sanctions designed to repulse unwanted outsiders. Floor surveillance committees, aware of these techniques, are charged with the mandate to detect flagrant examples of such behavior and step in to restore unmanipulated competition. The ease and subtlety with which such deviance can be accomplished, however, makes it nearly impossible to forceably eradicate.

On the macro level, Abolafia (chapter 7) also recognizes the enormous profits speculators can derive from manipulating the market into a noncompetitive condition. He argues that insiders, who rely on the market's positive public relations image to ensure lucrative commissions for themselves, are willing to accept temporary restrictions on their manipulative activities in order to maintain a market that will continue to be attractive to investors over the long-term. They voluntarily submit to surveillance rebukes and refrain from most flagrant forms of abuse. Outsiders, though, having no career stake in the market's credibility as a competitive arena, may opportunistically seek to establish and press manipulatively-gained advantages to their fullest limits. When this happens (as in the case of the Hunt brothers), a crisis occurs and formal boundary maintenance sanctions are invoked. Abolafia concludes that market competition is socially maintained by an array of continually applied controls ranging from informal norms, to rules of conduct, to formal structures.

Thus, Smith's (1937) classic notion that the laws of the market are guided by an "invisible hand," is shown by close empirical examination to be another romanticized construct. In today's financial markets the "private interests and passions of men" do not produce that "which is most agreeable to the interest of the whole society." What we see instead is a very visible hand, a hand which must constantly intervene to maintain the interests of society and which is criticized by many as being inadequately active: of intervening just enough to preserve appearances but not enough to truly maintain pure competition (chapter 9). By showing how the assumptions underlying pure competition are no more than idealized constructions, the analyses presented in this book cast further doubt on the perfection of the entire market system.

The Market in Socio-Cultural Context

Throughout this volume we have noted how financial markets are flawed by deviance and imperfections. Structural opportunities make it possible for a variety of insiders, whether they be market professionals or corporate management, to profit by virtue of their advantageous position. Illegal and/or immoral activities, such as trading on inside information, violations of fiduciary responsibility, market manipulations and outright fraud, are fairly commonplace in these financial arenas. As Lejeune (chapter 9) points out, the deviant aspects of financial markets are rooted in our socio-cultural context: they reflect the norms and values of our society. At a variety of levels and in a variety of ways, then, *the market is maintained by insiders for their own benefit at the expense of outsiders* (chapters 3, 8 and 9).

THE NATURE OF FINANCIAL MARKETS

These social dynamics form the base of a sociological model of financial markets. Let us now extract some overarching conclusions about the broader nature of financial markets and show how the sociological perspective on the market compares and contrasts with the economic perspective.

Economists' forte lies in their statistical analyses of the fluctuation of price levels. Unfortunately, the magnitude of this economic institution—the sheer volume of commodities and securities traded on the numerous financial markets that exist in our country alone—makes it impossible to calculate the precise nature of all price fluctuations in any single, unified study. As a result while many empirical investigations into the sequence of prices exist, no clear-cut, definitive answers have been reached; in fact, we find an arena rife with controversy (chapter 3). To date, economists have divided themselves on the issue of whether price fluctuations follow a random or nonrandom sequence, but Tarascio argues that a combination of these two conditions more accurately describes the nature of price series. Generally, he concludes, future levels cannot be predicted from past price behavior. However, on some occasions, a predictable patterning or sequence of serial correlation can be observed in price fluctuation, thus effecting a reconciliation of the EMH's weak and semi-strong forms.

While sociological analyses of financial markets have found fault with the assumptions underlying these economic models and their implications for human behavior, some consensus can be reached between these two fields regarding their conclusion about the broader scope of financial markets. From a sociological perspective, we agree that market price fluctuations are generally unpredictable. This predominant lack of foreseeable patterning is not caused by the random character through which information becomes available to the public; it is lodged in the impulsive, subjective and fundamentally unpredictable nature of human behavior. Yet human behavior is not random. As the Adlers (chapter 5) conclude, people's actions in the market, although occasionally irrational, are predominantly understandable responses to the social structure, social organization, perceptions and collective beliefs of this complex arena. Thus, at times, collective movements become launched, based on a group belief about how the market will act (or react). In these instances, market trends develop which can be recognized, identified and anticipated to continue for some (short-term) period. Sociological insights into human behavior can thus be used to supplement economists' expertise in the area of price fluctuation, to provide a more inter-disciplinary understanding of both how and why financial markets operate.

DIRECTIONS FOR FUTURE RESEARCH

Although we have attempted in this work to offer some insights into specific dimensions of financial markets, this still only begins to scratch the surface of dimensions of this field ripe for social scientific analysis. There are several directions we would propose for future research.

On the micro level, social psychological analyses are needed of the type of people who both work or dabble in this profession. While some studies have been conducted describing personality profiles of successful participants (cf. Baker, 1971; Blotnick, 1979), there have been few[2] which look at social correlates of success: how successful participants can be sociologically differentiated from their unsuccessful counterparts (for both floor and off-premises traders). More studies of the interactional dynamics of financial markets would also be welcome, focusing on such topics as the language of the market, non-verbal communication in the market, the emotions of the market and the micropolitics of the market. Lastly, an examination of the careers of market participants would be of interest, describing recruitment into the field, various types and degrees of involvement with financial markets, stages in members' careers, and modes or motivations for retirement from this field.

From a more macro perspective, an intriguing area for future research are the social movements and collective trends in the market. One such burgeoning trend ripe for study is "social investing:" a politically conscious investing strategy through which participants seek to support companies whose products, employee relations, environmental stance and international politics they endorse, by acquiring their stock. Brokerage firms have already sprung up which set up portfolios of this kind, oriented toward "doing good while doing well."[3] Further analyses of financial markets from a traditional structural-functional perspective are also needed. Here, the market can profitably be analyzed as a social institution, in terms of its functions within the social system and its interaction with (and mutual influence by) other societal institutions.

Finally, the findings of this volume implicitly call for social policy analyses of financial markets which might point out ways to reduce the structural opportunities for the exploitation of outsiders by insiders and help to transform financial markets into the arenas of equal competitive opportunity which they formally purport to be.

NOTES

1. See Lyman (1978) for an excellent discussion of the role of greed in speculative behavior.
2. One notable exception to this void is provided by Glick (1957), who offers us a social psychological analysis of how members define success and failure as typologies in the Chicago Mercantile Exchange.
3. A more detailed discussion elaborating on social investing may be found in *The Futurist* (see Lowry, 1982), or in the new social investing advisement newsletter, *Good Money: The Newsletter of Social Investing and Inventing*.

REFERENCES

Baker, W. The successful investor. *Psychology Today,* November 1971, pp. 59; 84–86.

Blotnick, S. In search of a story. *Forbes,* April 2, 1979, pp. 24–125.

Glick, I. O. *A social psychological study of futures trading.* Unpublished doctoral dissertation, University of Chicago, 1957.

Lowry, R. P. Social investing: Doing good while doing well. *The Futurist,* April 1982, pp. 22–28.

Lyman, S. *The seven deadly sins.* New York: St. Martins, 1978.

Smith, A. *The wealth of nations.* New York: Modern Library, 1937.

Smith, C. W. *The mind of the market.* Totowa, N.J.: Rowman & Littlefield, 1981.

BIOGRAPHICAL SKETCH OF THE CONTRIBUTORS

Mitchel Y. Abolafia received his Ph.D. in Sociology from the State University of New York at Stony Brook. He is currently an Assistant Professor at the Graduate School of Business and Public Administration, Cornell University, Ithaca, New York.

Patricia A. Adler received her Ph.D. in Sociology from the University of California, San Diego. She is currently Research Associate, Department of Sociology, University of Tulsa.

Peter Adler received his Ph.D. in Sociology from the University of California, San Diego. He is currently Assistant Professor of Sociology at the University of Tulsa.

Wayne E. Baker received his Ph.D. in Sociology from Northwestern University. He is currently Assistant Vice President of the Synectics Group, Inc., a financial consulting firm based in Washington, D.C.

Michael Klausner received his Ph.D. in Sociology from the University of Illinois at Urbana. He is currently Assistant Professor of Sociology at the University of Pittsburgh at Bradford.

Robert Lejeune received his Ph.D. in Sociology from Columbia University. He is currently Professor of Sociology at Herbert Lehman College, City University of New York.

Ritchie P. Lowry received his Ph.D. in Sociology from the University of California, Berkeley. He is currently Professor of Sociology at Boston College and Co-Director and President of the Center for Economic Revitalization and Co-Editor of *Good Money: The Newsletter of Social Investing and Inventing*.

Robert Parker is a doctoral student in the Department of Sociology at the University of Texas, Austin.

David A. Snow received his Ph.D. in Sociology from the University of California, Los Angeles. He is currently Associate Professor of Sociology at the University of Texas, Austin.

Vincent J. Tarascio received his Ph.D. in Economics from Rice University. He is currently Professor of Economics at the University of North Carolina, Chapel Hill and Editor of the *Southern Economic Journal*.

Index